Richard Littlejohn is an award-winning *Daily Mail* columnist and broadcaster, and No. 1 bestselling author. In 2012, he was given the prestigious Edgar Wallace Prize for fine writing by the London Press Club.

He was voted one of the most influential journalists of the past forty years by Press Gazette, has been Fleet Street's Columnist of the Year and was named Irritant of the Year by the BBC's *What The Papers Say* for his unrivalled ability to get up the noses of the great and good. His satirical books and his highly-acclaimed novel *To Hell in a Handcart* have all been best sellers.

Richard has written for the *Sun*, London's *Evening Standard*, *Punch* and the *Spectator*. He has presented his own TV series and documentaries on LWT, Sky, Channel 4 and Carlton, winning a Silver Rose of Montreux. As a radio presenter he has worked for London's LBC and the BBC, receiving a Sony Award for his football phone-in show *6-0-6*.

Littlejohn's Lost World

RICHARD LITTLEJOHN

arrow books

3 5 7 9 10 8 6 4 2

Arrow Books
20 Vauxhall Bridge Road
London SW1V 2SA

Arrow Books is part of the Penguin Random House group of companies
whose addresses can be found at global.penguinrandomhouse.com.

Copyright © Richard Littlejohn 2014

First published by Hutchinson in 2014
First published in paperback by Arrow Books in 2015

www.randomhouse.co.uk

A CIP catalogue record for this book
is available from the British Library.

ISBN 9780099569282

Per

For Margaret Kathleen

This edition is also dedicated to
the memory of Paul Sidey (1943–2014)

Acknowledgements

Thanks to my editor Paul Sidey and my wife Wendy Littlejohn for their tireless support and enthusiasm. To my mother, Margaret Littlejohn, my sister Vivienne McCracken, my uncle Ken Littlejohn, for the family history. To Geoff Allen and Andrea Allen for the guided tour of the multicultural metropolis formerly known as the Soke of Peterborough.

Others who deserve a mention include John Lodge and Kirsten Lodge, Deke Arlon, Jill Arlon, and Colin Dunne. Thanks also to Jocasta Hamilton, Rose Waddilove and Neil Bradford at Random House and Martin Soames at Simons Muirhead & Burton.

Most of all thanks to my mum and dad, who made it all possible.

Any mistakes and memory lapses are my sole responsibility. In mitigation, I shall claim it was all a long time ago.

Part 1

The eighteenth of January, 1954, Bill Littlejohn found himself in the garage of his parents' end-of-terrace house in Ilford, Essex. It was bitterly cold and he was painting a midwife's bike.

His wife had gone into labour and was about to give birth to their first child. Bill was banished from the makeshift maternity ward in an upstairs bedroom. Nothing to see there.

Having made himself scarce, he decided he might as well make himself useful. The midwife said her bike would benefit from a lick of paint. Bill figured it was the least he could do.

Almost ten years earlier he had been hunkered down in the backstreets of Marseilles, directing the bombardment of France's biggest port by ships belonging to the Allied Fleet in the Mediterranean. He was put ashore with a cumbersome, battery-powered wireless backpack with a whiplash aerial, a tin helmet, a sidearm and a canteen of water, and instructed to take a strategic position behind enemy lines, from where he could relay the coordinates of German targets back to the gunners on board the mainly American warships anchored offshore.

One false calculation, one slip of the slide rule, one salvo of stray ship-to-shore ordnance; one German sniper, for that matter, and his war would have been over. Kaput, just a couple of weeks after his twentieth birthday. When he signed up in 1941, he hadn't bargained on being part of the land forces invading southern Europe three years later.

Bill joined the Royal Navy, despite the fact that he couldn't swim and had a phobia about water. He was determined not to end up part of the poor bloody infantry like his father, William Henry Littlejohn, also called Bill, who had served in the trenches and killing fields of the First World War, fighting in both the first battle of Mons, where he sustained arm and stomach wounds, and later at Ypres, which was for ever known to him and his comrades as 'Wipers'.

When Bill Sr volunteered for the army, some neckless NCO who thought he had a sense of humour posted him to serve with the Sherwood Foresters, a Midlands regiment stationed at Warwick, in preparation for embarkation to France.

If generations of Littlejohns had a pound for every

time someone had asked: 'Where's Robin Hood, then?' they'd have been as rich as the Rockefellers.

In 1942, Young Bill trained as a radio operator, at the cutting edge of communications technology but hardly the sharp end of the fight against fascism. He served on the Russian convoys before being transferred to the Med. His weapons training was rudimentary, since no one imagined that navy wireless technicians would ever have to slug it out on the front line, where the bullets fly.

A life on the ocean waves wasn't without risk, but it had to be safer than braving anti-aircraft fire while parachuting from a glider over occupied Belgium; fixing bayonets for hand-to-hand jungle combat with the Japanese in Malaya; trying to take out a German machine-gun nest with a hand grenade; or serving as a rear gunner on a Lancaster bomber over Berlin.

That was the plan, anyway. On his maiden voyage in the Irish Sea his ship collided with a fishing boat and instantly started to sink.

Back in Vine Gardens, Ilford, Bill's mum, Amelia, known to all as 'Min', woke up in a cold sweat at the precise moment the ship began to sink. She always maintained that from the day he joined the navy she had a premonition that her son would be lost at sea.

As you will already have gathered, Bill didn't drown. He managed to clamber into the last of the lifeboats and was rescued by a passing frigate. But only after making his first vital contribution to the war effort on active service. It was his job to send out the distress signal.

After the outbreak of war with Germany, the Littlejohn family – Bill Sr, Min, Young Bill, younger brother Ken – was evacuated to Fairlie, on the west coast of Scotland. Bill Sr was a stevedore at the Royal Docks, on the River Thames in London, and was seconded to the naval dockyard at Fairlie, which has a sheltered harbour and was home to the Anti-Submarine Experimental Establishment during the Second World War.

The transfer may well have been fixed by Min's youngest brother, Walter French, who had been the Royal Navy's Chief Engineering Artificer. During the Second World War he was recalled to the reserve and posted to the RN test laboratories at Teddington, where he was in charge of the tanks used to develop Barnes Wallis's famous 'bouncing bombs' which were employed with such devastating effect in the Dambusters' raids.

Being transplanted from east London to the Scottish seaside must have been a rude awakening for the Littlejohns. Young Bill was bored silly, but soon found himself a profitable sideline shipping fresh Scottish seafood by rail back to a neighbour in Vine Gardens who had a stall on Billingsgate Market. Skate was especially plentiful in the waters of the West of Scotland and was in great demand in London, where it had been in short supply since the start of the war. Bill would buy it off the local fishermen, box it up, packed in ice, and his neighbour would meet the cargo off the train at Euston. The enterprise kept Bill sane and in pocket money until he was old enough to join up. Fried skate wing would become his favourite fish for the rest of his life. He'd even eat the bones.

Although life in Fairlie was safer than east London, which was coming under regular bombardment from the Luftwaffe, the Littlejohns never really settled in Scotland. They had rarely ventured further than Clacton and Southend on the Essex coast, even though they were one of the first families in Vine Gardens to own a car. Their end-of-terrace house stood out from the rest by virtue of its garage.

Stevedores, who worked on the ships unloading cargoes, considered themselves a cut above mere dock labourers. They had their own union, the NAS&D, known as the 'Blues' – named after the colour of their membership cards – to distinguish themselves from their bitter rivals, the 'Whites', in the much larger TGWU. To reflect this enhanced status, Bill Sr bought himself a Wolseley – an exclusive marque usually associated with middle-class doctors and solicitors, not hairy arsed manual workers – which he later traded in for a brand new Ford 8. But dock work was arduous, dangerous and involved long and what we would call today anti-social hours. Stevedores' pay reflected that and the Littlejohns lived well by the standards of the 1930s working class. They owned their own home in leafy Ilford, then a distinctive town in its own right before metropolitan sprawl turned the eastern fringes of Essex into part of suburban Greater London.

Their exodus from the East End to Essex, from the inner city to the suburbs, was the beginning of a trend which began in the late 1920s, accelerated after the war and continues to this day. The Littlejohns were part of the aspirant working class, determined to get up, get on and get out. Half a century later these were the kind of people, the so-called C2s in marketing speak, who had once supported Labour but who switched to Mrs Thatcher and the Conservatives in search of a more affluent tomorrow.

In 1987, the Labour leader Neil Kinnock made a speech to his party's conference in which he tried to explain the reasons for Labour's third successive defeat at the handbag of Mrs Thatcher.

Adopting a cod Cockney accent intended to mimic the then TGWU general secretary Ron Todd, Kinnock posed a rhetorical question which nailed the failure of Labour's clapped-out collectivist model:

> *'What do you say to a docker who earns £400 a week, owns his own house, a new car, a microwave, as well as a small place near Marbella?*
>
> *'You do not say,' he continued, '"Bruvver, let me take you out of your misery".'*

OK, so in the 1930s microwave ovens hadn't been invented and second-home aspirations stretched no further than a beach hut in Margate, rather than a villa in Marbella.

But that aside, Kinnock could have been talking about Bill Littlejohn Sr. Vine Gardens was a considerable step up from the cramped terraced house a few miles west in East Ham where they started married life.

Young Bill was born in that house, in Grosvenor Gardens, in July 1924, a long throw-in from West Ham football ground. His parents met in the wake of the First World War and were married soon afterwards. Min French grew up in Poplar, east London, and after leaving school at fourteen went into service, like so many women of her class and generation.

Her father was the butler and sometime food taster for a rich American sewing machine manufacturer who kept a house in central London, in wealthy Belgravia. Family legend has it that he died after tasting poisoned food intended for his master. Whatever the cause of his premature death, he was given a full East End 'state funeral' cortège complete with plumed horses and elaborate floral tributes. It was way beyond the modest means of the French family and was the kind of send off later reserved for bare-knuckle fighters, 'diamond geezers' and, later, East End gangsters such as the Kray Twins.

This wasn't the first tragedy to befall the French family. Min's paternal grandfather ran a fleet of horse-drawn hackney carriages, which provided him with a comfortable income in the mid-to-late 1800s. But as fate would have it, one night the stables in Fulham burned down, destroying all his cabs and killing the horses. Needless to say, he was not insured and was left destitute. Had her grandfather prospered, had her father not died young, perhaps Min would have enjoyed the life of a well-to-do young lady and would not have been forced into service. She would probably have gone through life being called by her above-stairs given name of Amelia, not the below-stairs diminutive, Min. She certainly wouldn't have wed a docker, who would have been considered below her station.

If Amelia French hadn't married William Henry Littlejohn, Bill Littlejohn wouldn't have been born.

And neither would I.

Despite being dumped in the Irish Sea on his maiden voyage, shelled by his own side in Marseilles and getting paralytic drunk for the first and only time in his life on dark rum in Casablanca – an episode of which he had no memory and involved him being carried back on board ship by his shipmates and left to stew in his bunk – Bill managed to survive the war unscathed. In fact, while he was onshore in Marseilles, orchestrating the bombardments over ship-to-shore radio, his ship, *Verity*, suffered a direct hit and sank to the bottom of the Med.

At the cessation of hostilities, he ended up in Gibraltar, where he learned he was to be demobbed. On the day he was to be transported back to England, he decided he needed a souvenir of his adventures.

Some men return home from battle with an enemy bayonet, some with a shell case, some with a dose of the clap. Bill wanted something to demonstrate to his family that his sacrifice – and theirs – had not been in vain. Fruit and vegetables had been in short supply in England during the war and bananas, in particular, were virtually nonexistent. People craved bananas, which had become an almost forbidden delicacy.

So he visited a local market and bought a stem of bananas. Not a bunch of bananas, or a hand of bananas – a *stem* of bananas. A stem contains up to twenty hands, each of which in turn can contain up to ten individual bananas.

He returned to his ship carrying what was in effect a small tree, laden with up to two-hundred bananas, weighing over 100lb. He must have looked like a two-legged version of Carmen Miranda's hat.

By the time he left Gibraltar the bananas were already beginning to ripen. When he arrived in Portsmouth in full naval uniform they were turning brown and giving off a pungent odour. He managed to manhandle the bananas and his seabag, or duffel bag, on to the train to Waterloo, where he was given a wide berth by other passengers and secured a carriage to himself on account of the sweet, suffocating stench of the ripening fruit.

From there he took the bus to Liverpool Street, where he was to catch the overground train home to Ilford. The conductor helped him on board with his six-feet-tall tree and joked that he should charge him double fare. Bill paid him in bananas.

His family knew he would be home that day, but not when. Consequently, no one was waiting to greet him at Ilford station.

It was late afternoon, there were no cabs on the rank, so he decided to walk the mile home along Ilford Lane, his seabag over one shoulder, his stem of bananas over the other.

As he approached Vine Gardens, he spotted red, white and blue bunting draped across the entrance to the street, complete with a huge banner reading: 'Welcome Home Bill'.

He was horrified. Bill was essentially a shy man, never one for ceremony, and certainly had no intention of playing the returning hero. So he turned tail and ran as fast as his load would allow him, taking refuge in the garden of the church hall on the other side of the road.

Passers-by out walking their dogs must have wondered

about the strange fruit tree that had sprouted, apparently from nowhere, among the bushes. He eventually returned home under cover of darkness, bearing his bruised and battered bounty. Despite the fact that the bananas were ripe to the point of rotting, they were instantly transformed into the focus of a homecoming feast – mashed with Carnation evaporated tinned milk and caster sugar, liberated from the Royal Docks. While family, friends and neighbours filled their boots, Bill sloped off for a quiet cigarette. He'd completely lost his appetite for bananas.

In the eighteen months after VE Day 1945, nearly four and a half million servicemen and women were demobbed. Most returned home to an uncertain future. Bill Littlejohn was no exception. Before the war, he had hoped to go to art college and become a graphic designer, an ambition he never realised. By 1945, it was a bit late. He needed a job, but wasn't prepared to take just any job. His father offered to fix him up with work as a docker.

Generations of Littlejohns had worked the river and the jobs were traditionally handed from father to son, like the print, where other members of the family worked. Prior to joining the army and before he started at the Royals at the end of the First World War, Bill Sr had been apprenticed to a printing firm in Moorgate, in the City of London. Before the war, it was possible that Young Bill would have followed his dad and grandfather into the Royal Docks. But the Second World War changed everything, broadening the horizons of those who fought.

Most had no intention of returning to the old ways. So Bill told his dad 'thanks, but no thanks' and set about launching himself in a new direction. Although he had acquired experience of working with wireless while in the Royal Navy, there wasn't much call for a ship-to-shore radio operator in peacetime. Like millions of other young men who had joined up in their teens, he'd never had a proper job before he went off to war. There was a four-year gap where further education and training might otherwise have been.

He still harboured hopes of making a career in graphic design and decided to pitch himself to print firms and advertising agencies in the City of London. But he faced two pressing problems: available jobs were in high demand and short supply. There were chronic shortages of materials and firms weren't hiring. And now he was living back home, it meant there was an extra mouth to feed in the Littlejohn family and Bill would be required to contribute to his keep.

While he looked for work, he would pay his mum housekeeping out of the small stipend he was given when he was demobbed. Depending on length of service, demobbed personnel received an average lump sum of between £65 and £150 on leaving the armed forces.

Every morning he would set out to walk the eight and half miles into the City in search of gainful employment. He even told his mother and father he had found a job, rather than admit that he was still unemployed.

It was a pretence he kept up for months, leaving the house suited and booted, trudging into London, knocking on doors, returning home every evening after a fruitless seventeen-mile round trip hike.

So why didn't he just come clean and tell his parents his search for a job had proved fruitless? The main reason was that his dad would have insisted he took a job in the docks, something he was determined to avoid, not out of any kind of snobbery, or because he was afraid of the kind of back-breaking manual labour which had always put food on the Littlejohns' table, but because he felt that his contribution to the war effort had earned him a tilt at a better future.

The second reason was that memories of the mass unemployment during the Great Depression still lingered and there was a residual stigma attached to being without work, even when it was through no fault of your own. I shudder to think what he would have made of modern Britain, where the welfare state has shamelessly institutionalised idleness as a way of life and six million people sit at home claiming an assortment of out-of-work benefits, while jobs they could be doing are filled by foreign immigrants imbued with the work ethic.

Shortly before the last of his demob money ran out, Bill noticed a recruitment advertisement for the Metropolitan Police. On a whim, he walked into Ilford nick and volunteered his services. His application was successful and overnight Young Bill became Old Bill.

A couple of weeks later he was undergoing basic training at Hendon Police College in north-west London. At the end of his probationary period he was told to report to Fulham Police Station in west London.

In those days, it was the policy of the Met to transfer new recruits as far as possible away from their home turf. The view was that coppers working their old stamping ground might be unduly influenced by local villains they may have grown up with. Fulham was about as far away from Ilford as it was then possible to get within the Metropolitan Police district. In 1945, Fulham was a scruffy suburb, not the swanky, up-itself Sloane Ranger overspill area it has since become.

It was while working at Fulham that Bill discovered the delights of cat racing. On his first night patrol, the sergeant instructed all beat officers to round up a stray cat and assemble at midnight on Parsons Green, the village green next to the home of the Vicar of Fulham. How were they to know which cats were strays and which were domestic pets enjoying a night on the tiles? Use your initiative, the sergeant said.

At the appointed hour, half a dozen of London's

finest boys in blue congregated on the green, each armed with a squealing cat concealed beneath their rain capes. On the command 'Pre-*sent* cats' they were ordered to form a line while holding their moggie by the tail at arm's length.

They were then instructed to unsheath their truncheons and on the order 'On your marks, get set, GO!' whack the cats on the backside and let go of their tails.

The first cat to screech its way across the park was declared the winner and the losing cat 'owners' would have to stand the 'winning owner' a full English breakfast back at the canteen. White City Dog Track it wasn't.

After a couple of years of dealing with drunks, kerb-crawlers and pickpockets, Bill became an aide to CID and spent some time at Scotland Yard. But his heart wasn't in it. He'd already spent four years in a disciplined service, as a naval rating, and had tired of taking orders. It was time to move on. That's his story, anyway. His kid brother insists that Bill's decision to leave the Metropolitan Police was influenced by the discovery of a dangerous liaison he was having with the teenage daughter of a disapproving Assistant Chief Constable at Scotland Yard.

Whatever the reason, Young Bill resigned from the Old Bill and joined the newly nationalised British Railways as a clerk.

Which is where he met my mum.

*

Margaret Kathleen Sparke was the eldest daughter of Albert Edward Sparke, known as Bert, and Hilda Louise Moxham. Bert was nine years older than Hilda and brought with him to the marriage a son, Ron, by his first wife, who died from complications shortly after the boy was born. Milk fever, they called it.

Bert and Hilda's relationship was not untypical of the time. Nor was the age gap. After the First World War, young men were in short supply. The trenches and the subsequent influenza pandemic had drained Britain's pool of eligible bachelors.

Hundreds of thousands of 'pals' who responded enthusiastically to Lord Kitchener's exhortation to fight for King and Country at the start of the war had perished or come home horribly disfigured.

Bert had been luckier. He spent the war as a farrier, looking after the horses that pulled the gun carriages for the Royal Artillery but never saw active service in France.

There's a sepia-tinted photograph somewhere of Bert and his favourite horse, Blackie, taken around 1916. Anyone who called a horse Blackie today would be damned as a racist and find himself charged with a hate crime.

Plenty of women of marriageable age, like Hilda, who was born in 1900, faced the prospect of marrying older men who had escaped the hostilities, on account of their age or because they worked in reserved occupations. Either that, or they would remain spinsters for the rest of their lives.

That isn't to say all these marriages were unhappy. By all accounts, Hilda fell on her feet. Bert was a bit of a catch, a handsome, hail-fellow-well-met character, who liked a drink and smoked like the *Flying Scotsman*. He was a pipe man, but not averse to a cigarette.

Bert was a dapper chap, always in a suit and tie: the heart and soul of every party, from the office party to the Labour Party; chairman of every society going, from the bowls club to the billiards team; member of Essex County Cricket Club; and active in the Railway Clerks' Association, the trades union which represented white-collar rail staff.

Bert and Hilda married in 1926. Unlike most newly-weds, who had no alternative but to move in with their parents, Bert already had a home. So Hilda swapped her job in a lampshade factory for that of housewife in Hockley, Essex, complete with ready made family.

In 1928, the family expanded with the birth of their first daughter, Margaret, followed three years later by her younger sister, Olive. They moved into a new home in a cul-de-sac in Gidea Park, what we would now call an 'upwardly mobile' suburb of Romford. Bert's garden at Gidea Park was his pride and joy. Every morning in the summer he'd tap the barometer in the hall, step outside and pick one of his prize roses for his buttonhole.

Margaret was a pretty, clever girl, who everyone thought was destined for grammar school. But her education was interrupted by an illness she contracted from drinking unpasteurised milk, a virulent strain of tuberculosis in her glands, resulting in frequent hospital visits.

At one stage she had to wear a fearsome wooden brace from her neck to her feet and was taken for regular treatment at the specialist Great Ormond Street children's hospital.

Margaret left school at fourteen and her dad fixed her up with a clerical job in his office. Towards the end of the war, Bert and Margaret returned home to find their cul-de-sac had taken a direct hit.

Until that time, Gidea Park had escaped relatively unscathed as German bombers passed overhead destined for London's docks and the Ford motor factory on the Thames at Dagenham. One day in 1944, that luck ran out.

While Bert and Margaret were at work, a V1 rocket known as a 'doodlebug' had come down short of its target. Hilda and Olive were home at the time and were propelled across the room by the explosion but neither was seriously injured, save for a few cuts and bruises. Their house suffered only minor damage but other properties were completely destroyed. Such is the random nature of war.

When peace was declared in 1945, Margaret and Olive took the train to London to join the celebrations in Trafalgar Square. The Sparke family resumed their routine.

Three years later, Margaret was working as a secretary in the offices of British Railways at Stratford, east London, then as now a major rail hub, complete with its own workshops.

It was here she met her future husband, ex-Royal Navy, ex-Met. policeman and amateur cat jockey, Bill Littlejohn.

At first, she wasn't sure where the relationship was going. During the early weeks of their courtship, Bill had an unnerving habit of falling asleep during all the movies and West End shows he took her to see. Margaret interpreted this either as narcolepsy or a lack of interest. It turned out that Bill had seen them all before, with a previous girlfriend.

Their love affair survived this early setback, they became engaged and in 1951 they married. By the standards of the day their honeymoon was spectacular. Most couples had to settle for a weekend in Brighton but Bill and Margaret embarked on married life with the adventure of a lifetime.

Working on the railways wasn't the best paid employment around. Bill would almost certainly have brought home twice as much every week had he chosen to follow his father into the docks. But British Railways managerial staff were entitled to one important perk – free first-class rail travel, including on mainland Europe.

Bill and Margaret set off across France for an idyllic honeymoon in Switzerland, which had remained neutral in 1939–45 and thus escaped the ravages of war. The contrast with bomb-scarred London couldn't have been more pronounced. They spent a week in a pristine Alpine hotel, breathing the mountain air. They felt as if they were in another world.

Returning to England, it was back to reality. Although they'd spent their three-year engagement saving for their own home and collecting for Margaret's 'bottom drawer', they moved in with Bill's parents in Ilford.

On reflection, it seems strange writing that last sentence, which really does belong to another world. How many couples are 'engaged' for three years these days before getting married? Does anyone get engaged any more? And if they do, they remain engaged and don't bother getting married. I suppose it saves them joining the 50 per cent of modern married couples who end up getting divorced after about five minutes.

In an age of instant credit and 110 per cent mortgages, does anyone actually save up for their own home in the twenty-first century? A Conservative-led government, which supposedly believes in thrift, will even underwrite your mortgage, despite the fact that excessive borrowing and reckless lending were the main causes of the biggest banking crash since the Great Depression.

As for a 'bottom drawer', that's probably where most young women keep their Rampant Rabbits today.

In 1951, rampant rabbits were what my grandad shot on the allotments round the corner from Vine Gardens.

It was supposed to be a temporary billet. Bill and Margaret had bought a plot of land in Shenfield, Essex, intending to build a chalet bungalow. Chalet bungalows were all the rage in the fifties. I wonder if they were hoping to recreate the romance of their Swiss honeymoon in the Essex countryside.

The total cost, including construction, came to approximately £1500, which, adjusted according to official government inflation statistics, is equivalent to just under £40,000 today.

If you want a better guide to the astronomical rate of house price inflation over the past six decades, ask an estate agent. In the summer of 2013, a three-bedroom bungalow (not even a chalet bungalow) in Crossways, the same street as the house Bill and Margaret built, was being advertised for sale at £550,000. A four-bedroom home round the corner was up for £1.4 million. No wonder so many young couples struggle to get a foot on the housing ladder today.

Still, in 1951 even £1500 was a small fortune on a British Railways salary. They chose Shenfield because it was the last station on the electrified railway line into Liverpool Street, via Stratford. Beyond Shenfield, it was steam all the way and a slower journey time to work.

Prices, therefore, were a balancing act, reflecting both the speed of journey and the relatively long distance into Town. As you moved nearer London, the cost of housing increased accordingly until you reached the run-down East End.

They'd hoped that their new home would be completed within a year, if not less. But Britain was still suffering from post-war shortages. All available skilled men and materials were diverted to providing homes for those who had been bombed out.

So Bill and Margaret were destined to spend the first three years of their married lives in the spare bedroom of his parents' house in Ilford. It can't have been an ideal arrangement, especially with a younger brother also living at home, but it was far from uncommon.

Whatever the privations, they must have had some time to themselves. Margaret became pregnant twice. The first time she miscarried early in her term. The second was in 1953, the year of the Coronation.

When she went into labour, they weren't taking any chances. Bert, in particular, was concerned for his daughter. His first wife had died as a result of complications caused by childbirth and Margaret had already miscarried.

It was obviously going to be a big baby and a long haul. In those days, most babies were born at home, not in hospital.

The midwife was summoned early and Margaret was attended by both her mother and her mother-in-law. And probably, if truth be told, by an assortment of aunties and most of the women in the street, clucking in anticipation.

Kettles were boiled.

Back in the 1950s, the birth of a child was considered women's work. Fathers were not wanted on voyage, unlike today when men are expected to do everything except actually having the baby.

Which is how Bill found himself banished from the scene of the 'happy event' and ended up in the garage, painting the midwife's bike.

They weren't kidding when they said Margaret was carrying a big baby. I weighed in at 10lb 8oz when I was born. Mum said it was like giving birth to a Christmas turkey.

Grandad Littlejohn was especially delighted that his eldest son now had a boy of his own to keep the dynasty going. Panatellas all round.

The eldest son of the eldest son had always been christened William Henry. Dad was William Henry Littlejohn VII. I was destined to be William Henry VIII. As the old Harry Champion music-hall song, later turned into a pop hit in the sixties by Herman's Hermits, might have put it:

Every one was William 'Enery.
They wouldn't have a Jimmy or a Sam . . .

Margaret had other ideas.

For clarity's sake I have up to now referred to my dad as Bill, Young Bill or Bill Jr. While technically correct, that's not entirely accurate. Within the family he was more usually known as Johnny, to distinguish him from all the other Williams in the family.

To add to the confusion, other branches of the Littlejohns also favoured the name William. And a couple of my grandad's sisters had married men called Bill. By the time I arrived, there were several of them. Bill, Old Bill, Young Bill, Billy, Young Billy, Will . . .

Years later I laughed out loud at the scene in *The Sopranos*, in which Tony tried to explain why his cousin was also called Tony. To tell them apart Tony Soprano was known as 'Tony Uncle Johnny' and his cousin was called 'Tony Uncle Al', after their respective fathers.

If the Littlejohns had followed that principle I could have ended up being called 'Billy Uncle Johnny' or even 'Billy Uncle Bill'.

The only derivative of William left by the time I entered the world was 'Willie'. And Mum was determined – much to my subsequent relief – that her first born son wasn't going to be called Little Willie.

A stand-off ensued, with my dad stranded in

no-man's-land between his traditionalist father and his determined wife. For the first couple of weeks I was known as 'Buster', the name they'd given me while I was still in the womb.

It was a period of intense negotiation and shuttle diplomacy before a compromise was reached. For all I know, my maternal grandfather Bert Sparke was drafted in to bring his experience of trades union collective bargaining to bear. I'm surprised the matter wasn't referred to binding arbitration. Certainly both sides threatened to walk out.

Eventually, a deal was struck. Over beer and sandwiches, I like to think. Towards the end of January 1954, Bill and Margaret finally registered the birth of their son, Richard William Littlejohn.

Where she got 'Richard' from remains a matter of conjecture, lost in the mists of time. The original story was that I was named after the American actor Richard Widmark, who starred in a string of gung-ho, post-war movies, including *The Halls of Montezuma* and *Hell and High Water*. Another version has me named for the young Richard Burton, who had just finished giving his *Hamlet* and *Coriolanus* at the Old Vic.

Mum's story has changed over the years. My guess is that I wasn't named after anyone in particular. Richard was simply plucked from the 'anything but Willie' files.

I've always liked to think that the real inspiration was Richard Greene, who played Robin Hood in the popular

TV series, especially given the Little John connection. Unfortunately, that theory collapsed when I realised that the first series didn't appear until 1955, the year after I was born.

I'm not sure Grandad Littlejohn was ever reconciled to the name Richard. What I do remember is that he was ecstatic when my son was christened William Richard Littlejohn in 1979. There's a treasured picture of the four of us Littlejohn eldest sons of eldest sons sitting on a fireplace in the early 1980s. Grandad is grinning from ear to ear with pride. I'm the odd one out.

My birth was registered at Ilford Town Hall, a neo-classical Grade II Listed building opened in 1901. Happily, it is still used today as the headquarters of Redbridge Council, unlike many other Edwardian and Victorian municipal offices, which were replaced by bland, jerry-built 'Civic Centres' in the name of modernity in the sixties and seventies. The romance of Ilford Town Hall was commemorated in song by the brilliant surrealist comedian Marty Feldman, one of a series of compositions imagining London architectural landmarks as a range of jewellery:

I'm sending you this little gift of Ilford Town Hall,
To wear around your neck till I return.
It isn't very much,

Just a homely touch,
To remind you that the flame of love will always burn.
The Albert Memorial doesn't match your eyes.
And West Ham Baths, I know you'd spurn.
So please accept this little gift of Ilford Town Hall,
Till I return!

Genius. Pure genius. They don't make 'em like that any more.

With the Shenfield chalet bungalow not yet complete, the first six months of my life were spent at Vine Gardens. Food was still on the ration and there was another, ravenous mouth to feed.

Rationing, which was introduced in January 1940, four months after the outbreak of the Second World War, didn't officially end until fourteen years later, on 4 July 1954, Britain's very own Independence Day.

Not that anyone went hungry in our house. Dockers probably had the best diet in London, given their easy access to imported food from all over the Empire.

I'm told the men who worked at the docks always wore long coats, even in the hottest weather, complete with deep poachers' pockets to carry their contraband home.

My grandfather, like his own father, worked for a company called Scruttons, which was based at Prince

Albert Dock and imported frozen meat. New Zealand lamb chops were never in short supply in Vine Gardens.

Grandad was an uncomplicated man, built like a brick outhouse. He might have been the better looking big brother of the actor Bernard Bresslaw, the gentle giant from the *Carry On* films.

Every week he'd plonk his pickings and his pay packet on the kitchen table. His wife would give him his pocket money and he'd head off to the pub for a pint.

There was a clear division of labour in the Littlejohn household, as there was in just about every other home in the land.

Min, my nanna, was the brains and the powerhouse of the operation, managing the finances and family welfare. Her slight frame belied a fierce intellect. She had a voracious appetite for books, which she would pass on to me when I was old enough to read.

Vine Gardens would feature in my life for the next fifteen years, but in the summer of 1954, Bill and Margaret and their baby son finally took possession of their own home.

When we moved in, Mum and Dad had little more than hand-me-down furniture. Every spare penny they had they sank into buying the land, building the house and paying the mortgage.

Shenfield railway station was only a couple of hundred yards' walk away. Each morning my dad would take the train to work at Stratford, leaving Mum to play house and look after me.

She wasn't short of support. My maternal grandparents, Bert and Hilda Sparke, were six miles down the road in Gidea Park. Bert was still working on the railways, too, like just about everyone else in his family.

Bert's eldest brother, Joseph Fuller Sparke, Uncle Joe, was the most successful, rising to superintendant at King's Cross station, in charge of the entire London North Eastern region. He wore a bowler hat and pinstripe trousers to work and lived in a grand company house on the Caledonian Road – then a desirable address, today a scruffy, inner-city slum full of transients.

Grandad Sparke never ascended to the same dizzy heights as Uncle Joe. His ambitions lay closer to home. But he had a responsible job, respected by all.

Bert's world extended in all directions way beyond Gidea Park and the Stratford railway depot. He was well known on the manor, as the saying goes. Bert knew everyone and everyone knew Bert.

He arranged our first family holiday that year, using his Essex CCC connections to fix up my dad with a job as a car park attendant at the annual Southend cricket festival.

While Bill called on his police point duty experience to marshall the Morris Oxfords and Austin A40s, Mum and Nanna would take me to the beach and feed me Rossi's ice cream. Dad's wages paid for the hire of a caravan for the duration. It was to be the first of many happy family holidays, but the last we spent with Grandad Sparke.

It was only a matter of time before the smoking caught up with him. It didn't help that he spent every working day inhaling the coal-fired fumes of the steam locomotives in the engine shed next to his office. In December 1955, he was taken into hospital with a rasping cough and severe breathing difficulties. Days before Christmas he died, officially of heart failure. He was sixty-four.

Today, he would have been diagnosed with lung cancer or emphysema. But even back then, no one was in any doubt. It was the tobacco that killed him. His doctor warned him, his wife warned him, his family warned him, his friends warned him.

The dangers of smoking were already widely accepted, even though practically everyone smoked, including most doctors.

I grew up well aware that pipe tobacco and cigarettes had killed my grandad. Cigarettes weren't known as 'coffin nails' and 'cancer sticks' for nothing.

So why have successive modern governments felt it necessary to spend millions upon millions of taxpayers' money on intelligence insulting campaigns to 'educate' us about the dangers of smoking?

As more and more people quit, they've even had to invent 'passive smoking' to justify their nannying excess. If 'passive smoking' really did exist, no one of my generation would have lived beyond their teens.

What always puzzled me was that my other grandfather seemed to smoke just as much as Bert. Grandad Littlejohn rolled his own, but with apparently little ill effect. He eventually gave up smoking when he was seventy-five and lived into his nineties. There was a school of thought that if he hadn't rashly given up smoking, the nicotine might have prevented the onset of Alzheimer's, which finally robbed him of his faculties.

Perhaps everyone who reaches seventy-five should be prescribed cigarettes on the NHS. At that advanced age, you won't have long enough to contract lung cancer but the nicotine may stop you going doolally.

When Bert was taken into hospital, my Aunt Olive, Mum's younger sister, was in Canada. It took days to contact her and arrange passage home. Today, she'd have a 4G mobile phone with international roaming. It would take as long to find her as it took to dial the number or send a text. She'd be home in hours, not days, on the first plane out overnight.

But that was the end of Olive's North American adventure, at least for a few years. She moved back to Gidea Park to look after Nanna Sparke.

Yet Nanna was just fifty-five when Bert died. In the twenty-first century, it might seem strange that a woman of fifty-five would be considered old. She certainly didn't need anyone to 'look after' her. But that was what families did in the fifties.

I'm assuming that Bert left her reasonably provided for, with a small British Railways pension and probably some kind of modest life insurance policy, which would have paid out a small lump sum on his death. There would have been no help from the government. Nanna wouldn't qualify for her state pension for another five years. Even then, pensions were set at subsistence level. A few months earlier, thousands of elderly people took part in a rally in London demanding a raise in the single person's pension to £2 10s. (£2.50). So no doubt Olive's regular wage packet was welcome and helped with the bills. She was only doing what was expected.

We had a large extended family. When I say 'family' I don't mean they were all blood relatives, although plenty were. Social mobility hadn't reality taken off and most people lived and worked within a few miles of where they were born.

Moving to Shenfield made Margaret and Bill frontier folk, the furthest outpost of the immediate Littlejohn/Sparke clan. Maybe we should have travelled from Ilford in a covered waggon. The Littlejohn branch was still centred around east London, the Sparkes a few miles further east, in Essex.

Grandad Littlejohn was the eldest of ten brothers and

sisters. Grandad Sparke also came from a large family. I couldn't keep track of them all.

In addition to all those related by blood or marriage, I also inherited an assortment of affiliated 'aunties' and 'uncles'. Everyone was Uncle This or Auntie That. To make matters even more baffling, some of them had the same first name, like the William Henry Littlejohns.

There were at least two, possibly three, Auntie Mays, a smattering of Uncle Arthurs and more Bills than you could shake a stick at.

My favourite uncle was Mum's cousin Eddie, a bit of a wide boy who turned up at their wedding wearing a George Raft-style, double-breasted, pinstripe suit and spats. All that was missing was the violin case.

Eddie looked like the George Cole 'Flash Harry' character in the *St Trinian's* movies. He was a ducker and diver, but he'd give you his last farthing. Eddie lived in nearby Brentwood and was always at Crossways, helping with odd jobs.

He was a fabulous uncle and would have made a great father but neither of his marriages produced children. When I was older, I can remember overhearing the men talk about Eddie 'firing blanks'. I assumed this was something to do with his National Service in the army.

Although he effected the swagger of a spiv, Eddie was soft as newly churned butter. Later in life he worked as a driver for the torch singer and sometime gay icon

Kathy Kirby, who had a smash hit in the sixties with 'Secret Love'.

Every day Eddie would drive Kathy from her home in Essex to a clinic in London, where she was being treated for chronic alcoholism. And every day on the way home, they would stop at the same off-licence where Eddie would nip in and buy her a bottle of gin for the return journey.

Olive was working as a hairdresser in a salon in Brentwood, then a fairly staid, respectable, unspoilt Essex coaching town on the main road from London to Colchester and the port of Harwich. A 'permanent wave' and a blue rinse was about as adventurous as it got in the 1950s.

Today, the salons of Brentwood specialise in nail extensions, tanning treatments, vajazzles and 'Brazilians' of every stripe, catering to the peroxide, perma-tanned slatterns of the ghastly TV 'reality' show, *The Only Way Is Essex* and their low-rent *TOWIE* wannabes.

Goodness only knows what Nanna Sparke would have made of the modern breed of Essex Girl.

Still, who am I to grumble? Thirty-five years later, together with my friend Mitch Symons, I co-wrote the best-selling *Essex Girl Joke Book*, under the pseudonyms Ray Leigh and Brent Wood, with a foreword by Professor Theydon Bois, from the Romford Library of Video. 'Reem', as they say on *TOWIE*. Whatever the hell that means.

★

In the fifties, fresh air was the cure-all, the essential require-
ment for good health. Before the Clean Air Act was passed
in 1956, smog – a lethal mix of smoke and fog – was
commonplace, even in suburban areas such as Ilford. The
act was a response to the Great Smog of December 1952.
A foul-smelling, yellow-brown blanket descended on
London, which left four thousand people dead and brought
road, rail and air transport to a standstill. It lasted several
days and was so widespread that it was even reported to
have choked cows to death in the fields.

Factories, homes and steam trains were all coal-fired,
filling the air with a rancid cocktail of carcinogenic pollut-
ants. Combined with low cloud and wet fog, the air quickly
turned toxic. Not surprisingly, respiratory illnesses were
commonplace.

Shenfield was far enough from London to offer respite
from the frequent smogs. I was one of the chief benefi-
ciaries, spending much of my early life in a pram in the
garden in all weathers.

Few modern mums would dream of leaving their
babies in the garden for hours on end, for fear that the
child would be carried off by the 'peed-io-files' who lurk
behind every hedge. Either that, or they'd face a dawn
raid from social services for child abandonment.

With Dad away at work, or attending evening classes
studying for his diploma in purchasing and supply, Mum
was left alone with me.

Not that she was alone, alone. Olive came for lunch every day, in the grey sit-up-and-beg Ford Popular which Nanna had never bothered to learn to drive while Bert was alive.

Most days I'd be taken for a long walk in my pram, to the park, to the shops. Shopping was part of the daily routine, since few homes had a refrigerator to keep food fresh.

Shenfield shopping parade boasted butcher, baker and, if not candlestick-maker, every commodity a housewife needed. The shopkeepers knew all their customers by name.

Mum would have been 'Mrs Littlejohn' even though she would have seemed little more than a slip of a girl to the long-established purveyors of goods various to the gentlefolk of Shenfield.

This was before supermarkets started eating into independent retailers. It would be another five decades before the advent of the internet would turn suburban shopping parades into identikit wastelands, littered with hideous coffee chains, charity shops and cut-price establishments offering a cornucopia of tat for a pound.

The daily shop afforded regular adult human contact and stopped young mothers with only a mewling, puking infant for company from climbing the walls or seeking solace in a bottle of Harvey's Bristol Cream.

Pushing a pram for miles every day also meant that

women of my mother's generation had no need for expensive Pilates and spinning classes to keep them young and beautiful. Housework provided all the stretching and aerobic exercise they needed.

When I was presenting a mid-morning radio show on London's LBC in the early 1990s, I asked Barbara Castle, feminist and former Labour Cabinet minister, what she thought had made the greatest single contribution to women's liberation.

Expecting her to answer 'The Pill' or 'Universal Suffrage', she surprised me with her answer.

'The washing machine,' Castle said. It had freed women from the daily drudgery of washing clothes by hand, created time for them to pursue education and self-improvement. The fridge came a close second, removing the necessity of the daily shop.

In the mid-1950s, however, in common with around four out of five homes, we still didn't have what you'd call a proper washing machine. Mum had a 'copper' in which she boiled the washing in Dreft, her detergent of choice, before rinsing it in the sink. Terry-towelling nappies would be left to soak in a bucket in the bathroom.

As I got older, she turned washday into an adventure. I looked forward to it. My job was to turn the mangle, squeezing the surplus water out of the wet washing before it could be pegged out to dry in the garden in summer, or arranged on a wooden clothes horse in front of the coal-fired Potterton boiler in winter.

No doubt, if I'd thought to ask her, Barbara Castle would have agreed that the invention of disposable nappies in the 1970s was another giant leap for womankind. I'm sure my mum thought washing dirty nappies should be filed under: 'What's the worst job you ever had?'

Strange, then, that a quarter of a century later local councils were appointing legions of 'Real Nappy Co-ordinators' to coax women to dump disposables and embrace old-fashioned, reusable cotton nappies in the name of the 'environment' and saving the polar bears.

That's progress for you. One step up, two steps back.

My early years were dominated by women. Although the men were the breadwinners, they were largely absent except at weekends. Whatever modern feminists tell you about the oppression of women, family life in fifties Britain was a *de facto* matriarchy. My world revolved around my mother and my grandmothers, who were regular visitors to Crossways. Despite having little formal education, both nannas devoured books, had beautiful handwriting and an immaculate grasp of grammar, which they were determined to pass on to me.

The three of them would take turns reading to me from the moment I could sit up in my cot. Mum would spend hours teaching me phonetics – A is for Apple, B is for Ball, C is for Cat, D is for Dwarf, etc. I could recite the alphabet when I was two years old. By the time I went to nursery school, before my fourth birthday, I had the reading age of a much older child.

One of the greatest scandals of my lifetime was the abandonment of phonetic teaching by the educational establishment in favour of the trendy 'word recognition' method, which betrayed millions of schoolchildren, condemning them to leave school virtually illiterate.

Thanks to my mother and grandmothers, when I started primary school I had a greater level of literacy than many sixteen-year-old comprehensive school leavers in the late twentieth and early twenty-first centuries. Glib politicians who boasted that their priorities were 'education, education, education', in that order, robbed generations of youngsters of the vital tools of self-expression and comprehension. Employers despair of job applicants who can't spell and have never even been taught how to write a formal letter.

I was taught how to write 'thank you' letters before I started school. They didn't care what I read, either. Books or comics, every printed word was equally valid. I can remember my excitement when Nanna Sparke bought me the very first edition of *Harold Hare's Own Paper*.

Harold originally featured in the *Jack and Jill* comic, before being granted his very own eponymous publication. It cost 5d. (2p today) and was in such popular demand that it had to be ordered in advance from the local newsagents.

From Harold Hare, I graduated to the *Beano* and *Dandy*, and later to the *Boy's Own Paper*, *Hotspur* and *Hornet*, which were packed with tales of derring-do from the war. My heroes were Matt Braddock VC, an intrepid flying ace; Gorgeous Gus, an aristocrat who owned a football team; and the working-class athlete Alf Tupper.

Braddock practically won the Second World War single-handed, from what I could gather. Gorgeous Gus would turn up late, wander on to the pitch with five minutes left and score a sparkling hat-trick to snatch victory from the jaws of defeat. Alf Tupper, the Tough of the Track, would devour a pre-race meal of fish and chips before breaking yet another world record. 'I ran 'em all' was his catchphrase.

The big prize was finding one or more of these comics' bumper annuals in my Christmas stocking. That was enough to keep me quiet until dinner time.

My other Christmas treat was a 'Junior Smokers' Kit', a box of sweet cigarettes, chocolate cigars, matches and pipes. God alone knows what the modern health Nazis would make of any parent who gave their children a confectionery-based smoking kit these days. In 2014, we'd be raided by social services, my parents prosecuted and I would be taken into care, screaming and kicking and puffing on my pretend pipe.

On reflection, I was probably thoroughly ruined, not that I realised it at the time. Although Mum's half-brother Ron had two children, my older cousins, Jackie and Russell, who lived in nearby Harold Wood, I was Nanna Sparke's first grandchild by her own daughter. I was also Bill and Min's first grandchild and the eldest son of the eldest son had always enjoyed special status in the Littlejohn family, even if he was called Richard, not William Henry VIII.

My grandmothers would take me on day trips to give Mum a break from the ordeal of trying to keep her boisterous son entertained.

One of my earliest memories of London is being taken up to Town by Nanna Sparke. I couldn't have been more than about four, but I vividly recall the train journey to Liverpool Street and ascending the stairs to the top deck of a red Routemaster bus. This was the first time I can remember riding on a double-decker. The buses in Shenfield were all single-deckers.

Most of all I remember what I had for lunch. And where. J. Lyons and Co. began running tea shops in London in 1894. The first Corner House, built in the art deco style, opened the same year. The restaurants spread throughout the West End and were famous for the 'Nippies', waitresses in neat uniforms who served the tables. After the war, table service ended and the Corner Houses converted to cafeteria-style, self-service.

They were the nearest thing Britain had to Parisian working-class brasseries, specialising in affordable meals and fancy pastries.

I couldn't say in which Corner House we had lunch, but the memory of what I ate is vividly, indelibly, etched on my subconscious.

Proust had his madeleine. I have my knickerbocker glory. Invented in the 1930s, a knickerbocker glory is an ice-cream sundae, served in a tall glass, packed with layers of jelly, fruit, merangue, ice cream and topped with whipped cream, nuts and a cherry. The Lyons' version was also rumoured to contain a generous shot of sherry.

It was the biggest dessert I'd ever seen, eaten with the kind of long spoon usually recommended for supping with the devil. It cost half-a-crown (2s. 6d. in old money, twelve and a half pence today), a considerable sum of money in the fifties, but worth every penny, as far as I was concerned. Talk about the nectar of the gods.

The knickerbocker glory fell out of fashion from the sixties onwards and pretty much disappeared from menus following the closure of the last Corner House in 1977. But the memory never left me. As I write this, I can still taste it.

Fast forward thirty-five years to 2012, and TV's queen of baking, Mary Berry, is demonstrating her recipe for a traditional knickerbocker glory on the BBC's *Great British*

Food Revival, introducing the delights of this sumptuous, calorific dessert to a whole new generation.

Now that's what I call public service broadcasting.

When I was three, I was enrolled in a nursery school run by a middle-aged woman called Mrs Pritchard, in the front room of her home round the corner from Crossways on the way to the railway station. Come to think of it, it might be the same house being advertised for sale at £1.4 million in the summer of 2013.

There were maybe a dozen of us pre-school boys and girls in the class, which was held three mornings a week. It was more than just a glorified child-minding service. Mrs Pritchard took her responsibilities seriously and was pretty strict. She was getting on a bit and my mother thinks she may have been a retired teacher.

Although lessons were fun, lots of modelling with Plasticene and papier mâché and such, she did her best to prepare us for education proper. She read a story to us most mornings and those of us with rudimentary literacy skills were expected in return to read to the class as best we could.

Mrs P was also big on drama and made all her own props. Mum recalls her meticulously fashioning balsa-wood replica swords and cardboard armour for a play about King Arthur and his knights. Unfortunately, by the time the parents arrived to watch the performance, myself and another boy had gone at rehearsals a little too enthusiastically. The set had been smashed to smithereens, the cardboard castle was in ruins and all that was left of our swords were the handles.

By all accounts, I enjoyed being the centre of attention. In fact, it seems I enjoyed it rather too much.

One day, I was given a note to hand to my mother when she came to collect me at lunchtime. Mrs Pritchard requested that Mum ceased including a bottle of orange squash in my packed elevenses because, after drinking it, I insisted on burping loudly and repeatedly, setting an undesirable and frankly disreputable example to the rest of the class.

I'm assuming the offending drink was diluted Robinson's Orange Barley Water, as the only other orange juice that came into the house was provided by the fledgling National Health Service, established in 1948 and still in its infancy when we lived in Shenfield.

My generation of children was the first to benefit from 'free' healthcare. The emphasis was on prevention and from an early age we were subjected to a series of inoculations against everything from measles to polio.

There's no doubt that these inoculations led to a drastic reduction in disease and, especially, infant mortality.

Before the war, it was quite common for families to lose fairly young children to illnesses which, by the time the 1950s came around, were preventable and today are virtually nonexistent.

Bill and Min Littlejohn lost their second son, Dad's little brother Ronnie, in 1929. Ronnie went into isolation hospital suffering from diphtheria, a fiercely contagious upper-respiratory disease, and never came home. There was no vaccine available in the twenties.

Ronnie was just two and half years old when he died. Dad was only five at the time. He retained a life-long terror of doctors and hospitals, which he always associated with terminal illness.

We will never know for certain whether this morbid fear ultimately contributed to his own premature death from colon cancer, aged seventy-one, in 1995. Although he was exhibiting all the classic symptoms of the disease, he kept cancelling a series of doctor's appointments which my mother made for him, until it was too late. His doctor told me subsequently that if the cancer had been caught earlier there was every chance that it could have been treated successfully.

Our family GP in Shenfield was Dr Davidson. Unusually for the era, Dr Davidson was a woman. While nursing and midwifery were almost exclusively female occupations, few women advanced to become surgeons, consultants or general practitioners.

Her practice was within walking distance, in the shopping parade opposite the station. You didn't need an appointment; you just rolled up and took your turn.

Today, it's almost impossible to see an NHS GP the same day. You have to start ringing an automated number at 8 a.m. and hope you'll be allocated an appointment within the next couple of weeks, if you're lucky.

Even the fire-breathing dragons from whom the ranks of doctors' receptionists have traditionally been drawn were less frustrating to deal with than a computerised switchboard diverted via Delhi.

Dr Davidson also made home visits, day or night and at weekends, too. All GPs did until fairly recently. It was considered a normal part of their vocation.

That, of course, was before the 1997–2010 Labour government set about 'improving' the NHS. Despite Labour 'investing' billions of pounds of taxpayers' money in the health service, securing a home visit from a doctor is about as easy as getting seats for the Royal Box at Wimbledon on Men's Singles Final Day.

Labour awarded GPs handsome new, six-figure salaries and agreed, absurdly, that they could abandon evening and weekend cover. This led to an influx of dubious foreign locums and a crisis at overloaded accident and emergency departments.

If Dr Davidson is still alive, which is entirely possible given that she was probably still only in her twenties in the mid-to-late fifties, she must be horrified at the callous indifference towards patient care shown by her successors.

We were regular visitors to her surgery, for inoculations

and minor ailments. On other occasions, such as when I was confined to bed with German measles, she'd come to the house. Vaccination didn't always prevent you catching transmittable diseases, but it did mitigate the effects and render them non-lethal.

Mum also had to call out Dr Davidson to tend wounds I sustained when I dived head-first through our plate-glass front door, probably pretending to be Superman. These days, Mum would have to drive me thirty miles to the nearest casualty unit, where I'd spend six hours waiting to be seen before being sent home with an aspirin by a junior physician with English as a second language.

Dr Davidson also dispensed the free, sickly-sweet, syrupy orange juice for the under-fives, which had been made available on the NHS to ensure Vitamin C intake and strengthen immune systems.

It was a sensible precaution, but the only problem was that it was packed with corrosive levels of sugar. The orange juice may have warded off coughs and colds but it provided plenty of work for the expanding NHS dentistry service.

At weekends, Dad would be given the keys to the Ford Popular and, in summer, we'd head for the seaside. I'd ride in the back with Mum and Olive. Nanna Sparke would sit in the front passenger seat. There were no fancy child safety seats in those days.

Southend was just twenty miles away, down the Arterial Road from Gallows Corner, an ancient place of execution once popular with highwaymen who would lie in wait for passing coaches. Today it's a retail park, anchored by Tesco. It could be anywhere.

We'd set off as if equipped for a polar expedition, with enough tartan travel rugs, blankets and towels to service a small refugee camp.

We carried picnic hampers packed with Thermos flasks full of tepid tea, ham and egg sandwiches, fairy cakes and, Mum's favourite, Dairylea cheese triangles in a circular box. Base camp was established on the beach at Shoeburyness, the eastern Southend suburb later immortalised by the Bard of Upminster, Ian Dury, in his definitive love song to Essex, 'Billericay Dickie'.

> I know a lovely old toe-rag,
> Obliging and noblesse,
> Kindly, shoremaid shag from Shoeburyness.

The East Beach is considered one of the finest in the country, a mixture of sand and pebbles extending way out into the Estuary, where the mud begins.

Deckchairs and windbreaks were hired from a hut on the sea front. No British summer holiday would be complete without a windbreak, especially at Southend, where gale-force winds come roaring up the Estuary.

In what other country would a seaside town like Skegness seek to attract visitors by boasting that it was 'So Bracing'? Southend could certainly give its East Coast rival a run for its money in the 'bracing' stakes.

We always came home from the coast with ruddy complexions, not so much sun-tanned as wind-chafed. I don't recall ever being smothered in suntan lotion, if such a thing existed in the fifties. Sunburn was treated with liberally applied calamine lotion. Mum swore by Nivea face cream.

Long before Ian Dury saluted Shoeburyness in song, the artist Joseph Mallord William Turner, who gave his name to the modern Turner Prize, committed the town to canvas in his oil painting *Shoeburyness Fishermen Hailing a Whitstable Hoy* in 1809, part of his Thames Estuary series. For some unfathomable reason, the painting now hangs in the National Gallery of Canada.

In Keith Waterhouse's marvellous play *Jeffrey Bernard Is Unwell*, Bernard laments the fact that his architect father's celebrated Art Deco entrance to the Strand Palace Hotel is on display at the Victoria and Albert Museum:

In any other country it would still be outside the Strand Palace.

Precisely. In any other country, Turner's painting of Shoeburyness would be on display in Shoeburyness, or Southend Town Hall. At the very least, it would hang in the National Gallery in London, not the National Gallery of Canada in Ottawa. I've never understood why we cling stubbornly to foreign treasures such as the Elgin Marbles but display such a cavalier attitude towards our own heritage.

Often we'd have a stretch of the beach pretty much to ourselves. This was partly on account of the fact that most day-trippers tended to congregate close to Southend's main attractions: the Golden Mile, the Kursaal amusement park, the world's longest pier, and the Southend Cliff Railway, a funicular built in 1912.

The Kursaal opened in 1894 on a four-acre site near the sea front and became the largest permanent fairground in the south of England. It was the world's first theme park, beating Coney Island in Brooklyn, New York, by several years. By the fifties it was famous for its exhilarating rides, like the Waltzer, the Cyclone, the Dive Bomber and the Wall of Death. Imagine a proto-Disneyland on the Essex coast. It was a magical place.

The entrance hall, with its distinctive dome, is still there, a sad reminder of an almost forgotten golden age of British seaside holidays. But the outdoor amusements shut in 1973 and the site was redeveloped for housing.

Southend pier is one and a third miles long. It had its own miniature railway and in the 1950s attracted five million people a year. My friend Lou Manzi's father ran the lucrative fruit machine concession on the pier. In summer, the machines had to be emptied several times a week.

There was also a variety of other machines designed to part holidaymakers from their money. I was particularly fascinated by the hand-operated crane which promised to deliver valuable prizes but 99 times out of 100 came up empty. The pier was a magnet for holidaymakers from Essex and London's East End. In 1959 fire destroyed the pier's pavilion and a couple of years later it was replaced with a tenpin bowling alley. Another fire claimed the bowling alley in 1976 and the railway was closed the following year. By then, the resort was already in terminal decline as a result of the popularity of continental package holidays, which coupled the 'Kiss Me Quick' vulgarity of Southend with reliable weather.

I can remember being taught to sing a little ditty:

> *Saaarf-End, all the way through,*
> *From the cockles and welks,*
> *To the queue for the loo.*

My nanna didn't approve. She thought the word 'loo' was terribly common, especially coming from the lips of a young boy. The ladies in the family never used the loo, or went to the toilet. They 'spent a penny', an allusion to the cost of admission to the cubicles in public conveniences.

The other reason the beach was often sparsely populated was that Shoeburyness was home to a Ministry of Defence firing range, sited at the charmingly named Pig's Bay. In the Second World War a boom was built to prevent enemy ships and U-boats sailing up the Thames to London. In the 1950s, the artillery barracks were still active. Our lazy afternoons on the beach were punctuated by frequent shellfire from the practice range next door. We should have packed tin hats as well as travel rugs.

Mum and Olive taught me to swim, without the aid of a rubber ring. Dad would never go in the water, presumably a hangover from being sunk in the Irish Sea on his maiden voyage with the Royal Navy.

On the way home, we'd stop for fish'n'chips and Rossi's famous ice cream. I'd always be given a saveloy to chew on. For the unitiated, a saveloy is a type of highly seasoned sausage, made from ground intestines apparently mixed with gravel and sawdust and forced into a bright red, vulcanised condom. Some chip shops fry them in batter, just to be on the safe side.

Deranged, risk-averse, misanthropic modern food inspectors have tried to ban everything from medium-rare hamburgers to scrambled eggs, but, miraculously, saveloys have somehow escaped their attention and are still freely available, if you know the password.

There is a café at Shoeburyness called Uncle Tom's

Cabin which survives to this day. I'm amazed it hasn't fallen foul of the 'diversity' police.

Looking at black and white photos of family excursions to the seaside, what also strikes me is the fact that no one is dressed for the beach. The women are wearing frocks, the men suits or sports jackets and cavalry twill trousers. For the purposes of paddling, frocks were tucked in knickers and trouser legs rolled up.

My dad's idea of 'casual' was to wear an open-neck shirt. I don't think I ever saw him in shorts, even in the hottest summers. He wouldn't have been seen dead in some of the clothes modern males mistakenly believe appropriate. My old man would rightly have considered those ludicrous, three-quarter-length cargo pants a hanging offence.

My grandmothers always wore hats when they left the house and Grandad Littlejohn was never seen outside his own home without a jacket and tie. 'Leisure' wear was still a distant, alien concept.

We were frequent visitors to the Littlejohn family home in Ilford. They'd moved there from East Ham after Dad's little brother Ronnie died of diphtheria. The doctor told Bill that Min needed a complete change of scenery. She was understandably suffering from severe depression brought on by the loss of her son. Melancholia, they called it in the twenties.

It was a typical three-bedroom, between-the-wars home, a step up from the cramped Edwardian terrace in East Ham. Vine Gardens had an indoor bathroom and separate upstairs lavatory, unlike Grosvenor Gardens, which had an outside toilet in the backyard.

Each property had individual architectural quirks to distinguish it from the otherwise identical house next door.

When I got older, I would sleep in the tiny front box room, which featured a distinctive triangular bay window, the shape of which lent itself to endless adventures in a boy's imagination. This bay window doubled as everything from the bow of a boat to the gun turret on a wartime Lancaster bomber.

There were reminders of war all over the house: pictures of Dad in his Royal Navy dress uniform and Grandad in his Sherwood Forester fatigues.

Most ex-servicemen from the two world wars had brought back souvenirs from the front line. Grandad still had his service revolver and his bayonet, which he kept in the garage in his toolbox. On the mantelpiece in the back parlour there was a letter opener fashioned from a German shell casing.

How times have changed. In the summer of 2013 an SAS sniper, Sergeant Danny Nightingale, was given a suspended two-year military detention sentence for possessing a 9mm Glock pistol and 338 rounds of ammunition smuggled back from Iraq.

He had originally been jailed for eighteen months, a sentence which was quashed by the Court of Appeal. The weapon and ammo were found by civilian police in a bedroom at his shared army house. It is not known who grassed him up. Military judges said they wanted to give him an immediate custodial sentence but were constrained by the appeal court ruling. The case was reported to have cost Sergeant Nightingale £120,000 in legal fees.

Just as well the authorities haven't always taken such a hard line on military 'souvenirs', otherwise my grandfather and hundreds of thousands of other ex-soldiers would all have been banged up in jail after the two wars. There wouldn't have been enough prison cells to detain them all.

When I was a boy, military uniforms on the street were commonplace. Men and women wore them with pride. Old soldiers sported their campaign ribbons and regimental crests on their blazers. Servicemen were respected. Their sacrifice had ensured the nation's enduring freedom.

Today, we rarely see serving military personnel wearing their uniforms in public, except on ceremonial occasions.

There have been stories of soldiers in uniform being refused service in pubs because it might 'offend' other customers. At Birmingham airport, soldiers returning from Afghanistan were told to change out of their uniforms and into civilian clothes before they were allowed into the terminal.

After the grisly, ritual murder of Drummer Lee Rigby by Islamist terrorists in Woolwich in May 2013, orders were issued from the Ministry of Defence to all servicemen and women not to wear their uniforms outside their barracks.

Fortunately, this craven order was quickly counter-manded by the Prime Minister, but it illustrates starkly what a strange country Britain has become. Fear of causing 'offence' to anyone has perverted and paralysed public policy.

There are times when I'm grateful that my dad's no longer around to see it. And I can just imagine how Grandad's generation would have reacted.

Fix bayonets!

Britain used to be a liveried society. Everyone from bus conductors to road sweepers wore some kind of uniform, generally topped off with a peaked cap.

It can't be a coincidence that, with all these symbols of authority on the streets, the incidence of crime and anti-social behaviour was remarkably low.

These days only the Corps of Commissionaires maintains the old standards. Even the police wear scruffy pullovers and baseball caps. Just about the only uniform on Britain's streets today is the hideous, ubiquitous hi-viz jacket. You can't tell the coppers from the car park attendants.

When I was growing up, some of the smartest authority figures were the park keepers. These 'parkies' were often ex-servicemen, who took great pride in maintaining discipline and preventing vandalism on their patch.

There were two parks in striking distance of Vine Gardens. Just round the corner was Loxford Park, with its children's playground and bowling green. Slightly further afield was the larger Barking Park, which boasted a magnificent open-air swimming pool and its own light railway. In the 1950s it also featured a Mississippi-style paddle steamer on the boating lake.

Practically every town had a lido, but few now remain. They were closed when councils embraced the concept of shiny new 'leisure centres' in the 1960s and 1970s – most of them grim concrete and glass monstrosities which started to fall apart from the day they were opened.

Councils also started sacking park keepers when they decided they'd rather spend taxpayers' money on political posturing and ridiculous job creation schemes, such as setting up nuclear-free zones and hiring legions of 'diversity' outreach coordinators.

They made their priority pandering to the 'community', roughly translated as noisy minorities and special interest groups, rather than providing proper public services for the whole community.

Parks were neglected and condemned to fall into disrepair. Excited children once played innocently in clean paddling pools, on properly maintained swings and roundabouts, surrounded by immaculate landscaping. By the turn of the twenty-first century many of these oases had become dystopian urban wastelands, infested with derelicts and druggies.

The good news is that Barking Park has been restored with the help of a Lottery grant. The bad news is that the last time I walked from my grandparents' old house down the alleyway leading to Loxford Park, the bowls club had metal grilles on the window, a razor wire fence round the outside and was covered in graffiti.

I can't imagine any old-fashioned 'parkie' letting that happen.

Bill Fraser was a prominent television actor who, later in his career, appeared regularly as Judge Bullingham in *Rumpole of the Bailey*. In the fifties he was one of TV's most celebrated stars.

Fraser played alongside the comedian Tony Hancock in *Hancock's Half-Hour* and his big break came when he was cast as Sergeant Major Claude Snudge in *The Army Game*, which aired for four years from 1957 on ITV. He went on to star alongside Alfie Bass in a hugely popular *Army Game* spin-off series called *Bootsie and Snudge*.

When I was a boy, Bill also ran a sweet shop and

tobacconist's in Ilford Lane, just round the corner from Vine Gardens.

It wasn't unusual to find him serving behind the counter, weighing out a quarter of mint humbugs or handing over a pouch of ready-rubbed. Grandad bought his tobacco from Fraser's shop.

This was at the height of his fame, when millions were tuning in to watch the antics of Bootsie and Snudge. Given that one of ITV's founding fathers, Lew Grade, is said to have described commercial television as a licence to print money, Fraser can't have been short of a few bob.

Perhaps his decision to invest in a small confectionery and tobacconist's business was merely a reflection of the traditional precariousness and uncertainty of the acting profession, where 'resting' was a way of life.

Even so, can you imagine any of today's television stars moonlighting as an assistant in a sweet shop? They have batteries of agents, lawyers and accountants with property portfolios and offshore tax avoidance schemes to protect their wealth.

If you wandered into a sweet shop and found, say, David Walliams serving behind the counter, you'd assume it was one of those hidden camera set-up shows, designed to coax unsuspecting members of the public into making complete fools of themselves.

Ilford was a thriving shopping centre. When I was barely out of nappies my grandmothers, mum and aunt would amuse themselves by taking me into C&A and posing me in a selection of women's headgear. They thought it was hilarious and by all accounts I was happy to go along with it. For years, I believed my dad when he told me that the initials C&A stood for 'Coats'n'Ats'.

As I became more aware of the world around me, I used to love being taken to the old Pioneer Market in Ilford Lane. It was an old-fashioned indoor market hall, stalls piled high with fruit and veg, fresh and cooked meats, bread and sweets, buttons, wool, lengths of cloth. It seemed to me that you could buy anything here, from musical instruments to toys and cameras. There was non-stop banter between the traders and their customers, a real buzz about the place, street theatre at its finest.

The Pioneer Market has long since been demolished. It has been replaced by a ghastly thirty-one-storey glass and steel tower block, which looks as if it has been transplanted from downtown Dubai and is utterly out of keeping with its surroundings.

But the fond memories of the old building linger. Local legend has it that the Hollywood cowboy Roy Rogers once turned up at the Pioneer Market with his horse Trigger. Others claim it was the singing cowboy Gene Autry, who had a number one hit with 'Rudolph the Red Nosed Reindeer'.

Unfortunately, it was neither of the above. The cowboy in question appears to have been one Cal McCord, rumoured to be a former American officer who settled in England after the war and went on to become a bit-part actor specialising in rope tricks.

If you wanted to see a real star in the flesh in Ilford, you had to go to Bill Fraser's sweet shop.

We didn't have a television at Crossways. The only time I got to watch TV was when we visited either of my grandparents' homes. Nanna Sparke had an impressive mahogany set with a tiny black and white screen, which she and Bert had bought to watch the Coronation in 1953. Half the street piled into their front room to share the experience.

My earliest TV memories are programmes like *Watch with Mother*, which first aired the year before I was born and ran, astonishingly, until 1973. This introduced generations of youngsters to Bill and Ben, the Flowerpot Men; Andy Pandy and Teddy; Rag, Tag and Bobtail; and the Woodentops.

There was also *Picture Book*, a TV version of *Listen with Mother* on the wireless:

> *Are you sitting comfortably?*
> *Then I'll begin.*

Watch with Mother was originally broadcast between 3.45 p.m. and 4 p.m. three days a week, after pre-school children had their afternoon nap and before older children came home from school.

Bill and Ben lived in clay flowerpots with their friend Little Weed, who only had one word in her vocabulary:

'Weeee-eed.'

They would come alive when the man who worked in the garden went in for his dinner, which is what most people called lunch in the fifties. Bill and Ben spoke a strange language called 'Flob-a-dob'. At the time, some educationalists expressed concern that this incoherent dialogue might influence impressionable young children and restrict their development.

All I can say is that it didn't inhibit my speaking skills, although later in life I have been known on occasions to lapse into fluent 'Flob-a-dob' after a few sherberts.

Andy and Teddy lived in a toy box with a rag doll called Looby Loo, who was obviously an early role model for a large number of contemporary female politicians and *Guardian* newspaper columnists. Looby would perform a little dance to her very own theme tune:

Here we go Looby Loo,
Here we go Looby Light,
Here we go Looby Loo,
All on a Saturday night.

As for Rag, Tag and Bobtail: Rag was a hedgehog; Tag a mouse; and Bobtail a rabbit. And, from what I remember, that was about it. Nothing much ever happened.

Daddy Woodentop, Mummy Woodentop, Jenny Woodentop, Willy Woodentop and Baby Woodentop were a middle-class family who lived on a farm. Jenny and Willy were twins. The BBC intended the show to 'educate' young children about family life.

The Woodentops were assisted on the farm by Sam Scrubbit, who looked after the animals, including Buttercup the Cow; and his wife, Mrs Scrubbit, who helped Mrs Woodentop around the house. Obviously the assumption at the BBC was that every family had some kind of domestic help.

Star of the show, to my mind, was Spotty Dog, billed as 'the biggest spotty dog you ever did see'. He was an early prototype of Hector from *Hector's House*, who appeared in the sixties, although his vocabulary was even more limited than that of Bill and Ben, consisting mostly of growling.

Daddy Woodentop was permitted a 'Zummerzet' West Country accent, since that's clearly how the programme makers at the BBC believed all farmers spoke.

But the narrators of these programmes delivered their lines in 'Received Pronunciation', defined by the *Concise Oxford Dictionary* as 'the standard accent of English as spoken in the South of England'.

Not in the part of the South of England where I lived, it wasn't. Grandad Littlejohn sounded like the Cockney actor Arthur Mullard, my grandmothers like Kathleen Harrison, from *Here come the Huggetts* and, later, *Mrs Thursday*. The only women I ever heard speaking in 'RP' were BBC continuity announcers and the Queen.

Oh, and those products of the Rank Studios charm school chosen to play 'working-class' women in post-war movies such as *London Belongs to Me*.

They managed to make Dick van Dyke's hilarious accent as the chimney sweep in *Mary Poppins* sound as if he'd been born directly beneath Bow Bells.

Incidentally, 'Woodentop' quickly became CID slang for a uniformed beat copper and was the original title of the pilot episode of the police series *The Bill*, which made its debut in 1984.

Most of the time, when I wasn't at nursery school, Mum managed to keep me amused: encouraging me to read, write, bake cakes, paint pictures and make models. We had one game where she would arrange the kitchen chairs in rows, like the seating on a bus. She'd pretend to be a passenger and I'd dispense tickets from a toy machine round my neck. There was a serious purpose to all this. It taught me how to handle money, do basic sums and give change.

I had a wooden fort, complete with miniature tin

soldiers, and a garage, which had an ingenious winch to lift my model Dinky cars on the top deck. I wish I knew where it went. It's probably worth a small fortune today.

Dad built me a counter and some shelves so I could play shopkeeper, pretending I was one of the stallholders on the real-life Pioneer Market.

Unfortunately, my very own 'shop' had a rather short shelf life. My dad took a fireman's axe to it when he came home from work one day to discover that I'd flooded the house.

It happened not long after I was allowed to take myself to the toilet in the bathroom, which was upstairs on the first floor.

I'd remembered what Mum told me about always washing my hands. I put the plug in the basin, ran some hot water and used the soap as instructed. Sadly, I forgot to take the plug out. And, worse, I also forgot to turn off the tap.

This only became apparent when water started dripping through the kitchen ceiling and cascading down the stairs.

When the story was related to Mrs Pritchard at nursery school, she asked me: 'And what did your daddy say?'

Putting on my most angelic, butter-wouldn't-melt, expression, I replied:

'Little bugger.'

*

That Christmas, I got a pedal car with police insignia and a little blue light on the bonnet. One fine day, I was nowhere to be seen. The car was missing, too. Mum went looking for me in the street. I'd been known to wander off before.

She found me about a hundred yards away, at the junction of Crossways and the main road. There had been a minor traffic accident and she caught up with me at the scene, standing behind a patrol cop and pretending to take notes, just like Jack Warner in *Dixon of Dock Green*.

Although we had no TV, we did have a wireless and an ancient gramophone: one of those wind-up jobs with a metal horn, like the famous HMV advert with the attentive dog, Nipper. It would only play 78s. My favourite record was 'The Laughing Policeman', by Charles Jolly, a music-hall standard. I'd play it over and over again, cranking the handle, dropping the needle on to the heavy acetate disc, and driving my mother to distraction.

As I got older, my grandfather tried to teach me the banjo, but I had little dexterity when it came to musical instruments. But I did fancy myself as a singer and knew all the words to Lonnie Donegan's hit record, 'My Old Man's a Dustman'. Or, at least, I thought I did.

When it came to the line: 'One old man got nasty, He to the council wrote': I'd sing:

> *One old man got nasty,*
> *He chewed the council's rope.*

Sounds good to me. Better than the original. Years later, I rewrote 'My Old Man's a Dustman' for my *Daily Mail* column as a satire on the complete pig's ear politicians have made of the straightforward business of emptying the bins.

At Shenfield, we had two corrugated metal dustbins: one for general rubbish and the other for ashes from the boiler. Every week, the dustmen would walk round to the back of the house, hoist the bins on their broad backs, carry them to their truck and empty them. They'd then put the bins back where they belonged. Once they'd finished, another man would follow on behind with a huge broom, sweeping up any spillage and scooping it into a giant shovel.

Job done.

Last time I drove down Crossways, the street was littered with an assortment of torn rubbish sacks, ugly wheelie bins and multi-coloured recycling receptacles. Councils have managed to turn the simple business of refuse collection into a complicated form of torture, complete with an exciting range of fixed penalties for the most minor infractions of the rules.

A friend who lives in Crossways, a couple of doors down from our old home, tells me he regularly has to walk to the station through piles of garbage on pavements strewn with everything from used nappies to discarded pizza boxes ripped apart by scavenging urban foxes.

Chewing the council's rope doesn't sound like a bad idea.

There always seemed to be someone coming to Crossways to collect or deliver something or other. If it wasn't the dustmen, it would be the coalman, the milkman, the fish man. The ice-cream man would ride along Crossways, ringing a handbell, on a modified grocery delivery bike with a cool box fitted to the front. In the summer, the coalman would leave his young son with us so that we could play together while he went about his round.

The boy was a bit older than me but we got on like best pals. The coal bunker was our command post, standing in for an air raid shelter; a German gun emplacement, which we'd attack by lobbing lumps of coal like hand grenades; or a US Cavalry fort. It was whatever we designated it to be.

Mum would make us orange squash and sandwiches for lunch. By the time the coalman had finished his round, we were absolutely filthy, like a couple of tar babies, but exhausted and happy.

How many modern mothers would let their young son play in a coal bunker all day with an older boy they barely knew?

Come to that, how many mums would let their husband take her son on his coal delivery round and dump him on someone who, if not a complete stranger, could hardly be described as a close friend of the family?

Today we'd both be confined to our bedrooms with computer games. But these were more innocent times. I learned to mix with different people, use my imagination and work off all my excess energy in the fresh air, even if half the time I was breathing in pure coal dust.

When I was about four, my dad and his father must have thought I needed toughening up. They decided to teach me to box. Not that I needed much toughening up, as I was always in the wars. My young body bore the self inflicted battle scars which resulted from running at doors with my head; falling out of trees; and clattering down the stairs on a tea tray doubling as a toboggan.

Learning to box was part of most boys' rite of passage, a life skill passed down from father to son with varying degrees of success.

They bought me a pair of junior boxing gloves the size of a football and a Freddie Mills punchbag. Frederick Percival Mills was considered something of a male role model to men of my grandfather's generation. He had fought his way up from a milk round to win a world title.

In 1946, he took a terrible battering from the American heavyweight Joe Baksi, who entered the English language as rhyming slang for hackney carriage. Joe Baksi = taxi.

Mills recovered from that setback to capture the

British version of the World Light-Heavyweight Championship in front of 46,000 spectators at the old White City stadium in west London. He was renowned as much for his ability to absorb heavy punishment as for his two-fisted aggression.

Mills held the title for two years before retiring in 1950 after a brutal clattering by another American, Joey Maxim. He remained in the public eye as a bit-part actor in a number of movies, including a couple of *Carry On* films, and became a presenter of the BBC's first pop music show, *Six-Five Special*, alongside the disc jockey Pete Murray. As fate would have it, I worked with Pete Murray as a presenter on LBC radio in the nineties. I forgot to ask him about Freddie Mills.

After he retired, Mills opened a night-club in Soho, which brought him into contact with the notorious London gangsters the Kray Twins. In 1965, he was found dying in his car in a cul-de-sac behind his club. A rifle was on the seat beside him and a verdict of suicide was recorded.

Over the years there have been a number of bizarre theories about his death. One has it he fell out with Krays, who had him murdered. Another that he was killed by Chinese gangsters who were seeking to take over the club.

There were also suggestions that he was about to be revealed as a serial killer called 'Jack the Stripper' and that he was involved in homosexual relationships with the singer Michael Holliday and Ronnie Kray, even though he was married with two daughters.

One of the more lurid theories was that he took his own life after being arrested in a public toilet and charged with gross indecency.

If all this had been known earlier, I doubt my grandad would ever have bought me a Freddie Mills punchbag.

Please don't get the impression that my dad's only contribution to my early upbringing was teaching me to fight and taking a fireman's axe to my 'shop' after I flooded the house. He had his sensitive side.

As I mentioned earlier, he was a talented artist and had hoped to go to art school and train as a graphic designer. The Second World War intervened and, after he was demobbed, jobs in his chosen field were in short supply.

Throughout his life he loved to doodle. Knowing my appetite for comics, Dad even created his own cartoon character, Freddie Fieldmouse, and made up stories to entertain me. He'd sit me down for hours recounting the adventures of Freddie Fieldmouse, simultaneously drawing Freddie and his friends on a sketch pad to go with the stories.

In another life, he'd have found work as an illustrator and Freddie Fieldmouse might have ended up with his own comic, just like Harold Hare. Who knows?

I'm convinced it would have been a roaring success. Many's the night I fell asleep dreaming about the escapades of Freddie Fieldmouse.

My dad smelt of Old Spice aftershave lotion and manly sweat, but not in an unpleasant way. Well, not until bri-nylon came along.

In the fifties, most men wouldn't dream of wearing an underarm deodorant. Even aftershave was considered a bit risqué in some circles. Dad wouldn't have a fresh shirt every day, he'd simply change the collars.

Once a week a square cardbox box would arrive at the house, containing a consignment of white collars, presumably from the laundry. Men with office jobs always wore detachable white collars, whether their shirts were white, blue or striped.

I would imagine that's the origin of the expression 'white-collar worker'. It was used to distinguish clerical and managerial staff from manual workers, who wore blue shirts and overalls. The distinction no longer applies but the terminology endures.

This was before the advent in the late 1950s of bri-nylon shirts. Dad was an early adopter of this new, cutting-edge technology, which promised to stay fresh longer and remain wrinkle-free.

What the manufacturers didn't tell you was that this miraculous material generated copious amounts of static electricity and was an absolute nightmare to wash. The first time I sat on my dad's lap when he was wearing a bri-nylon shirt I got an electric shock. He glowed in the dark.

I can remember my mum cussing quietly to herself as she scrubbed the armpits with carbolic soap in a vain attempt to remove the unsightly and apparently indelible brown understains, which appeared after the first wearing and stubbornly resisted all attempts at removal.

The other drawback was that bri-nylon, a petroleum by-product, didn't allow the skin to breathe properly. So the wearer was inclined to sweat profusely. And not in a good way.

After travelling to work and back in a crowded railway carriage, and spending all day at his desk in a stuffy office, Dad came home smelling, in the unforgettable words of the folk singer Roy Harper:

> *Like a Chinese wrestler's jockstrap*
> *Cooked in chip fat on a greasy day.*

Bri-nylon was also virtually indestructible, like the controversial fabric in the Ealing Studios' 1951 satire *The Man in the White Suit*, directed by the brilliant Alexander Mackendrick and starring Alec Guinness.

Men of my dad's generation tended to hang on to their shirts, having come of age in the war when everything was in short supply and no one threw anything away unless it was utterly beyond salvation.

One unanticipated side effect of this remarkable longevity was that, after strong initial sales, demand dropped away dramatically since no one ever needed a new one, provided they could conceal the brown patches under their jacket.

Naturally, this was a problem for the various manu-facturers who were strangling their own golden goose. They spent years seeking an alternative, eventually coming up with the more hygienic poly-cotton mixture.

But not before they churned out all manner of nylon garments, from pyjamas and nightgowns to frocks and smoking jackets, and an assortment of highly charged bed linen capable of turning any home into a tinder box.

One upside of the 1973 OPEC oil crisis was that it finally sounded the death knell for bri-nylon by raising the cost of the raw materials to uneconomic levels.

And that should have been that. But recently I read that bri-nylon shirts were making a comeback, via the vintage clothing market on eBay.

It would be wiser to bury any remaining bri-nylon shirts deep underground in lead-lined concrete tombs; they obviously have the afterlife of nuclear waste.

My sister Vivienne was born on 10 January 1958, eight days before my fourth birthday, in the maternity ward at Chelmsford hospital. This relieved my father of the possibility of having to paint another midwife's bike. They brought her home in a carrycot, bearing a birthday present for me – a toy soldier in a sentry box for my fort. Funny the tiniest detail you remember from more than five decades ago. I wasn't aware of receiving any less attention as a result of the new arrival in our household, but by then I was of an age to amuse myself.

I was still attending nursery school three times a week and later that year began school proper, enrolling at St Mary's Church of England School, a short walk from Crossways. The plan was that I'd gain my primary education at St Mary's then move on to Brentwood, one of the country's leading independent schools, which numbers among its old boys the former Labour Foreign Secretary Jack Straw, the author Douglas Adams and the broadcaster Robin Day. Had I gone on to Brentwood my contemporaries would have included comedians Keith Allen and Griff Rhys Jones.

Looking at the Brentwood website today, I also learn that its more recent pupils include the topless glamour model Jodie Marsh, so it's obviously co-ed now. In my day it was boys only.

As it turned out, I never made it to Brentwood. This wasn't the last time I dodged the independent school bullet, either. I was only at St Mary's for a year and, curiously, can remember almost nothing about my time there.

Frankly, I find my lack of memories of St Mary's quite puzzling since I can recall vividly so many other aspects of my early life. Maybe it's because I could already read and write quite proficiently by the time I started primary school and was treading water in the reception class.

For instance, I can remember a good deal about my Auntie Olive's wedding reception in 1959. It was held in an ivy-clad hotel near Ingatestone on the day Vivienne first walked unaided.

I can see my kid sister clambering up and down the steps of the main entrance, clearly delighted with her new-found ability.

According to my mother, it was also the first time she saw me drunk, aged five. While the adults were on the dance floor, I was touring the tables draining the dregs from their glasses. There was a widespread suspicion that my Uncle Eddie had egged me on. Eddie naturally denied any involvement but it was precisely the kind of mischief he enjoyed.

Dad was making his way up the British Railways' LNER (London and North Eastern Region) management ladder. He'd moved on promotion from Stratford to Liverpool Street and then across London to King's Cross.

When his next promotion came around it was clear he would have to leave London. The choice was between York, Doncaster or Peterborough. After talking with my mother, he picked Peterborough. It was the nearest, an hour up the East Coast Main Line by train and within striking distance of Ilford by rail and road.

Following Olive's marriage to Ford tractor salesman Tom Millar, she had moved out of Nanna Sparke's house in Gidea Park. Olive and Tom had their own house built on a plot of land at Ingatestone.

Mum was reluctant to move so far away from her mother. After much agonising, it was decided that Nanna would sell her own home and move with us to Peterborough. She was just fifty-nine, as old as the year.

It must have been just as big a wrench for her as it was for my parents. It had taken three years to build their own home and they had lived there for just five. They had put a lot of themselves into the property. They'd certainly left their mark on it. Dad had built a stone fireplace and Mum had decorated the front room with an unusual wallpaper, patterned colourfully with motifs of paint palettes and brushes, that she'd spotted on a visit to the Ideal Home Exhibition. Very 1950s.

In truth, with two children the family would probably have outgrown the chalet bungalow sooner rather than later. That didn't make it any less of an upheaval. If they ever did anticipate leaving Crossways it would only have been for a larger house in the same area.

Peterborough might just as well have been another planet. It was an industrial city on the edge of the agricultural East Anglian Fens, which owed much of its prosperity to the decision in the nineteenth century to route the main London to the East of Scotland railway line through it.

That same railway was now responsible for the arrival of part of the extended Littlejohn family. In the summer of 1959, both Crossways and Gidea Park were sold and our possessions packed on to the same Pickford's removal van.

We squeezed into the sit-up-and-beg Ford Pop, like the Beverly Hillbillies, and headed up the Great North Road to the future.

Our new home really did feel as if it was in the middle of nowhere. It was built on a new estate right on the outskirts of town, fairly typical of the type of housing developments which sprung up all over Britain from the 1950s onwards. It backed on to a vast playing field, known locally as the Grange. The Netherton Estate had originally been farmland and, opposite our house, still was. We looked out on cornfields which stretched to the local dairy and beyond.

Ours was one of the first houses completed, a four-bedroom, flat-fronted property with a bay window and its own garage. Most of the rest of the street was a building site. The planned shopping parade hadn't been built yet and our road, Ledbury Road, wasn't on a bus route. The grass verge hadn't been laid and the garden, front and back, was a mixture of rough soil and builders' waste.

In everything but location, location, location, it was a step up from Crossways. Ledbury Road was larger and partially centrally heated. There were a couple of radiators downstairs and a heated towel-rail in the bathroom. The kitchen boasted a decent-sized pantry and was big enough to accommodate a table and chairs.

What had been intended as a dining room, opening on to the back garden, was turned into a parlour for my grandmother. My bedroom was at the front, overlooking the road and the cornfields which were to become my playground.

While Mum and Nanna settled us into our new home and Dad went off to work at the railway offices every morning, I was pretty much left to my own devices, free to explore the neighbourhood, such as it was.

A few other families had moved into the area and there were always kids kicking footballs or playing cricket on the Grange, so I soon made friends. Until the cornfields were concreted over for more housing, they were a paradise of endless adventures. At harvest time, the straw would be bailed and stacked, providing ready-made building blocks for the construction of forts and castles. Come dinner time, all the mothers would appear out front as if on cue and summon us in unison. From all over the cornfields, hungry little heads would pop up, like meerkats.

Even though I wasn't yet six years old, my parents clearly weren't that concerned about me coming to much harm, just so long as I didn't venture too far afield. Independence was encouraged and I quickly adapted to my new surroundings.

Mum must have thought she'd moved to the Little House on the Prairie. She admitted later that she hated Peterborough at first. Unlike Shenfield, the nearest shops were a good mile away, consisting of a small Co-op, a sub-post office, a cobbler's, a men's barber, a fish and chip shop and a multi-purpose *Open All Hours* family-run business called Rolph's. It opened at 6 a.m. and stayed open until late, which was rare in the late fifties and sixties.

Mrs Rolph was a formidable woman, a local legend who looked like Granny from the Giles cartoons in the *Daily Express*, only with fewer teeth. When she smiled, which she was rumoured to do intermittently, her mouth resembled that of the duelling banjo player in the movie *Deliverance*. She had a shock of grey hair and seemed always to be dressed from head to toe in black, as if in permanent mourning. I don't know if there was a Mr Rolph, but she did have two sons, Walter and Graham. Walter was a kindly soul who spent his working day out the back of the shop, presumably trying to avoid his mother's ferocious tongue. Graham ran a greengrocery stall under the front awning of the shop.

Mrs Rolph had a voice like a blowtorch. It could strip paint at twenty paces. Even when she was expressing her gratitude for your business – *'Thankinyewlaydee'* – she made it sound as if she was asking you outside for a fight. I was terrified of her.

At the front of the shop, she sold cigarettes, newspapers, comics and magazines, loose sweets and broken biscuits. The broken biscuits fascinated me. There was never a shortage. Did they break the biscuits deliberately? And if so, why?

Custard creams, garibaldis, bourbons, chocolate digestives, shortbread, ginger nuts. All smashed to smithereens. Take your pick, a penny a pop.

The broken biscuits barrels at Rolph's weren't unique. Most shops seemed to have bargain bins of defective goods of some description or other. Where did all this junk come from?

The cobbler next door to Rolph's even had a bucket of reconditioned second-hand shoes for sale. People were quite happy literally to wear dead men's shoes.

Over the years, Rolph's had expanded and been knocked through into the shop next door. It sold everything from groceries to paraffin, in those days widely used in lamps and heaters.

There was no attempt at sophisticated marketing. Cornflakes would be displayed alongside rat poison, fresh vegetables next to disinfectant and fire-lighters.

Mum had a standing order from Rolph's for her household essentials, which would be brought by a boy on a delivery bike once a week.

It was a magnificent machine and must have weighed a ton. After dropping off his load, the delivery boy would treat the younger kids to a ride in the giant metal basket over the front wheel.

I must have eventually overcome my terror of Mrs Rolph, because, when I got older, I briefly had a job at her shop, delivering newspapers and groceries on that same bike, which probably dated back to before the First World War.

Peterborough must have come as a real culture shock for my mother, a sophisticated woman who from a relatively young age had been used to travelling up to London to shop for clothes and go to West End shows.

Apart from the sense of isolation, she especially hated the local accent, which was a strange hybrid of East Midlands industrial and East Anglian agricultural. Mrs Rolph's accent was a particularly grating example of the dialect.

For instance, ice cream was pronounced 'horse crim', as in: *'Wanna horse crim, Mooriel?'*

'Ayyup, me duck' was the standard greeting, as it was in Leicester, Nottingham and Derby to the west. Peterborough also had its own colourful variants.

'*Ayyup, corey bollocks*' was one popular colloquialism.

'*Ayyup, spunk bubble*' was another. I believe it is still used to this day. Only in Peterborough would '*spunk bubble*' be a term of affection.

Mum hated it if I lapsed into the local dialect. If I ever told her I was going outside to 'roide moy boike deown the doike' I'd get a clip round the ear and a sharp reminder that 'We don't talk like that.' Throughout the years we spent in Peterborough, my mum always led me to believe we were just visiting.

Not long after we moved into Ledbury Road, it was time for me to start at my new school, West Town Juniors and Mixed Infants, in Williamson Avenue, about a mile away if you took the short cut across the Grange. We'd walk, with Viv in her pram. It took a good twenty minutes there and back.

The school was housed in a purpose-built Edwardian brick building, established in 1909, with separate 'Boys' and 'Girls' entrances. West Town had a strict uniform policy. Grey shirts and green striped ties; bottle-green or grey jumpers; grey socks and navy-blue blazers. Grey shorts for boys, grey pleated skirts for the girls. Shoes had to be black.

West Town was much like thousands of other schools built around the turn of the century. They could be quite intimidating institutions, with long corridors and tall ceilings, obviously designed to instil the serious purpose of education in our impressionable young minds. West Town carried a permanent, pungent aroma of floor polish and disinfectant.

Headmistress of the infants' school was Miss Davey, a spinster with a withered foot. Because of her reinforced, built-up boot we could always hear her coming. Although she was big on discipline, she adored her pupils and we adored her back.

In overall charge of the school was the headmaster, Eric Sutton. For four years, from when I was seven years old, he was probably the most important man in my life, after my father.

I certainly saw more of him than my dad, who was often away on business. Mr Sutton – never Eric, heaven forfend – was there five, sometimes six, days a week.

He was a major – in every sense of the word – influence in my formative years. Mr Sutton had the air of a Regimental Sergeant Major and ran the school with military efficiency – not surprising, really, given that he'd served as an NCO in the Army Education Corps during the Second World War.

West Town wasn't a Church of England affiliated school, but every morning we had a muscular Christian assembly, including the Lord's Prayer. Mr Sutton would lead us in the singing of hymns – everything from 'All Things Bright and Beautiful' to 'Hills of the North Rejoice' and 'I Vow To Thee, My Country', the words of which I still know by heart.

In these multi-cultural times, hymn singing is increasingly frowned upon. The nearest most school assemblies come to a song of worship is 'Morning Has Broken', by the former sixties pop star Cat Stevens, who changed his name to Yusuf Islam when he converted to the Muslim faith.

And is it any wonder, when sections of the Church of England frown upon traditional hymns? Two days before Remembrance Day, on 9 November 2013, the *Daily Mail* reported:

> A leading Church of England vicar yesterday condemned the words of one of the country's best-loved hymns as obscene, offensive and unfit to be sung by Christians. The Reverend Gordon Giles, one of the Anglicans' leading authorities on hymns, declared that 'I Vow to Thee, My Country' should be rewritten if it is to be sung by modern congregations.
>
> His verdict was delivered in advance of the Remembrance weekend when the hymn, which is especially valued by military families, will feature in thousands of services across the country and the Commonwealth.
>
> Its patriotic words, written in the final year of the First World War, speak of the 'final sacrifice' made by those that love their country, and end with a promise of peace in heaven.
>
> The hymn has been among the most popular since the 1920s.

It was a favourite of both Princess Diana and Margaret Thatcher, and was sung at Lady Thatcher's funeral at St Paul's in April.

But Mr Giles – a former succentor responsible for hymns at St Paul's – called 'I Vow to Thee, My Country' 'dated' and 'unjust'. He said in an article in the Church Times: *'Many would question whether we can sing of a love that "asks no question", that "lays on the altar the dearest and the best" and that juxtaposes the service of country and that "other country" of faith.*

Should we, undaunted, make the sacrifice of our sons and daughters, laying their lives on the altar in wars that we might struggle to call holy or just?

'The notion of vowing everything to a country, including the sacrifice of one's life for the glorification of nationhood, challenges sensibilities today.'

Obscene? Offensive? I'd have thought the real obscenity, the real offence, was a 'leading' Church of England priest choosing Remembrance weekend to pour scorn on the memory of millions of British war dead.

Mr Sutton had a piercing parade-ground bark that would halt small boys in their tracks up to a hundred yards away. That said, his bark was worse than his bite. He was a disciplinarian with a fearsome cane on the wall of his study. I can't remember him ever wielding it in anger. Maybe I've simply forgotten. But the prospect was deterrent enough.

If he did have to administer corporal punishment, it would have been in the spirit of the old adage: this is going to hurt me more than it is going to hurt you, boy.

I don't recall him wearing a mortarboard, but he didn't need any props to convey his natural authority. To my young mind, he was the living embodiment of the headmaster played by Jimmy Edwards in the TV series *Whacko!*.

West Town had a wide catchment area, taking in kids from a variety of different backgrounds: the sons and daughters of factory workers, railwaymen, shopkeepers, doctors, solicitors, bank managers and bus drivers. Eric Sutton treated everyone equally.

It would be fair to say that the teaching methods at West Town were 'traditional': plenty of learning by rote and tests at the end of every week. They certainly wouldn't have met with the approval of modern 'child-centred' educationalists.

Class sizes were huge, too, by the standards of today's schools. There were forty-eight pupils in the top class, preparing for the 11-plus. None of the teachers took any nonsense from their young charges, who tended to behave reasonably well because they were terrified of being told to stand in the corridor, where they might come to the attention of the headmaster.

I can remember being sent out a few times, usually

for disrupting lessons by talking or laughing, although on one occasion I was exiled for flicking ink pellets. This was a popular pastime. For our essays, we used old-fashioned fountain pens, which were refilled from inkwells on our desks. If you dipped folded pieces of paper in the inkwells, they made formidable projectiles, which could be propelled accurately across the room, using your ruler as a miniature trebuchet.

Years later, memories of being sent out to stand in the corridor came flooding back when I was working a Saturday shift on the *Sunday Express*, then edited by the legendary Scottish Presbyterian John Junor. It was approaching 5 p.m. and deadlines were looming. I was at the back of the newsroom, sharing a joke with my colleague Colin Adamson, a brilliant reporter known throughout Fleet Street as 'The Animal'. Bert Pack, the delightful but terminally nervous news editor – apparently he once shat himself on the spot after a bollocking from JJ – approached and asked us if we'd like to adjourn to the pub. Of course we would, but I pointed out to Bert that our shifts weren't due to end until 6 p.m. Early departure was generally frowned upon. 'Don't worry about that, old boy,' Bert said. 'Off you go and have a drink on expenses. The editor doesn't like jollity in the office.'

*

Although Mr Sutton was determined to pursue academic excellence, he also held the view that all work and no play made Jack a dull boy.

We were herded outside at breaktimes in all weathers, encouraged to play football and cricket against goalposts and stumps chalked on to a wall. Eric Sutton would regularly referee these scratch games, occasionally joining in himself to make up the numbers, like the PE master played by Brian Glover in the film *Kes*.

Cuts and bruises were commonplace on the concrete surface but we were discouraged from making a fuss. Mr Sutton saw a few battle scars as character-building. Half the time, the first-aid room looked like Emergency Ward 10. Twisted ankles, sprained wrists, scuffed knees, split lips, black eyes, scraped elbows, the odd fracture: these were all occupational hazards.

Once the nurse had carried out some rudimentary running repairs, it was straight back outside to continue whichever hazardous activity had caused the damage in the first place. Barely a week went by without me limping home from school with a blood-spattered handkerchief wrapped round my leg or a sticking plaster on my forehead. You try slide-tackling on concrete without getting hurt.

According to my mum, I was always in the wars. She should have taken out shares in Elastoplast.

But she didn't blame the school. Boys will be boys.

My mother would never have dreamed of suing the local education authority for negligence. A few scrapes and the occasional visit to casualty were part of the currency of childhood. I still bear the scar of a conker-related penknife incident on my left knuckle.

How times change. We now live in a litigious age where all risk must be eliminated and 'where there's blame, there's a claim'.

In 2010, nine-year-old Lewis Pierce cut his thumb and damaged a tendon after a bust-up with his seven-year-old brother George in the playground at their primary school in West Sussex.

It started when George sprayed his big brother with a jet of water from a newly installed drinking fountain. Lewis lashed out, but George ducked and Lewis hit the fountain instead.

His damaged tendon was patched up in hospital and he was left with a one-inch scar. Even though Lewis was said to be 'completely unconcerned' by his self-inflicted misfortune, his mother Annette had other ideas.

No doubt inspired by those spiv law firms who tout for business on daytime TV, promising free foreign holidays and new cars in exchange for minor 'slip and slide' accidents, Mrs Pierce decided that there might be a nice little drink in her son's injury.

She sued West Sussex Council for damages, claiming

breach of duty and negligence. Her lawyers alleged that the school had not carried out a proper risk assessment before installing the drinking fountain. A court in Brighton upheld the claim and awarded £3215 in com-pen-say-shun. If the verdict had been allowed to stand, every school in Britain would have had to remove drinking fountains from their playgrounds or open themselves to the possibility of thousands of opportunist claims for damages.

West Sussex appealed, maintaining that schools could never be completely safe. The council's lawyer said: 'Any part of the premises, for example the corner of a brick wall, could be perceived as sufficiently sharp as to cause a laceration if punched.'

In a welcome outbreak of sanity, the judge agreed to uphold the appeal. Lady Justice Sharp said schools obviously had to take reasonable steps to ensure pupils safety 'bearing in mind that children are inclined to lark around'. But she said that they were not under a duty to safeguard children in all circumstances, adding: 'The law would part company with common sense if that were the case.'

And she awarded all legal costs of the original hearing and the appeal against Mrs Pierce. The amount hasn't been revealed, but, with any luck, this will deter other parents from trying it on in future.

Unfortunately, the law parted company with common sense years ago, when 'no win, no fee' arrangements were introduced, sparking an avalanche of unwarranted compensation claims. Far too many greedy chancers have been encouraged to believe that they are entitled to a bumper payout for the most trivial accidents at no potential cost to themselves, just so long as they can find someone to blame.

Over the years, I've made a good living monstering the elf'n'safety and com-pen-say-shun culture. Much of it is down to overcautious insurance firms terrified of being sued and hiking premiums accordingly. If any activity carries the slightest risk, far easier to ban it.

Elsewhere, a private school in Belgravia, London, asked parents to stop giving their children peanut butter, or cereal containing nuts, for breakfast for fear it could spark an allergic reaction in other pupils. Other schools had already banned nut products from lunchboxes. But this was the first time parents had been told what their kids can eat for breakfast before they go to school.

Look, I know that some people can experience serious reactions to nuts. But I do find it suspicious that the number of sufferers from peanut allergies is alleged to have doubled over the past decade. When I was growing up, no one suffered from food allergies. Is it seriously being suggested that children will go into anaphylactic shock because they smell peanut butter on their classmates' breath?

My guess is that this diktat will have been forced on the school by its insurance company, in the same way that airlines have been forced to stop serving packets of salted cashews just in case an 'allergic' passenger in cattle class slaps in a multi-million dollar lawsuit for attempted murder.

If my old school had to face all this madness in the sixties, they wouldn't only have had to ban us from playing football in the playground, they'd have had to stop us bringing Cadbury's Fruit and Nut on the premises, too.

If I wasn't playing football outdoors, I was indoors playing Subbuteo, invented in 1946 and unveiled in the *Boy's Own Paper*. This involved flicking miniature footballers with your fingers across a green baize pitch, like the surface of a snooker table. The pitch was designed to be table-mounted, but more often than not we spread it out on the floor, so we could crawl around on our knees. Originally the figures were one-dimensional and cut from cardboard, like the dollies' dresses my sister used to cut out of comics. Later they were moulded from plastic and came in the colours of all major teams. We had leagues and cup competitions, just like the real thing. Subbuteo was a relatively crude concept, certainly nothing as sophisticated as the myriad realistic football games available today on computers and consoles like Xbox and PlayStation. Yet if you lay on the floor, lowered your head to pitch level and squinted, you were transported in your mind to White Hart Lane, Old Trafford or Wembley. You could make the sound of the roar of the crowd in the back of your throat. Today's computer games, although brilliant, leave nothing to the fertile young imagination.

Subbuteo still survives but, inevitably, has fallen foul of the 'diversity' police. In September 2013, plans to erect a full-size statue of a Subbuteo referee in a famous Cambridge open space were abandoned. The sculpture was designed to commemorate the 150th anniversary of the compiling of the rules of Association Football, which were drawn up on Parker's Piece. But 'diversity' campaigners protested that the six-foot seven-inch figure, on a half-moon Subbuteo base, was too white and too male. One member of the steering committee had 'issues' with the 'race of the figure and the perceived gender'.

What is the matter with these people? How many black or female football referees were there in 1863? Come to that, how many black or female referees are there on the Premier League list today?

None.

For all the FA's anti-discrimination ribbons and Kick It Out badges, there hasn't been a black referee at the top level of English football since Uriah Rennie retired in 2009. The only woman official, Sian Massey, has yet to progress beyond running the line. If they wanted a genuinely 'diverse' statue of a Subbuteo referee they could always have given him a white stick and a guide dog.

*

Whenever Mr Sutton caught anyone fighting in the playground, he would haul the combatants into the gym, make them wear boxing gloves and then they would slug it out over three two-minute rounds in the ring, in full accordance with the Marquess of Queensberry Rules. Goodness knows what modern elf'n'safety would make of primary schoolboys being forced to punch each other's lights out under the supervision of a teacher. These days, my old headmaster would probably have found himself up in court on child cruelty charges.

Mr Sutton was a great believer in the virtues of sport and physical education. Our Edwardian school building didn't have a playing field, so for organised games he'd march us in a crocodile to the local 'rec', rain or shine. In winter, we played football, in summer cricket. Eleven-a-side, too, even at age eight. And with hard cricket balls, not the sponge jobs used today.

After school and on Saturdays he'd take teams to compete in tournaments. And he expected us to win. Eric Sutton would never settle for second best.

When I revisited West Town while writing this book, the building hadn't changed much but there were padlocked steel gates across the entrance to the playground. Screwed to the gates was an official notice which read, 'No Ball Games', on pain of a £250 fine. Any council official who had tried to tell Mr Sutton that ball games were banned would have been hauled into the gym, handed a pair of boxing gloves and invited to explain himself over three two-minute rounds. Seconds away, lights out.

All this team sport was in addition to several sessions of vigorous PE (physical education) every week and trips to the local open-air swimming pool.

Mr Sutton may have placed great importance on our physical development, but he gave equal – if not more – weight to nurturing our intellectual capacity.

These days, 'passion' is a much-abused cliché. Every inept reality TV contestant professes their 'passion' for everything from fairy cakes to break-dancing. But Mr Sutton really was passionate about education in general and literacy in particular.

It was his ambition to get as many of his pupils as possible into grammar school, which he saw as the gateway to a better future. He succeeded spectacularly, his school regularly topping the table of 11-plus passes.

West Town was what we would now call a 'bog standard' state school. But there was nothing 'bog standard' about the ethos instilled by Eric Sutton, who could have held his own in any exclusive fee-paying establishment.

He was a dapper man who always wore a sports jacket, complete with leather patches on the elbows, and cavalry twill trousers. He wouldn't have been seen dead without a shirt and tie – unlike some of the slovenly scruffs on parade at the teachers' union conferences every Easter these days.

For forty-odd years, the feminisation and politicisation of state education has been a disaster. There are more than 4250 schools in Britain where not a single male teacher can be found in the staff room. The Eric Suttons of this world are as extinct as the stegosaurus.

Coupled with the trendy, 'child-centred' teaching methods indoctrinated by Marxist training colleges, this has been responsible for a collapse in discipline and an alarming increase in illiteracy.

But in 2012 came some good news: a report that there had been a significant increase in the number of men training as primary school teachers.

Generations of boys have been utterly betrayed by the system set up to educate them – many written off as suffering from a bewildering array of fashionable 'hyperactivity disorders' and pumped full of mind-bending drugs simply because young female teachers have no idea how to control or inspire them.

Mr Sutton didn't need Ritalin to bring an unruly child to order, just a well-aimed blackboard eraser.

With no competitive sport to channel their physical excesses – a consequence of the pernicious 'all-must-have-prizes' culture – and zero intellectual stimulation, young men are leaving school unsuited to the adult world.

The rise in single motherhood and absentee fathers, coupled with a monopoly of female primary school teachers, means that countless thousands of boys reach puberty without having encountered a male role model, apart from the local 'gangstas'.

Our sick, suspicious society, which considers any man who wants to work with children to be a potential paedophile, has helped to turn primary schools into testosterone-free zones. A male teacher who volunteered to take young boys and girls swimming would be lucky to escape without a knock on the door from the nonce squad or a petrol bomb being lobbed through his front window.

Those hardy male souls who have taken the plunge report hostility and 'intimidation' from all-female staff rooms – which tends to suggest they are probably not cut out for dealing with a class full of seven-year-old savages, either. All this combined with relatively low pay has conspired against encouraging any young family man to become a primary school teacher.

Changes introduced by the Conservative Education Secretary Michael Gove, which allow teachers to earn a salary while they train in school, have begun to attract more men into the profession.

The government also launched a campaign to persuade male graduates to take up a career in primary education.

As a direct consequence, the numbers applying have risen by 51 per cent, albeit from a low base.

Eric Sutton would have approved.

Mr Sutton was also big on music and drama and encouraged his pupils to perform in front of the school. He was active in the world of amateur dramatics, appearing in many local theatrical productions. Once, when he was starring in *Seven Brides for Seven Brothers* at Peterborough's Embassy Theatre, a gang of us sneaked into the Saturday matinee via the emergency exit and heckled him during his big number. He knew we were out there but couldn't identify us because he was blinded by the footlights.

I'm sure his enthusiasm for the performing arts must have rubbed off on some of us. One of my former West Town classmates is Andy Harries, the television and film producer who made the movie *The Queen*, which saw Helen Mirren win an Oscar for Best Actress. I've bumped into Andy a few times over the years and I'm sure he'd endorse my admiration for our old headmaster.

As I mentioned earlier, there were kids from all types of social backgrounds at West Town. Peterborough has always attracted immigrants from across the British Isles and beyond. After the war, Polish servicemen and freed Italian internees settled there, many of them finding jobs in the Fletton works of the London Brick Company. Other

Italians soon arrived from Italy, attracted by the available, reasonably well-paid work. The rich clay indigenous to the area was especially suited to manufacturing house bricks. Demand peaked in 1967 at the height of the post-war housing boom. Others arrived to work in agriculture and at the many factories in the city. At one stage, the Perkins Engines company's Peterborough plant was the biggest diesel engine factory in the world, employing seven thousand workers turning out 75,000 engines a year. Even before the city was officially designated 'New Town' status in the late sixties, it was a magnet for newcomers.

Immigration from the Indian subcontinent and the West Indies had yet to become a significant factor, but there were children from Italian and Polish backgrounds in our class.

I remember a bright, pretty Italian girl with callipers, which she had to wear after contracting polio when she was an infant. There was a polio epidemic in the 1950s, which affected 45,000 people. Callipers were quite a common sight back then.

Outside Woolworth's stood a life-size statue of a girl in callipers, clutching a teddy bear in one hand and a collection box in the other. I think it was put there by what was then known as the Spastics Society. After 'spastic' became a term of abuse, the charity changed its name in the 1990s to Scope – which in America is a best-selling brand of mouthwash. This was part of a trend which saw the Marriage Guidance Council rebrand itself as Relate, which sounds like a condom.

Last thing I heard, 'spaz' was making an unwelcome comeback in the playground as a new generation rebels against the strictures of its 'elders and betters'. One thing you can always rely on is the cruelty of children towards other children.

Years later I was presenting the BBC's football phone-in show 606 on Radio 5 Live. We were discussing why England had no decent wingers. I happened to remark, distastefully but in jest, that it was because whenever we played football in the playground at school, the kids with the leg irons were always sent to play on the wings.

My young female co-host, Fiona Cotterill, was horrified. Minutes later we took a call from a Scottish listener which seemed to back her up.

'Richard, I really must take issue with your comments about making the kids with the legs irons play on the wings . . .'

Fiona looked at me and muttered, noises off: 'See, I told you so.' I immediately regretted the remark.

'Look, if you're offended, I apologise unreservedly,' I told the caller.

'Och, no offence taken, Richard. I just rang in to say that in Scotland in my day we always made the kid with the leg irons go in goal.'

★

The first black friend I ever made was the son of an American airman stationed at the giant USAF air base at nearby Alconbury. He must have arrived at our school around 1960 or 1961. Karl Hall was naturally a curiosity at West Town, where all the other pupils were from white British and European backgrounds. He was as much a curiosity for his accent as his colour. We'd only ever heard people talk like that on TV and in the movies. Karl wasn't at West Town for more than a couple of terms but quickly made friends by bringing American comic books to school, featuring superheroes like Batman, Superman and Green Lantern. He also brought something he called 'candy' and told us how he drank Coca-Cola and ate hamburgers, freely available on the USAF air base but otherwise exotic delicacies unobtainable in early 1960s Britain.

Peterborough has always absorbed immigrants, being one of the first cities to welcome Ugandan and Kenyan Asians fleeing persecution in Africa. But in the sixties, what we now call the 'ethnic minorities', even when they're in the overwhelming majority in some areas, were very much a tiny minority.

That was before Labour's deliberate decision between 1997 and 2010 to dismantle Britain's border controls and, in the words of Peter Mandelson, 'scour the world for immigrants'. Labour's stated aim was to 'rub the Right's faces in diversity'.

As a result of this cynical policy, the population of

Peterborough has been transformed irrevocably. Tens of thousands of Eastern European immigrants have settled in the area, seeking jobs in agriculture which bone-idle, welfare-cosseted British nationals refuse to accept.

I can remember a TV report a few years ago from outside the shiny new Jobcentre in Peterborough. It was around the time the influx from Eastern Europe began. The reporter stopped one young 'Jobseeker' as he left the building after signing on for his benefits cheque.

He was able-bodied, dressed in the latest 'street' fashions and swigging from a can of lager. The reporter was anxious to discover what kind of work he was out of. Why, for instance, didn't he volunteer for one of the minimum-wage agricultural jobs being snapped up by the newcomers from overseas?

The 'Jobseeker' looked at the reporter contemptuously, took another swig from his can of beer, and replied: 'You must be joking. I wouldn't get out of bed for a job like that.'

While this work-shy layabout continued to enjoy a subsidised lifestyle, no doubt in a rent-paid council flat, some of the new arrivals were forced to camp out in shanty towns in local open spaces, or were crammed into tiny terraced houses originally built for railway workers and now owned by unscrupulous slum landlords.

Let me emphasise: I don't blame anyone for emigrating to seek a better life for themselves and their families. It was a process that began in the fifties and in many respects has enriched and benefited Britain. Vital services such as the NHS and public transport would have collapsed without the efforts and dedication of staff from overseas, especially the Commonwealth. In a global economy, mobility is a plane ticket away.

The service economy, which has made London a thriving, modern world city, couldn't flourish without a plentiful supply of immigrant labour.

But successive governments have paid no heed to the impact on indigenous British citizens, especially in provincial towns and cities such as Peterborough, who can often trace their roots in an area back for centuries.

The sheer scale of the influx has changed communities for ever, nowhere more so than in Peterborough. Once white, working-class areas are now almost exclusively Muslim. The Peterborough to which we moved in 1959 is virtually unrecognisable.

All this happened without the electorate ever being consulted. Mass immigration was carried out by a deliberate policy of deception. Anyone who questioned the policy, or drew attention to the speed and the numbers, was despicably howled down as a 'racist'.

To get an idea of the impact, examine the 2011 Census. Only 56.7 per cent of people in Peterborough described themselves as Christian, despite the arrival of thousands of devout Roman Catholics from the Eastern European accession states.

Although Britain has become an increasingly secular society, this rapid decline in Christian worship is astonishing in a city which is home to one of Europe's great Anglican cathedrals, one of the most important twelfth-century buildings in Britain and resting place of Catherine of Aragon. Three years on from that Census, you can bet the percentage categorising themselves as Christian will have diminished still further.

Hardly surprising that many long-standing residents of Peterborough say they now feel as if they live in a foreign country. This doesn't make them 'racist', simply bewildered and betrayed by politicians.

When I was at West Town, we used to play football against our great rivals at Gladstone Street school, which was about a mile away across the main East Coast railway line. The school was slap in the middle of another of those housing developments originally built for railway employees in the late nineteenth century. The catchment areas of West Town and Gladstone Street overlapped halfway across the railway bridge. In the sixties, early immigrants from the subcontinent began settling there.

In February 2013, Gladstone Primary achieved the dubious distinction of becoming the first school in Britain in which none of its pupils speak English as their first language. Not one. The four hundred children have as their mother tongue more than twenty different languages, including Urdu, Portuguese, Czech, Polish, Pashtu, Arabic, several African languages, Russian and Dari, which is spoken in Afghanistan, Iran and Tajikistan.

Back over the bridge, and not to be outdone, West Town now also describes itself as a 'community' school. There, too, more than twenty different languages are spoken. Its mission statement says: 'As a multi-cultural community, we have unique opportunities to respect and understand cultures, religions and views which are different from our own.'

Better make that more than twenty-one different languages. The teachers obviously all speak fluent *Guardian* as their first language.

Not much room for Eric Sutton's muscular Christianity and 'traditional' teaching methods there, then.

What was once a 'community' in the true sense of the word is now a disparate patchwork of different nationalities, religions and languages. My old primary school is an educational Tower of Babel.

We are where we are. It is for Eric Sutton's successors to play the difficult hand they have been dealt.

We can only hope that the 'multi-cultural' social experiment foisted upon places like Peterborough by the politicians doesn't result in the Balkanisation of Britain.

The glimmer of hope is that surveys consistently show that despite the demographic upheaval, Britain is one of the most racially tolerant nations on Earth.

Let's pray that it stays that way for the sake of those

children who had no more say in being sent to West Town than I did as a five-year-old in moving to Peterborough in 1959.

Our school day kicked off at 9 a.m., with a break at 10.30, lunch between noon and 1 p.m. and 'home time' at 3.30 p.m. Since 1946, every pupil under the age of eighteen had been entitled to a third of a pint of free school milk a day. The miniature bottles were delivered every morning and were distributed by 'milk monitors' five minutes before the bell rang for morning break. At West Town, the job was awarded to model pupils, just as 'trusties' wangle cushy jobs in prison libraries.

Like prison 'trusties' who ingratiate themselves with the screws and the prison governor, milk monitors were drawn from the ranks of teachers' pets and were widely resented and despised by their fellow pupils, since they routinely became teachers' pets by grassing up their classmates for a variety of misdemeanours. The main disadvantage of becoming a milk monitor was being on the receiving end of regular roughings-up behind the bike sheds.

You won't be surprised to learn that I was never asked to become a milk monitor. Perhaps news of my prior abuse of the orange juice at Mrs Pritchard's nursery school in Shenfield had somehow managed to reach the ears of the staff at West Town.

The idea of handing out free milk was intended to combat calcium deficiency, which had become common among children because of dietary deficiencies caused by wartime rationing.

Britain, as I have said, came off the ration in the summer of 1954, by which time dairy products were freely available and milk rounds had long since resumed. But the politicians were so convinced of the efficacy of the scheme, especially for the deprived children of the less well-off, that they decided to continue it.

Had they actually bothered to inspect the scheme in action they might have concluded it was a monumental waste of money.

At West Town – and I've no reason to think it was any different at other schools – the milk was stacked in crates in the playground. This meant that in winter it froze, and in summer it curdled.

Milk technology was in its infancy and skimmed and semi-skimmed had yet to be invented. Full-fat was flavour of the month, every month. While the thick layer of yellow cream was a treat in the right circumstances – and much prized as a topping on everything from cornflakes to tinned pears – it could quickly turn into toxic waste.

In the winter, it would expand alarmingly, like a stripper's nipple, popping the silver cap and resisting all attempts to access the milk beneath. In summer, it formed a slimy, nauseous bung, which was enough to put even those with a strong constitution off milk for life.

Consequently, much of the milk delivered to schools was poured down the drain. The elder boys would amuse themselves by peeing into the empties and replacing them in the crates awaiting collection by unsuspecting dairy delivery drivers.

Occasionally the crates would get knocked over, showering the playground with shards of broken glass and puddles of urine. Today's 'risk assessment' obsessives would suffer a seizure if confronted with such a potentially lethal hazard to life and limb.

As any fule kno, it was the evil 'Fatcher' who put an end to free milk. When our greatest post-war Prime Minister died in 2013, almost every obituary made reference to 'Thatcher, the Milk Snatcher'.

In 1971, as Education Secretary, Margaret Thatcher withdrew free school milk from all seven- to eleven-year-olds. As far as the 'Ding, Dong, the Witch Is Dead' brigade was concerned, this was early, conclusive evidence of her cruelty to the working class, which would reach its bloodthirsty climax when she ordered the SAS to bayonet all babies and pregnant mothers in pit villages during the miners' strike.

When the measure was passed – to save taxpayers £9 million a year, more than was being spent on books –

Labour's then shadow education spokesman Edward Short described it as 'the meanest and most unworthy thing he had ever seen' in his time as an MP.

This was despite the fact that Short had himself served under Harold Wilson in the Labour Cabinet, which in 1968 scrapped free school milk for all secondary school pupils aged between eleven and eighteen.

Curiously, this aspect of the free school milk 'scandal' was overlooked by the 'objective' obituarists and 'historians' queueing up to dance on Mrs Thatcher's grave. These same 'experts' also choose to overlook the fact that Wilson's Labour government closed many more coal mines than Thatcher.

Still, the left have never let the facts get in the way of a good smear campaign. And 'Wilson, the Milk Snatcher' doesn't have the same ring to it.

No doubt if Mrs Thatcher had actually voted to continue serving full-fat milk to school children, the left would today be blaming her for the childhood obesity epidemic.

Incidentally, under-fives still receive free milk in nursery schools. When the Conservative-Lib Dem Coalition government came to power in 2010 plans to scrap free milk in nursery schools were considered, but were vetoed by Prime Minister David Cameron, the evil Old Etonian, Bullingdon Club toff responsible for the 'savage cuts'.

★

The classrooms at West Town had changed little since the school was built. The ceilings were tall and the walls half tiled, like public toilets. The only windows that opened were at least ten feet from the ground and had to be operated with a hook on a long pole. They provided little ventilation.

At some stage, central heating had been installed in the shape of enormous cast-iron radiators, which looked as if they may have been manufactured at the Cammell Laird shipbuilder's yards. While they were impressive in scale, they were useless in practice, giving out about as much heat as an electric light bulb.

In summer, the classrooms were sweltering. In winter, they were so cold that we often took lessons in our gaberdine macs and school scarves. Maybe that's why Eric Sutton was so keen on physical exercise. It kept our circulation flowing and stopped us freezing.

Thinking back, I can't remember a time when the school was ever closed, even in the coldest winters when snow and ice lay thick on the ground.

Be honest: how many times can you recall your old school being closed because of the weather? Once? Twice? Never?

I have memories of trudging through thick snow in a balaclava, wellies and short trousers, with wringing wet woollen gloves hanging from a piece of string knotted at the neck of my gaberdine mac.

My knees were red-raw, my nose was running and my heart was pounding with the thrill of snowball fights and sliding on treacherous sheets of ice created by tipping cold water on to the pavement and waiting for it to freeze.

During lessons we'd peer through frosty windows at the winter wonderland outside, willing the bell to ring so that the festivities could be resumed.

Maybe there was the odd day when the rackety radiator pipes froze or the ancient boiler gave up the ghost. But, frankly, I can't remember any school I attended ever being padlocked because of a light dusting of snow.

To the best of my recollection our school kept its doors open throughout the extreme winter of 1963, which was the coldest recorded since 1739–40. Average temperatures remained around 28°F (-2.1°C) for weeks. This was, of course, before global warming had been invented.

In fact, my abiding memory of that winter was going ice-skating with my dad on the Fens, which had been specially flooded for the purpose. The roads must have been passable, otherwise we would never have made it out there. The Fens near Eye and Whittlesey attracted thousands of people bearing ice skates and toboggans. It was a magical scene, which had changed little over the past three hundred years. Fen skating was introduced to Britain in the seventeenth century from the Netherlands. My dad was an accomplished skater, having honed his skills at ice rinks in east London before the war. I spent most of my time flat on my backside.

Certainly I can't imagine Eric Sutton ever letting a cold snap get in the way of our education. But he belonged to a generation of teachers who had been through the Second World War. Some of them probably served on the Arctic convoys. They weren't going to flinch in the face of a couple of inches of snow.

Come to think of it, I'm not sure my own kids were ever sent home from school because of the weather, either. And that doesn't seem all that long ago.

How times have changed. In the cold snap in January 2013, five thousand schools were closed across the country. According to the chairman of the local government association's 'Children and Young People' directorate:

'Ultimately, head teachers, in consultation with school governors, make the final decision on whether or not to close a school. This is based on a range of local circumstances including the number of teachers who can make it into work safely, dangerous road conditions, or problems with vital supplies such as food, heating or water.'

It may well have been that in some remote rural areas, roads were impassable. Some parts of the country were worse affected than others, especially in the North East. But in Barnet, close to where I live now, for instance, sixty schools were shut. Why? I was out and about in north

London that weekend and the gritters and transport companies had done a great job.

All the major roads were clear, the buses and Tubes seemed to be running normally. The only weather-related disruption in Barnet was the panic buying in Waitrose, where the car park was overflowing and shoppers were squabbling over trolleys as they stripped the shelves bare.

There really was no earthly reason why any teacher in Barnet couldn't get to work.

In fact, just a few miles away in Hackney, only one secondary school and two primary schools closed.

So why the discrepancy? My guess is that in Barnet, and elsewhere, the risk-assessment brigade pulled on their hi-viz jackets, consulted their insurers and decided to take the line of least resistance. If they shut the schools, there's no danger that anyone will slip over in the playground and sue for compensation.

Curiously, though, it's only ever the public services that seem to collapse with monotonous predictability whenever there's 'adverse weather'. Everyone else just gets on with it.

At White Hart Lane, the game between Spurs and Manchester United went ahead in the teeth of a snowstorm. And my local curry house, Tandoori Nights, was absolutely heaving.

People clearly weren't letting a few snowflakes get in the way of a chicken vindaloo. And I can't help wondering now how many of my fellow diners braving the elements that Saturday night are employed as teachers in the London Borough of Barnet and were enjoying an undeserved day at home in front of the fire.

Some people are made of sterner stuff. Mike, our postman, got through as usual. So did Mr Patel with the papers. Why was it, then, that councils all over Britain thought that opening the schools presented a uniquely hazardous proposition and was therefore to be avoided at all costs?

What was also utterly predictable was that Heathrow would go into meltdown at the drop of a snowflake, even though other airports soldiered on smoothly.

If Heathrow really has spent £36 million on cold-weather emergency kit, there wasn't much evidence of it - apart from a handful of new brooms and a couple of plastic snow shovels.

And while we're at it, I'm sick and tired of assorted officials and dopey birds on the weather forecast telling us not to go out unless our journey is essential.

TV weathermen - it was always men in those days - used to restrict themselves to delivering the weather forecast, not issuing dress codes and instructions 'not to go outside unless your journey is absolutely necessary'. Quite apart from the patronising nonsense, do they think we are imbeciles? Why would anyone go out in freezing weather unless they had to?

*'Oi, Doris, get your coat on, pet. There's a blizzard outside so
I thought we'd take a nice non-essential drive in the country.'*

Heaven knows what my dad, who served on the
Russian convoys, would make of the institutionalised
cowardice and knee-jerk prohibitionism of the modern
elf'n'safety commissars when confronted with a few snowflakes.

One of the many advantages of Nanna Sparke moving in
with us was that we now had a television. It sat on an
occasional table in my grandmother's parlour off the
kitchen.

When Bert and Hilda bought their 'box' in the early
fifties, only 350,000 homes had TV sets. By 1960, television
covered 90 per cent of the population.

I'll never forget the pent-up excitement on the first
day we plugged in the TV. It took an eternity as its cathode
ray warmed up. The heavy, lined curtains, which Nanna
had brought with her from Gidea Park, were pulled shut
to prevent glare interfering with the picture.

First, though, you had to get a picture, which wasn't
that easy. We had no roof-mounted aerial initially. The
signal was supposed to be sucked in by a pair of 'rabbit
ears' mounted on the set top, which could be adjusted for
maximum clarity.

I suppose it really was that simple if you lived in close

proximity to the BBC's Alexandra Palace transmitter in north London, or near to one of the expanding network of relay stations. But getting a decent signal on the outskirts of Peterborough in 1959 was fraught with as much difficulty as NASA Mission Control, in Houston, Texas, communicating with one of its early Mercury space capsules in geo-stationary orbit thousands of miles above the Equator.

We sat there . . . and sat there. Eventually the screen flickered into life. It was like watching someone throwing confetti in a snowstorm. The sound of static filled the room like a wire basket of wet chips being lowered into a vat of boiling fat.

My dad tried twiddling the rotary knob on the front on the rudimentary control panel. This featured an on/ off/volume switch, two smaller knobs to adjust contrast and brightness and another to change channels.

The channel control was marked 1 to 9, which was optimistic since Britain only had two channels, BBC and ITV. Perhaps the others were designed to contact space monkeys orbiting Earth as part of Russia's Sputnik programme.

'Why don't you try moving the aerial, Bill?' Mum suggested helpfully. As Dad raised the 'rabbit ears' above his head, the screen stuttered into life.

'Try a bit higher.'

Dad climbed on a dining chair and began rotating the aerial from left to right.

'That's it, Bill, perfect. Hold it there,' Mum said as the blurry moving image suddenly stabilised.

'No, it's gone again. Try moving left a bit. No, right. Down a bit.'

Mum could have been auditioning for *The Golden Shot*, an ITV programme which didn't appear until several years later and involved contestants instructing a man called Bernie the Bolt to fire a crossbow at a target in an attempt to win a Teasmade, or something similiar.

'Yes, yes, don't move, Bill. You've got it.'

'Am I supposed to stay here all bloody night?' Dad snapped, as he teetered on one leg on the dining chair with the 'rabbit ears' outstretched at the end of one arm, while he balanced himself with his other hand on top of my grandmother's antique display cabinet. He looked like the Eros statue at Piccadilly Circus.

Mum and Nanna dissolved with laughter. Dad scrambled down to safety and somehow managed to restrain himself from throwing the TV through the French doors.

The next day he went in to Radio Rentals and ordered a proper, roof-mounted aerial.

Muffin the Mule made his television debut immediately after the war, in October 1946. Muffin was a marionette, operated from above by strings. He used to dance on top of a piano played by the actress Annette Mills, the sister of John Mills and aunt of Hayley, who was to become one of my early teenage fantasies. Hayley, that is, not Annette. And certainly not Muffin.

By the time I started watching TV, Annette Mills had died. After her death, the BBC dropped Muffin as a mark of respect. A curious decison in retrospect, since Muffin was the real star of the show. Sooty soldiered on after Harry Corbett died.

The fledgling ITV picked up the franchise and broadcast *Muffin the Mule* from 1955 to 1957, which is when, I imagine, I first saw him. Muffin had a supporting cast of puppets, including Crumpet the Clown, Oswald the Ostrich and Monty the Monkey. You could buy Muffin puppets from a stall on the Pioneer Market, in Ilford.

Like Looby Loo, Muffin had his own theme tune, written by Annette Mills:

Here comes Muffin,
Muffin the Mule,
Dear old Muffin,
Playing the fool.

When his TV career came to an end, Muffin was forced to go out on the road to earn a living, touring provincial theatres and schools. Not long after we moved to Peterborough, one of these tours brought him to West Town school.

It was the first time I'd ever seen a TV star perform

live. The idea that Muffin was appearing on the same stage from which Eric Sutton delivered his address to morning assembly was beyond fantastic.

The whole school filed into the gym, and took our places on the wooden benches. Youngest at the front, oldest at the back. I was a couple of rows from the front. A warm-up man was sent out to whip up the crowd. Just before the curtains parted, he had worked us up into a state of frenzy, clapping our hands in unison and chanting:

We want Muffin!
We want Muffin!

These days, any entertainer who tried to encourage a hall-full of primary school children to chant 'We want Muffin!' would be woken at 6 a.m. to find his front door being kicked in by the Jimmy Savile squad. But this was a more innocent age. Can you imagine today's youngsters being captivated by a simple wooden puppet?

I honestly can't remember if Crumpet the Clown was on the bill that day. Mind you, if the warm-up man had led us in a chorus of 'We want Crumpet!' Eric Sutton would have frogmarched him straight off the premises and round to the nearest nick.

Muffin the Mule was a throwback to the early days of children's television. Until 1956, there had been a so-called 'toddlers' truce' when transmission ceased for an hour after tea to allow parents to put their kids to bed. By the turn of the decade, dozens of programmes aimed specifically at children were being commissioned.

Puppet shows were still popular, but had been transformed beyond recognition by puppeteers such as Gerry Anderson, who went on to produce *Thunderbirds*, *Stingray* and *Fireball XL5*. My favourite Anderson creation was *Four Feather Falls*. The hero of the series was Tex Tucker, sheriff of a fictional Kansas frontier town. His cowboy hat featured four magical feathers given to him by an Indian chief as a reward for saving his grandson. The magic feathers gave Tex's dog and horse the powers of speech and, best of all, enabled Tex's six-guns to swivel in their holsters and fire at will whenever he was forced to raise his hands by the baddies.

I was so fascinated by this wonderful power that, with the aid of some string, I rigged up a similar system of my own. Using the string to tie my wrists to my cap guns, they too would rise to the horizontal, as if by magic, every time I put my hands up.

Who needs computer games?

Anderson had cut his teeth on *Torchy the Battery Boy* and *Twizzle*, both fairly primitive by his later standards, but revolutionary at the time.

Torchy had a battery inside him and a button on his chest which powered a magic beam. Twizzle was able to extend his arms to infinite lengths to get him out of scrapes. Although Twizzle's limbs looked like bendy pipe cleaners, this first stab at special effects captivated a generation, including me.

Anderson went on to develop his unique, patented 'Supermarionation' system, later employed on hit shows like *Thunderbirds* and *Captain Scarlett*.

Thirty-five years later, Anderson managed to fall foul of the Commission for Racial Equality. This august organisation made some daft pronouncements in its time, before Trevor Phillips eventually restored some kind of sanity, but this one took the Jaffa Cake.

The Commission upheld a complaint from a Bristol City Councillor, Mohammed Khali Ahmed, that *Captain Scarlett* was 'racist'. Councillor Ahmed alleged that the puppet show was 'having a very negative effect on race relations in this country'. And the basis for this complaint? One of the characters was called Captain Black.

The day the story broke, I defended Anderson in print and invited him on to my LBC radio show to put his side of the story. Anderson was incandescent with rage, arguing that far from being 'racist', *Captain Scarlett* was in fact a model of racial integration.

He pointed out that two of the good guys in the programme were both black, which was enough to get *Captain Scarlett* banned from some segregationist Southern states in the USA in the 1960s. Advertisers refused to sponsor the show unless the characters were either dropped or their skin colour changed to white.

Anderson stuck to his principles, even though it cost him a considerable amount of money. He also wondered whether Councillor Ahmed or anyone at the Commission for Racial Equality had actually watched the programme.

As any *Captain Scarlett* fan could have told them, Captain Black is white.

Nanna Sparke's TV opened up this wonderful world of entertainment, especially since the new aerial also enabled us to pick up ITV transmissions. The emphasis was as much on education as entertainment.

I loved quiz shows, such as *Junior Criss Cross Quiz*, a general knowledge game based on noughts and crosses. It was, I suppose, the forerunner of eighties afternoon game shows such as *Countdown* and *Blockbusters*, both a clever mix of education and entertainment. Bob Holness, who went on to present *Blockbusters*, was one of the early hosts of *Junior Criss Cross Quiz*.

When I was watching *Junior Criss Cross Quiz*, I could never have imagined that I'd one day end up as a TV presenter and Bob Holness would turn up as a guest on one of my programmes in the 1990s. Or that I would be invited to be a panellist on the long-running *Call My Bluff*, then being hosted by a certain Bob Holness. And Bob wasn't the only one of my childhood TV heroes I'd encounter much later in life.

Blue Peter began in 1958 and survives to this day, the world's longest-running children's magazine show. Christopher Trace was the original presenter and the one I remember best, along with 'Auntie' Val, Valerie Singleton, who went on to have a distinguished career in radio journalism. Early in my broadcast career, in the seventies, I used to report on air occasionally for a regional BBC breakfast show based in Norwich. The first time I was due to go live, I was a bundle of nerves. The show's star presenter, with whom I was about to do a live 'two-way', was one Christopher Trace.

There were a couple of other shows which I tried not to miss, either: *Five o'Clock Club* and *Rendezvous*.

Five o'Clock Club was another attempt to mix education and entertainment, segueing from making models from sticky backed plastic to showcasing the latest pop music. It was introduced by Wally Whyton, Muriel Young and Gerry Marsden, from Gerry and the Pacemakers, then at the cutting edge of the Mersey Beat.

I can't imagine any self-respecting, image-conscious rock star today sullying their image by moonlighting as a children's teatime TV presenter, alongside a puppet. Can you? Having said that, I'm constantly amazed at the depths to which people will descend to appear on television:

And now, over on CBBC, it's Blue Peter, *presented by Ann Widdecombe, Plan B and one of the meerkats off the insurance adverts. Simples.*

The template had been created a couple of years earlier by *Rendezvous*, which was also presented by Muriel Young, who, before she was teamed with Wally Whyton, had to perform alongside three puppets: Fred Barker the dog, Olly Beak the owl and Pussy Cat Willum.

They say you should never work with children or animals. To that list, you can add puppets. I've often wondered if this was where Frank Oz got the idea for *The Muppet Show*.

Rendezvous also starred the legendary guitarist Bert Weedon, whose best-selling 'teach yourself' manual *Play in a Day* is credited as a major influence by everyone from Eric Clapton and Jimmy Page to Keith Richards and Pete Townshend.

My parents bought me a guitar and a copy of *Play in a Day* but I proved about as adept at the guitar as I had been on my grandad's banjo. I couldn't play after six months, let alone a day, and gave it up as a bad job. The nearest I got to rock guitar god was playing a cricket bat in front of the mirror.

Shortly before Bert Weedon died in 2012, I was intro-duced to him at a charity bash. I didn't have the heart to tell him that *Play in a Day* had proved beyond me.

Still, honour was satisfied. Bert won one of the raffle prizes, a signed copy of my book *Littlejohn's Britain*. I hope it baffled him as much as *Play in a Day* baffled me.

It was on TV that I watched my first ever FA Cup Final, between Wolverhampton Wanderers and Blackburn Rovers in 1960. I was particularly drawn to the tall Blackburn centre-forward, a Northern Irishman called Derek Dougan, even though he was on the losing side. I fancied myself as a centre-forward. By the age of six I was already playing regularly and taking a keen interest in the game. Apart from the FA Cup Final and England internationals there were few matches broadcast live, so this was a rare opportunity to see the professional game.

Most of the grown-up football I got to see was played on pitches at the back of our house on the Grange.

Every weekend there would be games between local league sides, mostly drawn from pubs and factories such as Perkins, Peter Brotherhood and Baker Perkins. I followed the fortunes of a team called BRAD, which stood for the British Railways Accounting Department. My dad knew a few of the players and they used to let me and some of the other kids warm up with them. To my young mind, they were every bit as good as the footballers I'd seen playing for Wolves or Blackburn. After the game on a Saturday, they'd leave the nets up for the Sunday morning games, a real treat. We were used to jumpers as goalposts, or the goal chalked on the playground wall at West Town.

Even in the depths of winter, we'd kick footballs on the Grange until it got dark.

Although he had played football as a boy, my dad wasn't especially interested in the professional game. Athletics was his passion and he had run for Essex as a schoolboy. According to his younger brother, Ken, Dad once ran the 100 yards in ten seconds flat in an inter-county competition. If that's true, Dad was certainly modest about his achievement. If he'd had his way, no one would ever have known.

When he was selected to run for Essex at Southend, he had no intention of telling his parents. They only found out because the athletics authorities demanded that parental permission was obtained before a boy could take part in the tournament. It was granted, but Bill made his parents swear not to go anywhere near Southend on the day.

In the event, Grandad and Ken did travel to the meeting and watched Bill win his race convincingly. I don't think Dad was aware at the time that they had been there, but when he had to bring the cup home to Vine Gardens the news was broken to him.

If Dad had any allegiance to a professional football team it was West Ham, whose ground was just round the corner from his original family home in Grosvenor

Gardens, East Ham. I've never worked out why a team from East Ham was called West Ham, but since the club are soon to move into the Olympic Stadium at Stratford I suppose it's academic now. Still, neither have I ever come to terms with the fact that a team named after Woolwich Arsenal, south of the Thames, play their football in north London. But that's another story.

On Saturday lunchtimes, Grandad and the other men would return from the docks. Saturday morning working was routine in most industries back then. He'd pick up Dad from Grosvenor Gardens and head off to the Anne Boleyn, the pub on the corner next to Upton Park, West Ham's ground. Upton Park is also known to locals as the Boleyn Ground – pronounced Bow-lin. Legend has it that the pitch stands on an old hunting lodge once used by Anne Boleyn before Henry VIII chopped off her head.

Dad and the other boys would sit on the steps outside the pub, drinking Vimto and feasting on arrowroot biscuits while their fathers drank pint after pint inside. Grandad later told me that it wasn't uncommon for him to sink eight to ten pints in a lunchtime session, with little intoxicating effect. Dock work was thirsty work.

Ten minutes before kick-off they'd collect their sons and file into the Chicken Run, an old wooden stand hemmed in by chicken wire. The boys would stand on beer crates borrowed from the boozer.

If we'd stayed in Essex, no doubt I'd have become a

West Ham fan, too. My Uncle Ron and my older cousins, Jackie and Russell, were season-ticket holders at Upton Park, as were several other members of the extended Littlejohn family.

The move to Peterborough scuppered that. Although Peterborough United, known as 'The Posh', had just been elected to the Football League my dad never took me to their London Road ground as a young boy. That would come later, when Ron and Russell came to visit.

In 1961, I started taking a real interest in football, following the results in the newspapers and on TV. Just like virtually every other household in Britain, we had a Saturday night ritual, gathering around the TV to check Dad's football pools coupon. It seemed as if everyone did the pools in those days, trying to pick the eight draws that would win them a fortune.

Agents from the respective pools companies – Zetters, Vernons and Littlewoods – distributed and collected coupons and entry fees, which I seem to think were about 2s. 6d. a week.

We never won anything. Few people ever did. The thrill was as much about taking part and dreaming about what you would do with the money if by some miracle you did win.

I don't know whether Nanna approved of gambling. I do know she took a dim view of a brash housewife from Castleford, Viv Nicholson, who that year won £152,319 (almost £3 million in today's money) and announced she was going to 'spend, spend, spend'.

Nanna was appalled at the vulgarity of it all. She was of the traditional view that 'money doesn't always bring happiness' and thought no good would come of it. Viv Nicholson proved her right, blowing the lot, getting deported from Malta for assaulting a policeman and ending up in a mental hospital. Nanna probably thought it served her right.

When the 1961 FA Cup Final came around, my allegiance was about to be settled. If Tottenham Hotspur beat Leicester City they would become the first club in the twentieth century to win the elusive league and cup double. They had already wrapped up the First Division title by the time they walked out at Wembley.

I discovered from my *Charles Buchan's Football Monthly* that you could send away for an official programme. I saved up and sent a postal order for a shilling (5p) and a stamped addressed envelope to The Secretary, Empire Stadium, Wembley Way, Wembley, London NW.

The week before the match the programme arrived. It was a work of art and I pored over it from cover to cover, absorbing the player profiles of both sides and studying the teams' routes to the final.

The front of the programme had Leicester City's name first, as if they were the home side. I hoped this was a simple case of alphabetical order rather than an omen.

On the day, I settled down in front of the TV for the BBC's coverage, which began at 11.15 a.m., even though kick-off wasn't until 3 p.m. Although ITV was also covering the game, for all big national occasions the BBC was the default option. National occasions didn't come much bigger than the FA Cup Final. I didn't budge. I even sung along to 'Abide With Me', words of which were included in the programme.

That programme was a modest twenty pages with just a handful of adverts for Double Diamond beer, Bovril and Senior Service untipped cigarettes. You could also send away for an official 1961 FA Cup Final football, made from vinyl, complete with reproduction autographs of the players from both sides, priced 7s. 6d. (37p). A modern Wembley-branded ball costs a tenner, surprisingly reasonable considering that a portion of fish and chips at the stadium is £7.50.

These days football programmes cost anything up to a tenner and are little more than glossy souvenir catalogues, flogging everything from overpriced XXXL replica shirts plastered with sponsors' names to hideous duvet covers in your team's colours. While no Premier League team would dream of accepting advertising from tobacco companies, today's vice of choice is celebrity endorsed online gambling, the crack cocaine of betting, snorted via an app on your mobile phone.

*

On Cup Final day, the cameras would follow the teams from their hotels, fans would be interviewed as they boarded trains and coaches and as they walked up Wembley Way. There was usually a TV feature, perhaps on a baker who had created a batch of cakes in the team colours.

Nanna had made me a navy blue and white rosette, with a little tinfoil FA Cup and 'Up The Spurs' written on it. When the game eventually kicked off, Tottenham seemed a little off the pace. Maybe the 'Double' was to remain a dream. In the thirty-eighth minute, they were handed an advantage when the Leicester left-back, Len Chalmers, broke his leg. Despite his injury, Chalmers didn't leave the pitch until ten minutes before the end, hobbling around on the wing to maintain numerical equality. Substitutes didn't exist in 1961, but the injury to Chalmers intensified the debate.

Second-half goals from Bobby Smith and Terry Dyson sealed victory and history was made. Spurs won the Double and that was me hooked for life. I can still reel off the 1961 team by heart:

Brown, Baker, Henry; Blanchflower, Norman, Mackay; Jones, White, Smith, Allen, Dyson

Cliff Jones was a thrilling Welsh winger who had a goal disallowed in the 1961 final. Between 1958 and 1968, he scored 135 goals in 318 appearances for Spurs and was widely considered the best player in his position in the world.

On the day I'm writing this chapter, 2 September 2013, the transfer has just been completed of another Welsh winger, Gareth Bale, from Spurs to Real Madrid for a world-record fee of £85.3 million and a reported salary of £256,000 a week.

I've been lucky enough to meet Cliff Jones a few times over the years. On one occasion, I asked him how much he thought he'd be worth these days.

Cliff just laughed and said: 'A bloody lot, boyo.'

Money has changed the game beyond recognition. One of the saddest aspects of modern football has been the downgrading of the FA Cup Final, once the prestigious pinnacle of the season.

That first final I watched in 1960 also saw a player, Dave Whelan, of Blackburn Rovers, break a leg. Fifty-three years later, Whelan was back at Wembley as owner of Wigan Athletic who were playing mega-rich Manchester City in the 2013 final.

Where once I would have settled down to soak up the atmosphere, I forgot the game was even being played and missed the first fifteen minutes.

That's because the climax of the world's greatest domestic cup competition has been shunted to a 5.15 p.m. kick-off to accommodate television schedules. It is no longer the season's finale, merely an early evening aperitif for the main event, the freak show that is *Britain's Got Talent*.

Far from being the only show in town, the FA Cup Final has been reduced to just another game, sandwiched between lower division play-offs and the Premier League. Wigan beat the multi-millionaires of Manchester City 1-0, one of the great cup giant-killing results of all time. But instead of heading off to the pub and the beach to celebrate, Wigan still had two more league games to play. They were subsequently relegated.

Relegation didn't entirely take the shine off their fairytale achievement in defeating Manchester City's cosmopolitan team of mercenaries, bankrolled by Arab oil riches.

There's no doubt, though, that the romance of the FA Cup has been diminished by football administrators who know the price of everything and the value of nothing.

It reminded me that these days I hate just about everything about professional football – except the football.

On reflection, perhaps my disillusion began when I was a boy. The captain of the 1961 Double-winning team was Danny Blanchflower, a Northern Ireland international right half. He signed for Spurs the year I was born and by the time of the 1961 final he was already thirty-five, relatively old for a top-level professional footballer by the

Dad in his Royal Navy uniform *c*.1942.

Bill and Min on their honeymoon in Weymouth, 1923.

Mum, Dad and me, 1955.

Sparke family photo, Ron's garden, Harold Wood, summer 1954. Grandad Bert (back second left, next to Dad); Hilda holding the baby.

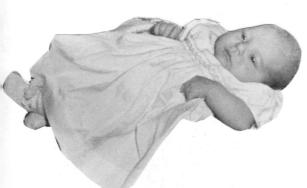

Who's a pretty boy then? My Christening photo.

The house that Mum and Dad built
Crossways, Shenfield, 1954

Shenfield serenade. Spot the fashionable
1950s paint palette motif wallpaper.

Stick 'em up. In the garden
at Crossways, 1956.

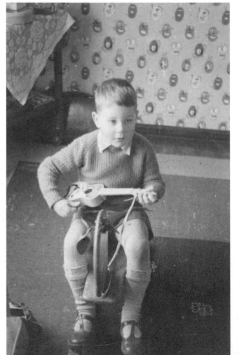

Viv and me and our new two-tone Ford Anglia 105E. Ledbury Road, Peterborough *c.* 1961.

My first bike.

Dad landscaped the back garden at Ledbury Road and built this wishing well.

The Littlejohns, 1958.

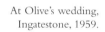

At Olive's wedding,
Ingatestone, 1959.

Viv and me go-karting
on The Grange *c*. 1962.

On the beach at Scarborough, 1963.

Santa's obviously been
on the sherry all day.

Muffin The Mule, live
at West Town School,
Peterborough *c.* 1959.

In the garden at
Ledbury Road, 1963

Bill Fraser. TV superstar and Ilford sweet shop proprietor.

TEX TUCKER'S FOUR FEATHER FALLS

THE CHILDREN'S OWN T.V. WESTERN

Danny Blanchflower and Jimmy Greaves with the FA Cup, 1962.

VESTA BEEF CURRY

AGRA INDIA

CHOPPED AND SHAPED BEEF WITH SOYA MINCE, VEGETABLES AND RICE

GENEROUS PORTION

SERVES ONE

ADD WATER EASY COOK JUST HEAT

standards of the day. Although footballers were not the big earners they have since become – the maximum wage was still £100 a week – Blanchflower supplemented his salary with advertising endorsements. For a while he was the face of the breakfast cereal Shredded Wheat, catch-phrase: 'Pass the hot milk, please' in his Belfast brogue.

When his playing career ended, Blanchflower stayed on as a coach. A few years after the Double victory – probably 1964 or 1965 – Blanchflower brought a reserve team to play at Peterborough.

In the days before first-team squads and a full set of substitutes, most clubs had proper reserve sides that played in a league called the Football Combination, fixtures which regularly attracted crowds of 10,000 and above.

I was thrilled. It would be the first time I'd ever seen a Spurs team in the flesh. OK, so it was a reserve side, but there were a couple of players who had turned out for the first team during the Double season – such as Frank Saul and Blanchflower's understudy, Tony Marchi – even if they hadn't played in the final. And, of course, I might get Danny Blanchflower's autograph.

In those days, teams often travelled by train, which was the case when Spurs came to town that day. Towards the end of the match, which I vaguely remember Posh winning, I left early and ran to the main railway station, bought a platform ticket and waited. I was determined not to miss my hero.

Three-quarters of an hour or so later, Danny Blanchflower and the rest of the team arrived and walked into the station buffet, which hadn't changed much since the 1930s: steaming urns of stewed tea, stale buns and curly cheese sandwiches under glass domes, and a fug of cigarette smoke that had turned the ceiling dark brown over the decades. All that was missing was Celia Johnson and Trevor Howard having a brief encounter in the corner.

Once they had paid for their tea and settled at their tables, I plucked up the courage to approach the great man.

Clutching my match programme, a team photo I'd brought from home and my autograph book, I went up to Danny and asked politely, 'Excuse me, Mr Blanchflower. Would you mind signing this, please?'

Blanchflower peered up from his mug of tea, gave me a quick once-over, and said: 'Fuck off, kid.'

With all the dignity I could muster, I somehow summoned a reply. 'In that case, I shall never eat Shredded Wheat again.'

My all-time football hero was not part of the Double squad but signed for Spurs later the same year. He didn't play in the 1961 final, but did appear on the back cover of the programme, advertising Bovril. James Peter Greaves was born at Manor Park, East Ham, in 1940, down the road from Grosvenor Gardens. Jimmy Greaves should have been spotted by West Ham's scouts but instead joined Chelsea, on the other side of London – making the same journey from east to west that my dad had made when he joined the police.

After scoring a record number of goals for Chelsea, 124 in 157 appearances, he was sold in April 1961 to the Italian side AC Milan. The young Greaves failed to settle and after a few months Tottenham manager Bill Nicholson brought him back to London, paying a transfer fee of £99,999 because he didn't want to burden him with the pressure of being the world's first £100,000 footballer.

I tried to model myself on Jimmy Greaves but could never emulate his innate elegance, explosive pace over short distances and instinctive ablity to bamboozle defenders and goalkeepers. As a schoolboy centre-forward I was more like his striking partner Bobby Smith, an old-fashioned English battering ram with the subtlety of a bull in a china shop. Crude but effective.

Greaves is still Tottenham's record goalscorer, with 266 in 379 matches. He scored 44 times in 57 matches for England, including six hat-tricks.

Jimmy went on to work as a TV and newspaper pundit. A few years ago I was invited to appear as a panellist on the show he presented with Ian St John, the former Liverpool player, another occasion when I've been fortunate to work alongside one of my boyhood idols.

As Michael Parkinson once said to me, when I inherited

his LBC radio show: 'The great thing about this job is that you get paid to meet your heroes.'

If Cliff Jones would have been worth 'a bloody lot' today, what price Greavesie in a market where Bale can command a transfer fee in excess of £85 million and more than a quarter of a million quid a week in wages?

Here's an indication of the changing value of money. In the mid-1980s, we were house-hunting in Highgate, north London. I walked into an estate agent's, said I was looking for a modest family home – four bedrooms, terraced would be fine – and asked to see some property details.

The agent inquired how much I had to spend. I might be able to stretch to as much as £100,000, I explained.

'I'm sorry, sir,' he said, condescendingly, 'but I don't think you'll find very much in that price bracket.'

'What do you mean?' I replied. 'A few years ago you could have bought Jimmy Greaves for a hundred grand.' And still had £1 in change.

There's a wonderful story about Greavesie from the 1962 World Cup. England were playing Brazil when a dog ran on to the pitch. Jimmy caught up with the dog and carried it to the sidelines, but not before the dog peed down his England shirt. The Brazilian winger Garrincha thought the incident so hilarious that after the game he took the dog home and adopted it as a pet.

In the 1980s my Spurs-mad friend Mike Collett commissioned a statuette of Garrincha's dog to be awarded each season to the fan who had shown most determination and dedication in following Tottenham away from home.

When I appeared as a manager on the first series of David Baddiel and Frank Skinner's *Fantasy Football League* show, I christened my fantasy side Garrincha's Dogs and took the trophy with me.

It sits on my desk to this day.

Part 2

*M*y bedroom at Ledbury Road was at the front of the house, with a large store cupboard over the stairs, which I used as a den. Out of the window I could look across the cornfields to the farm beyond. Long before anyone discovered the supposed phenomenon of crop circles, we kids would stamp our way through the fields in military formation to create a maze. From my room you could just about make out some of the elaborate patterns we had carved out. Years later, the lead singer of the Troggs, Reg Presley, spent the £1 million royalties he received from his song 'Love Is All Around' being chosen as the theme for the hit film *Four Weddings and a Funeral* on investigating crop circles. He was convinced the mysterious designs had been created by aliens from outer space. I could have saved him a lot of money.

The farm was home to Horrell's Dairies, a family firm with its own fleet of distinctive blue and white, horse-drawn milk floats. Milkmen wore peaked caps and white store coats and carried butter, eggs and cream, as well as milk – which came in one variety: full-fat. We'd often wander round the dairy, watching the cows being fed and milked, breathing in the pungent farmyard smells, stepping in cowpats, stroking the horses, admiring the skill of the resident farrier as he changed their shoes. We were welcomed, not run off the premises, as I suspect we would be today in the name of health and safety. Horrell's had its own bottling plant, steaming and sterilising the empties, refilling the clean bottles with milk, which only a few hours earlier had still been in the cow. The distance between land and table was a hop, skip and jump. People on the Netherton Estate were drinking milk produced in fields a few hundred yards away. Outside the dairy was an automatic vending machine which dispensed half-pint waxed cartons of milk for 3d. (just over 1p). The milkman would also carry half-pint bottles, which he'd sell direct from the cart. In many areas now, milk rounds have disappeared completely, put out of business by supermarkets that sell cheap milk imported from all over Europe. No doubt this makes sound economic sense, but unscrewing a plastic two-litre container of semi-skimmed from Holland can never replicate the sensous delight of popping the tinfoil cap on a glass bottle and glugging the full-fat contents direct from the cows grazing in the fields opposite your house.

Horrell's delivered to some of the houses in the street

but my mum preferred the Co-op, which gave her something called 'Divi'. This was an early version of modern supermarkets' loyalty card schemes. The Co-operative movement was a giant collective, run and operated by its members. Each member would be issued with a unique number that would be recited and recorded in a special book every time a purchase was made from any of the Co-op's many retail outlets, from grocery stores to dairies and undertakers. Your membership number entitled you to a discount, which could be claimed in cash twice a year, in time for the summer holidays and Christmas. I can remember queueing up with Mum and what seemed at the time like hundreds of other people at the main Co-op Department Store in Peterborough city centre, all waiting patiently in line to collect their cash 'bonus', which could run to several pounds. At the height of the scheme, in 1955, the Co-op had more than thirteen million members in over 30,000 stores. The 'Divi' was phased out in the 1970s when it became too expensive to administer. Fifty-odd years later, I can still recite my mum's 'Divi' number. It was seven-eight-six-eight.

The Co-op also operated its own abbatoir, which served its stores in Peterborough and surrounding towns and villages. Cattle, lambs and pigs were brought to market from farms within a radius of no more than thirty miles, so the provenance of the meat was always guaranteed.

How did we know this? The Co-op abbatoir was next

to the main railway line. Cows awaiting slaughter would graze in the fields alongside Westwood Bridge, where we used to go trainspotting, waiting for the *Flying Scotsman* to streak past on its way from King's Cross to Edinburgh. One day the cows were there, the next day they were mince, or steaks, or Sunday joints. We were well aware what went on in the building next door. It was part of the natural order of things. We weren't in the least bit squeamish.

Aged about seven, I was actually taken on a grand tour of an abbatoir during a summer holiday in Barnstaple, Devon. We called in on a cousin of my dad's whose husband was a slaughterman. It was with great pride that he showed us around his place of work, from live animals at one end to lifeless carcasses at the other. There was blood and guts and offal everywhere, like a medieval charnel house. I'd love to be able to tell you that I was deeply disturbed, that the plight of these poor animals stirred something sensitive deep inside me. The truth is: it didn't put me off meat for a moment. I still like my steaks medium-rare.

Never for an instant have I flirted with vegetarianism, although I don't go quite as far as a dear friend of mine who insists that if God had intended us to eat prawns he'd have put them on dry land, given them hooves and made them go 'moo'.

Today, the food chain stretches for thousands of miles.

It may have done wonders for availability but it has had a disastrous effect on quality and food safety. I simply refuse to believe that a battery chicken from Thailand, frozen and flown halfway round the world, is in any way comparable to, or as safe as, a free-range bird that has been bred, slaughtered, plucked and butchered on your doorstep.

We kids were never in any doubt where our food came from. The link between land and larder was there for all to see. Recent surveys have demonstrated that many modern schoolchildren have no idea of the origin of the food that ends up on their plates. They don't know milk comes from cows, or bacon from pigs, or eggs from chickens, or that fish don't actually have fingers. No wonder unscrupulous manufacturers have got away with passing off horse meat from Eastern Europe as prime hamburger.

Meat has always been relatively expensive, the best cuts at least. We only ever had a joint on a Sunday: beef or lamb usually, since I wouldn't eat pork. My dad maintained I'd inherited some Jewish genes from his Grandma Rauss, whose family had fled from Eastern Europe to escape the pogroms in the nineteenth century. By the time Emily married Great-Grandpa Littlejohn – William Henry V, the one who lost his hackney cab business to a fire – her dad had anglicised the family name and changed it to Rowse. She never ate pork either, apparently, presumably on traditional religious grounds.

Whatever the reason, I still can't even stand the smell of roast pork, or grilled pork chops, let alone the taste. Which is curious, since I love bacon, sausages, pork pies, any kind of smoked pork product. While my dad simply accepted that I didn't like pork, my mum saw it as a challenge. She'd serve me roast pork with thick Bisto gravy and try to convince me it was roast beef. As if I couldn't tell the difference. She'd even smother pork chops with mint sauce and swear blind it was lamb. Nice try, Mum, but you're not fooling me.

Mum deserved full marks for persistence. She was always trying to broaden my stubbornly conservative palate. When I got older she tried to persuade me that a duck she'd found in the bottom of the freezer was chicken. 'Don't be daft, Mum. It's not even the same shape.'

'It got flattened in the freezer,' she claimed. I still wasn't having any of it.

Despite my fondness for beef, I was never keen on my dad's favourite meal of boiled beef and carrots. This popular East End dish had been immortalised in the old music-hall favourite by Harry Champion. It was another song I was taught at an early age:

> *Boiled beef and carrots,*
> *Boiled beef and carrots,*

That's the stuff for your Derby Kell,
Makes you fit and keeps you well.
Don't live like vegetarians
On food they give to parrots,
Blow out your kite, from morn 'til night,
On boiled beef and carrots.

I had no idea initially what the words meant. 'Derby Kell' is Cockney rhyming slang for stomach. Derby Kelly = belly. Derby, or Darby, Kelly was reputed to be a music-hall singer, but I couldn't swear to it.

'Blow out your kite' is slang for 'fill your stomach', but not rhyming slang. One explanation is that 'kite' is derived from the Old English word 'kyte', meaning 'womb', which somehow evolved to mean 'stomach'.

Slang, and especially rhyming slang, has always fascinated me. Much of today's modern rhyming slang was made up in the 1980s by the writers of the TV series *Minder*. But a lot of it dates back to the nineteenth century. When I was a kid, my grandad gave me *Charlie Peace's Book of Slang*, named after a notorious Victorian burglar. I wish I still had it. Though many of the words are long extinct, plenty survive to this day.

For instance, I could never work out how 'kettle' came to mean 'watch'. I was sure it wasn't rhyming slang. Was it because you had to watch a kettle boiling on the stove? It continued to bug me, so when I was presenting the morning show on LBC radio I put out an appeal for anyone who could come up with the reason.

Within minutes, a cabbie called in. He explained that 'kettle' was an early example of double rhyming slang, employed in the East End to confuse the constabulary. It came from 'kettle and hob' = 'fob', as in fob watch, worn on a chain from a waistcoat.

Probably the best example of this mutated form of rhyming slang is still in common use today. I'm talking about 'Aris', as in 'backside'. To give someone a kick up the Aris is to administer a swift boot to their bottom. But where did it come from? Most people assume that 'Aris' is a derivation of 'arse'. Most people would be wrong.

Aris is short for 'Aristotle', the ancient Greek philosopher and polymath. Aristotle rhymes with 'bottle'. Bottle is short for 'bottle and glass'. Bottle and glass = arse. Geddit?

'Aris' is perhaps the only example of triple rhyming slang, although when this book is published I shouldn't be surprised if some readers don't write to me with a dozen others.

Anyway, back to boiled beef and carrots. Preparing it with a cheap cut of silverside or salt brisket, Mum would make her version in a pressure cooker to ensure maximum tenderness. I read recently that pressure cookers are making a comeback as people investigate economy cuts again. Silverside is back on the menu. In fancy French restaurants, they're calling boiled beef and carrots *'pot au feu'* and knocking it out at £30 a pop.

Even though I've never cared for the texture of boiled beef, it makes great gravy. Mum would serve it to me as soup, with chunks of crusty bread. We ate bread every day when I was a kid. I suppose it was a way of filling us up. My dad would have bread and jam after every meal. There was an advert which claimed: 'Four slices a day is the well-balanced way'.

On Sunday mornings, I'd go with Dad to his allotment, which he shared with my 'Uncle' Alan Brown, a friend who worked at W. M. Cory's, one of the local oil distribution companies in Midland Road, backing on to the railway line. Dad and Alan grew all their own vegetables: sprouts, carrots, cauliflowers, cabbages, potatoes, parsnips, turnips. We'd eat whatever was in season, fresh from the ground. I used to love shelling peas in a colander on the draining board. I'd eat them raw, straight from the pod, savouring their buttery sweetness. You don't see fresh peas in supermarkets so much any more and those you buy from surviving greengrocer's and farmers' markets are tough as tungsten-tipped bullets. Frozen food firms have cornered the market. Peas are one of the few foods that taste better from the freezer than from the pod. But you can't beat caulis and potatoes served within hours of being pulled from the earth, mud shaken off and boiled in salty water.

Unlike most cooks in the fifties and sixties, Mum didn't believe in boiling her vegetables to buggery, so that they resembled the sort of flavourless slop served up in prisons and school canteens. She was a pioneer of the *al dente* school in Britain.

Rare meat was still frowned upon, however, and our joints of beef and lamb were always well done. We'd have a couple of slices with fresh veg and Yorkshire pudding for Sunday dinner – never lunch – and another slice cold in a sandwich or with a salad at teatime, roughly 6 p.m. Mum even made Yorkshire pudding with lamb, because Dad used to like it after dinner with jam or golden syrup. Strange, thinking back, since Yorkshire pud used to be a strictly northern tradition and, to the best of my knowledge, Peterborough was as far north as any of the Littlejohns had ever settled, if you don't count the Scottish interlude during the war. And Peterborough is only seventy miles north of London, well short of 'eh bah gum' land. Maybe it's a habit my old man picked up in the navy. Either that, or it was just another way of making the meal go further.

Mum was certainly skilled at making meals stretch over more than one day. Waste not, want not was the catchphrase for women of her generation, who had grown up accustomed to the privations of wartime rationing. Nothing was ever thrown away. Monday night tea was always cold meat with bubble and squeak, leftover potato and veg fried to a crisp in the pan. If there was any meat still around on Tuesday, Mum and Nanna would have it for lunch with a tomato and a slice of cucumber.

She'd keep the beef dripping in a tub, covered with a muslin cloth, in the larder. It would be years before we owned a fridge. Dad would round off Monday tea with a large chunk of bread smeared with a thick layer of dripping.

Occasionally, Sunday dinner would be roast chicken, fresh from the butcher, never frozen, with roast spuds, cauli and white sauce. Again, we'd have it cold for tea and Mum would boil up the carcass and leftover vegetables to make a delicious soup, served with plenty of bread. We ate a lot of soup in those days.

We also ate a lot of rhubarb, which grew in vast quantities on the allotment. Stewed rhubarb, rhubarb and apple pie, rhubarb crumble, rhubarb and apple crumble, all smothered in demerara sugar and drowned in Bird's custard to mask the bitter aftertaste of this stringy, alleged 'fruit'. Rhubarb looks like crimson celery. It also tastes like crimson celery, even though it isn't related to celery. You might just as well stew celery and smother it with sugar and custard. Mum swore by rhubarb's laxative properties, force-feeding it to us in bulk if she suspected we were having a 'bit of trouble'. She was right. Eat enough rhubarb and you'll be as regular as clockwork. Every hour, on the hour.

★

As the sixties progressed, Mum would become more adventurous with the leftovers. She discovered the delights of Vesta curries, which came in a cardboard box, dehydrated, with rice, dried raisins and lumps of 'meat' which resembled a cross between Oxo cubes and a £1 deal of cannabis resin. On a Monday teatime, Mum would chuck in the leftovers with the Vesta mix, add boiling water and chopped apples and let it simmer, stirring occasionally. From what I recall, Vesta curries came in beef, chicken and paella varieties, but for some reason not lamb. Not that it mattered to Mum. She simply used a Vesta beef curry mix to spice up the lamb. If she'd had leftover roast pork, that too would have gone in the pot – no doubt served with mint sauce on the side to convince me it was lamb curry. Still, it was impossibly exotic, even if the reconstituted 'meat' that came in the packet was virtually indigestible. Later still, after she'd enrolled in a 'Continental Cookery' evening class, she started introducing pasta to our diet. Of course, it wasn't called 'pasta' then, it was all spaghetti, bought from a pioneering Italian deli in Gladstone Street, where many of Peterborough's early immigrants had settled. Up until that time, the only spaghetti we'd ever encountered came in tins from Heinz, swimming in saccharine-flavoured, tomato-style sauce. This was always served on toast, for added carbohydrate. Authentic Italian spaghetti came in three-feet-long packets, which presented a serious logistical challenge. You could always break it into two or three pieces, but that would be cheating. Cooking the stuff whole was half the fun. Mum would boil a pot of water on the stove and Viv and I would stand on a chair taking turns feeding in the stiff lengths of spaghetti, like steelworkers threading pig iron into a strip mill, until it wilted and disappeared below the surface. When it emerged a few minutes later, flaccid and steaming, Mum would cut it into bite-sized lengths with a pair of kitchen scissors.

This thrilling new ingredient opened up a world of opportunities for recycling leftovers. At Christmas, it really came into its own. What cold turkey remained after Boxing Day went into a giant casserole with spaghetti. Come New Year, we were still eating Mum's patent turkey noodle surprise long after the decorations had come down on Twelfth Night.

During the week, we always had three square meals a day. Before we left for school, Viv and I would be given porridge in winter and cornflakes in summer. We'd squabble over who got the cream off the top of the milk. Mum swore by Scott's Porage Oats, perhaps because I was convinced that the bloke on the box in full Highland Games rig, white vest and tartan kilt, putting the shot, was my dad. Looking back at old pictures, there was certainly a passing resemblance. I could never work out why Scott's Porage Oats was called 'porage' and not 'porridge'. Must have been a Scottish spelling. The TV commercial for Scott's is still etched on my memory. To the tune of 'Scotland the Brave', featuring the obligatory bagpipes, it went:

Start off the day with piping,
Start off the day with piping,
Start off the day with piping,
Scott's Porage Oats.

This was proper porridge, mind you, made with half-water/half-milk and a generous pinch of salt, and left to cook in a saucepan on the stove for a good half-hour, bubbling away like volcanic lava, before it was ready to serve. Not the instant microwave wallpaper paste you get today.

Cornflakes were always Kellogg's. I'm not sure you could buy any other. Supermarkets were in their infancy and own-brand lines didn't exist. Once in a blue moon, as a treat, we would get more expensive Weetabix or Shredded Wheat – probably the week Mum cashed in her 'Divi'.

In my early years at West Town, I stayed for school dinners. The school had its own canteen, staffed by a jolly bunch of dinner ladies from central casting, bosomy women of a certain age with hairnets and raucous laughs, a bit like the actress Peggy Mount. I imagine they'd all served in the NAAFI during the war. Certainly, the food hadn't progressed much. It was probably healthier when Britain was still on the ration. The menu was supposed to be different each day, but it was impossible to tell one meal from another. The main ingredients appeared to be suet and grisly, inadequately mashed potatoes marinaded in dishwater. As for the meat, was today's main course lamb, beef or pork? Who could tell? Without mint sauce or apple sauce to give you a clue, your guess was as good as anyone else's. The only common characteristic was veins running through every slice. Varicose veins, probably, judging by the lumps.

Every time I watch the Neil Simon movie *The Odd Couple*, starring Jack Lemmon and Walter Matthau as flat-mates Felix Ungar and Oscar Madison, my mind wanders back to school dinners. There's a fabulous scene in which the slovenly Oscar offers a guest some food:

> *What you got?*
> *I got, uh, brown sandwiches and, uh, green sandwiches. Which one do you want?*
> *What's the green?*
> *It's either very new cheese or very old meat.*
> *I'll take the brown.*

At West Town, we were offered either brown meat or grey meat. Or grey-brown meat. I took the browny-grey.

On Fridays, we were always given fish, a throwback

to the Christian tradition of meat-free Fridays, still observed by many practising Catholics. At least, that's what they told us. It wasn't like any fish I'd ever eaten. Perhaps they had some dried snoek left over from 1944 and didn't want to waste it. Pudding was always some kind of suet dish. If we were really lucky, they'd give us an anaemic jam roly-poly. Today's schools offer a variety of food to cater to religious and cultural differences. At West Town, the vegetarian alternative was to go hungry.

The day I was old enough to ride a bike unaccompanied, my number came up on the escape committee and I'd cycle home for lunch, a mile each way. Dad, too, would come home from his office in town, next to the station. This would be our main meal of the day: bangers and mash, mince and potatoes, shepherd's pie; steak and kidney pud (heavy on the kidney) with rich, glutinous gravy; braised steak, braised lamb, liver and bacon, liver and onions.

Every Friday, Mum bought fish from the Grimsby Fish Man, who did his rounds in an ancient Bedford van, with his catch packed in ice. By the time it got to our house, it was swimming in warm water. The Grimsby Fish Man couldn't afford a proper refrigeration unit, but he swore the fish was fresh and, to be fair to him, it tasted fresh. You could still smell the sea, although that might just have been the Grimsby Fish Man's natural aroma.

An occupational hazard, I guess. After the first twenty years, I imagine you don't even notice it.

We bought a lot of stuff from door-to-door salesmen in the early sixties. One Christmas, my present was *The Junior World Encyclopedia*, which came in sixteen parts, delivered once a month. My dad bought it from a travelling encyclopedia salesman and paid for it in instalments. It was first published in 1960 and was an eagerly anticipated monthly source of knowledge, much of it utterly useless but nonetheless fascinating. Thanks to the Junior World series, I discovered that Paracutin is a Mexican volcano (from Volume 12 – Paracutin to Quicksand). If I'm ever invited on *Mastermind*, that might come in handy one day.

The Man from the Pru (Prudential Insurance) came round to collect his premiums; as did the agent from the football pools. There were always people coming to the door, from men with suitcases containing dusters, brooms and assorted tins of polish, to gypsies selling lucky heather. That was before a knock from the 'travelling community' was accompanied by an offer to 'Tarmac yer droive, sor?'.

My favourite was the Corona Man, who delivered lemonade in bottles with swing-top stoppers. There was great excitement when Corona introduced Coola, a cut-price, own-brand cola to rival Coke and Pepsi. Up until then, the only people who had access to cola were those with contacts on the USAF base at Alconbury.

Another chap sold electrical appliances on tick from a suitcase, like George Mueller from HBO's *Boardwalk Empire*, an FBI agent on the run who flogged irons door-to-door on behalf of the Faraday Electrical Corporation of Chicago. I wonder if our chap had a hidden secret. I do know we had a second cousin by marriage who travelled in ladies' underwear and was rumoured to have gone over the side with one of his best customers. But we never talked about it.

I may have led a sheltered life, but as I got older I became aware there was such a thing as marital infidelity among adults. I have no idea how common it was, but married couples tended to stay together regardless, either out of economic necessity or for the good of the children. I don't think I knew of anyone in our family, or among our immediate circle of friends, who was divorced when I was growing up. There were a handful of kids at school being brought up by one parent, or their grandparents, but that was usually because one or both of their parents had died.

I'm not suggesting that anyone should stay in a loveless marriage or an abusive relationship. Sometimes divorce is the only sensible way out, for all concerned, including the kids. But married couples do seem to split up far too easily today. I was fortunate to have been raised in a loving, two-parent household, for which I will be for ever grateful.

When I came to the end of writing this book, in October 2013, one headline leapt out at me from the *Daily Mail*: 'Half of today's babies will see their parents split up'. Have you ever read a sadder statistic than the news that by the time they are fifteen, half of all children in England and Wales will have parents who no longer live together? There is no more damning indictment of broken Britain than the millions of kids condemned to be brought up in broken homes.

From the Grimsby Fish Man, we'd have cod or plaice, which would be steamed in parsley sauce, with mash, naturally, or fried in breadcrumbs. My nanna in Ilford used to fry her fish in matzo meal, but there wasn't much call for matzo in Peterborough in the 1960s. We always had 'afters', too, what we'd nowadays call dessert – although I notice the more demotic 'pudding' is enjoying something of a revival. We ate of lot of rice pudding, presumably because it was cheap, enlivened by a dollop of jam. Mum was always baking, too. A particular favourite was black-berry and apple. We'd pick the blackberries ourselves, on Sunday rambles in the nearby fields, and, as the garden became more established, Dad would grow our own apples. Cox's Orange Pippins, I seem to recall. I could never work out why an apple was called an orange. It remains one of life's enduring mysteries. As a special treat, we'd occasionally be given Mum's celebrated Dutch Apple

Pie, a delicious strudel for which she had won first prize in a city-wide 'Continental Cookery' competition and of which she was justly proud.

You might have thought that dinner would fill us up until next morning. But, no. Mum was terrified we might get hungry again. When we got home from school, we'd have tea – our third meal of the day. Eggs played a major part in tea. Boiled eggs with soldiers, fried eggs, poached eggs. Mum bought her eggs from a chap who lived further down Ledbury Road and worked on a poultry farm. Long before the Beatles came up with 'I Am the Walrus', he was the Egg Man. Once I week I was sent to collect them. These weren't ordinary eggs: they were huge. So enormous, in fact, that they wouldn't fit into standard-sized egg boxes, which meant he couldn't sell them to grocery stores and supermarkets. The good news was that they all had double yolks.

My absolute favourite tea was eggs in a bird's nest, a double poached egg in a hollowed-out mountain of mashed potato. Mixed with Heinz Tomato Ketchup, it was a psychedelic riot of red and yellow luxury, the colours of Noddy's car or Rupert Bear's jumper-and-trousers combo. If Tracey Emin submitted eggs in a bird's nest for the Turner Prize today she'd be the clear winner.

Talk about comfort food. Eggs in a bird's nest was a deep-filled duvet on a duck-down, sprung mattress – even though no one had ever heard of duvets in the 1960s. We still snuggled under eiderdowns until continental quilts came along a decade later.

And just in case we were peckish before we went to bed, we'd have one of Mrs Rolph's broken biscuits and a cup of cocoa, Ovaltine or Horlicks, the Food Drink of the Night.

In the years leading up to the Second World War, Ovaltine sponsored a show on Radio Luxembourg and launched a club aimed at children, called the Ovaltineys, which reached Britain via long wave. In the 1960s, Radio Luxembourg was to play an important part in my life, but in the 1930s Mum and her sister Olive both remember listening to the show on the wireless at their home in Gidea Park. Club members received their own badge and a special Ovaltineys comic. By the time war broke out, ending transmission, there were over five million Ovaltineys. In the sixties, the club was revived and relaunched, under the joint presidency of Eric Morecambe and Ernie Wise (more about Ernie Wise later). This intro- duced a whole new generation of children to the famous Ovaltineys' theme tune:

> We are the Ovaltineys,
> Little girls and boys;
> Make your requests, we'll not refuse you,
> We are here just to amuse you.

Would you like a song or story,
Will you share our joys?
At games and sports we're more than keen;
No merrier children could be seen,
Because we all drink Ovaltine,
We're happy girls and boys!

In August 2013, the British Heart Foundation issued an alarming report about childhood obesity. It estimated that almost a third of all children in Britain are clinically obese, a condition which could cause myriad problems in later life, including diabetes, breathing difficulties and heart disease. The study revealed that almost half of boys and over a third of girls go without breakfast. Some 80 per cent of children aged five to fifteen are not eating the recommended five portions of fruit and veg a day.

Around 85 per cent of girls and 73 per cent of boys do not undertake the recommended one hour of physical activity a day. A quarter of children aged two to fifteen are inactive for at least six hours a day at the weekend. The UK has the highest rate of child obesity in Western Europe, which is estimated to cost the NHS about £4.2 billion a year. In the ten years to 2013, a total of 20,885 young people were treated in hospital for obesity related conditions. And today this figure is showing a sharp, fourfold increase. Simon Gillespie of the British Heart Foundation said that children needed to 'get outside on a summer's day rather than sitting in front of the computer'.

Amen to that. When I was growing up, no one had ever heard the word 'obesity'. You might have thought that because we ate a high-fat, carbohydrate-rich diet, packed with spuds, bread and sugary puddings, we would all have been waddling around like hippos. The fact is: fat kids were few and far between. Those who were carrying a few extra pounds round the midriff were teased unmercifully – 'Piggy' or 'Bunter' being the most common nicknames.

We were told not be cruel because they couldn't help being overweight. It was down to their 'glands', whatever they were. Either that, or they had 'big bones'. Curious that, because the one thing all these kids had in common was that they ate more than anyone else and had an aversion to games. 'Greedy and lazy' would cover it. They weren't sent to child psychologists for counselling. They were put on diets and forced to take more exercise. There was no hiding place. At playtime, the fat boys were made to go in goal, thus freeing up those with callipers to play on the wing. Playing cricket in the summer, they volunteered to keep wicket since that required less running around than fielding at mid-wicket, next to the bike sheds.

The teachers weren't especially sympathetic. No one was excused PE because they were overweight. If they struggled to clamber over the vaulting horse or climb the wall bars, they were made to stay behind until they managed it. From a distance of fifty years, this may seem like child cruelty, but the ethos back then was very much that you had to be cruel to be kind. Children with what we would today call 'weight issues' were regarded as architects of their own flab, not victims of random misfortune to be indulged and patronised.

Let's consider the key findings of that 2013 study by the British Heart Foundation. One in three children now go without breakfast. Women of my mother's generation would be horrified. I've already described how we were never sent off to school without having eaten at least a bowl of cereal or porridge. At the weekend, we might get egg on toast or a fry-up on Sunday, with green back bacon sliced to order by the local butcher and double yolks from the Egg Man. Breakfast was the most important meal of the day. It still is, as far as I'm concerned, the key to a decent diet. As the old adage has it:

Breakfast like a king, lunch like a prince and dine like a pauper.

That still applies. There is no excuse today for any child having to go without breakfast, even in low-income households. Granted, the pressures of life mean that women have to go out to work to balance the family budget. But that shouldn't relieve them of the responsibility for ensuring that their kids start the day with a decent breakfast, even if it's only cereal or toast and jam. Microwave porridge takes two minutes. And in homes where no one works, parents have plenty of time to prepare breakfast.

Nor is there any reason why children shouldn't regularly be given fresh fruit and vegetables. Food doesn't come any faster than bananas and oranges and it's a darn sight cheaper than the processed, salt-heavy, microwaveable muck that mothers are content to shovel down their kids. Mind you, looking at the state of some of the tattooed XXXL monster mums propping themselves up on pushchairs outside school gates these days, it's hardly surprising. If these woman have no respect for their own bodies, how can they be expected to raise healthy children?

But quite apart from the slurry that passes for food in many households, the most worrying finding of the British Heart Foundation is that roughly three-quarters of school-age children take less than an hour's physical exercise a day. When I was at West Town, we had two hours of compulsory PE each week as part of the curriculum. Walking or cycling to school, and going home for lunch, took up at least an hour a day. That was on top of organised games and two playground breaks a day. There was no such thing as the 'school run' in the 1960s. Today, every town and city has its daily caravan of yummy mummies bringing their children to school in giant 4x4s, blocking the roads and parking on the pavements. What's even more absurd is that, having driven a mile or so to school, many of these women then head off to the nearest 'leisure centre' for their designer Pilates class or one-on-one personal training sessions. If they could be bothered to walk their kids to school, they wouldn't need to subscribe to expensive exercise classes. Their kids would be healthier, too.

As for many schools in England today, they are guilty of dereliction of duty when it comes to physical education. An Ofsted report published in February 2013 concluded that there is far too little strenuous, physical activity in schools. Over a four-year period, Ofsted visited 120 primary and eleven secondary schools. Its report stated: 'Pupils were not challenged to warm up vigorously or build stamina and strength by participating in sustained periods of physical activity. They were often prevented from exercising for extended periods because teachers interrupted their learning or took too long to introduce new tasks.' It also highlighted the scandal of schools scrapping competitive sport, as a direct consequence of the pernicious 'all must have prizes' culture in which no one is allowed to come second, let alone last, because it might damage the little darlings' 'self-esteem'.

As I have remarked before: what the hell would my old headmaster Eric Sutton have made of it?

*

Conkers were an essential element of every schoolboy's armoury, stuffed into satchels and blazer pockets along with half-sucked gobstoppers and dirty hankies. Conkers are horse chestnuts, best harvested from the trees by throwing sticks up into the branches, then drilled through the middle and suspended from lengths of string, knotted to keep the conker in place. At West Town, contests were held in the playground, competitors taking it in turns to try to smash their opponent's conker. In the version we played, you had three goes at demolishing your opponent's conker. After that it was his turn to try to shatter yours. Conkers was a boys' game. I have no recollection of girls being allowed, or even wanting, to take part.

The winner would take on all comers until either he prevailed or his conker was destroyed by a challenger. After the first victory, your conker becomes a 'oner', indicating its status and durability in battle. Subsequent wins moved it up the scale – a 'twoer', 'threeer' and so on. A 'sixer' was a badge of honour. Only once did I ever reach the giddy heights of a 'niner'. I retired it immediately and gave it pride of place on my bedroom windowsill.

We would go to elaborate lengths to harden our conkers, even marinading them in malt vinegar for months, like pickled onions. I even persuaded my mum to bake a batch in the oven to toughen the shells. In some parts of the country, this was considered cheating but we looked upon the toughening-up process as integral to the skill of the game. Drilling the hole through the middle of the conker required precision. If the points of entry and exit were not 'clean', the shell could fracture more easily, rendering it worse than useless in combat. One good clatter and it would disintegrate into a dozen pieces. After experimenting with my dad's manually operated hand-drill, I found that a meat skewer did the trick just as well.

The sport of conkers was not without its risks. In the wrong hands a 'sixer' could be a lethal weapon. Some boys' aim and hand-to-eye coordination left much to be desired. Bruised and cracked knuckles were common. Head injuries were not unknown. Occasionally a conker would fly off its string and hit a bystander. Even though the hazards were apparent, there was never any suggestion that conkers should be banned. Headmaster Sutton would patrol the playground, looking on approvingly as his pupils were locked in combat. Anything which brought out the competitive spirit was OK with him.

Fast-forward fifty years. A survey conducted in 2011 by the Children's Play Council revealed that conkers are now banned by one in six schools. It's not just the safety aspect: some schools prohibit conkers anywhere on the premises on the grounds that children suffering from nut allergies may suffer an anaphylactic shock if they are exposed to them. A few years ago, I heard from parents at one school in Cumbria where the head had allowed conkers to be played but insisted on the kids wearing safety goggles. The Health and Safety Executive tried to rubbish the story, saying it was a 'myth'. But it happened, if not as a result of an official edict but because in these risk-averse times schools are terrified of being sued if anyone gets hurt.

Tim Gill, the former director of the Play Council, said schools have forgotten 'how to give children a good child-hood'. He said: 'Bumps and scrapes and dealing with life's trials are part and parcel of growing into a confident and resilient person.' Precisely.

Some schools have even banned marbles from the playground, in case a child gets injured. Other games such as British Bulldog have also gone on the proscribed list. While it is, of course, sensible to take precautions, wrapping kids in cotton wool and eliminating all risk is absurd.

Yes, we suffered occasional cuts and bruises. But my generation was a damn sight fitter than today's pasty faced, flabby breed. We lived outside, close to the edge, always getting into scrapes – climbing, brawling; piling fifteen to the dozen on to rocking donkeys; trying to make park swings loop the loop; slide-tackling on cinders; attempting diving slip catches on concrete; and trying to dunk each other in ponds. And, yes, smashing each other round the knuckles – and, sometimes, the head – with conkers, which we had gathered by throwing sticks up into trees.

Even that's banned in some areas today. A few years

ago a reader from Nottinghamshire sent me a photograph of an official sign erected by Charnwood District Council at the base of a horse chestnut tree. In capital letters designed not to be ignored, it read: 'CONKER COLLECTION: Do not throw sticks etc. into this tree as it could cause injury to people walking beneath.'

What's even more depressing is that modern children are 'inactive' for six hours a day on Saturdays and Sundays. The only time I was ever 'inactive' at the weekend was when I was asleep or the rain was so heavy I couldn't play outside and had to stay indoors, watching professional wrestling or *The Cruel Sea* on black and white TV. The weekend was the time we were all encouraged to run wild: climbing trees, playing sports, riding bikes, exploring the outer limits of the local farmland.

Ledbury Road was still a building site in the early 1960s. It was a giant adventure playground. The shells of half-built houses looked like bombed-out buildings, the kind of devastation we'd seen on newsreels from the Second World War. Every windowless frame was a sniper's vantage point; every bare, wooden landing an enemy position to be captured. Wheelbarrows doubled as jeeps. My dad fashioned me a Winchester rifle from a discarded plank of wood. If we were thirsty we'd drink from standpipes or hosepipes.

Helpfully, the workmen would often leave the keys in

the ignition of their dumper trucks. It was an irresistible temptation. Some of the older boys quickly worked out how to drive them and it was not unusual for a dumper truck full of young hooligans to be spotted careering across the estate at full lick, diesel fumes spluttering out of an upright exhaust at the rear. Although we ran amok on the building sites, we were always careful not to smash anything which wasn't already broken to smithereens. Mindless vandalism simply wouldn't have occurred to us. We'd have been too terrified of the fallout when the site manager found out and told our parents. And, anyway, we didn't want to do anything which might jeopardise our chances of repeating our escapades the following weekend.

One time, we even set up a roadblock. Checkpoint Charlie was the name given to the most notorious crossing between East and West Berlin after the Berlin Wall went up in 1961. We'd seen it on TV and cinema newsreels. Every foot passenger and vehicle had to be checked before passing from the Soviet zone into the Allied zone.

This gave us a great idea. Why not build our own Checkpoint Charlie in Ledbury Road? There were plenty of materials to hand, so, with the aid of a couple of oil drums and a roof joist from a half-finished semi-detached, we were able to construct a barrier. There wasn't much through traffic back then, but we flagged down what vehicles there were and, armed with toy guns, asked the drivers to account for themselves. We did think about charging them 3d. for safe passage, but that would have been pushing our luck. You might have expected the drivers to be furious, but they were all happy to play along. Maybe growing up in wartime Britain they'd become used to being asked for their ID cards. Having established whether they were friend or foe, we raised the barrier, with some effort, and waved them through with a military salute.

Weekends had their own rhythm and routine. On Saturday mornings in the early sixties without fail we'd head for town immediately after breakfast. While Mum did her fruit and vegetable shopping on the open-air market, next to the cattle market behind the Embassy cinema, Dad would take us to the Public Library, on the Broadway. He'd escort Viv round the children's section, leaving me to explore the adult section. By the age of eight, I'd already graduated to grown-up literature. Or so I convinced myself. My favourite book was the historical parody *1066 and All That*, written by W. C. Sellar and R. J. Yeatman and illustrated by John Reynolds. It started as a serial in *Punch* magazine and was published in hardback in 1930. I must have borrowed it from the library at least a dozen times.

In the early 1990s, I wrote a column for *Punch*, then edited by David Thomas. And for the past twenty-five years, my newspaper columns have been peppered with parodies of dubious quality. I've often wondered how much of a debt I owe to the authors of *1066 and All That*.

I think we were allowed four books on loan at any one time. Each Saturday, we could return two, exchange them for two more. The librarian would date-stamp a sheet in the front of the book, take our tickets and place them in a card index. Failure to bring back the books on time incurred a fine of a shilling (5p).

The library was a typically solid, red-brick Edwardian structure, which had first opened in 1906. Like most municipal buildings of its era it was intended to inspire a sense of awe and reverence. It cost £6000 to build and was donated to the city by the Dunfermline-born American steel magnate and philanthropist Andrew Carnegie, of New York's Carnegie Hall fame, via his libraries foundation. Between 1883 and 1929, Carnegie's money paid for 2509 libraries throughout the British Empire and in the USA. Peterborough was just one of 660 built in Great Britain and Ireland, many of them in the Beaux Arts style. Carnegie was given freedom of the City of Peterborough on the day the library opened. The library's northern elevation featured a striking bay window decorated with stained glass and the building wouldn't look out of place among some of the fine architecture in London's Kensington at the back of the Albert Hall. In fact, the

West Front of Peterborough Cathedral is depicted on the frieze running around the Albert Hall.

It remained the city's library until 1990, when it was converted into a night-club. The new library looks less like a temple of learning and more like a cut-price sports goods warehouse in an out-of-town retail park. When I retraced my childhood footsteps while refreshing my memory for this book, the old library had been abandoned and was boarded up. I was overwhelmed with sadness. So much for Carnegie's philanthropy.

Around the corner from the library was the joke shop. We'd often visit it on the way home. Stink bombs, false fangs, plastic dog turds, farting powder, whoopee cushions, exploding cigars, the 'nail through the finger' trick, invisible ink, little battery-powered buttons you placed in your palms and which would administer a mild electric shock when you shook hands with someone. All could be yours for a few pennies of your pocket money.

Stink bombs were especially unpleasant, the mildest of which contained ammonium sulphide, which smells of rotten eggs. They came in little glass phials, which detonated when smashed. You could make them at home with your junior chemistry set and set them off discreetly on crowded buses, taking care to jump off before the stench became overwhelming. Can you imagine setting off a stink bomb on a bus today? It would be a job for the anti-terrorist squad.

On Saturday mornings we'd also call in at David Greig's grocery emporium, opposite the Bull Hotel, in Westgate. Greig opened his first store in 1870, in London's Brixton, and by the 1960s the company had 220 shops across Britain. At one time Greig's was considered to be the main rival of J. Sainsbury.

This was a shop which always fascinated me. It seemed set in aspic, frozen in time as if nothing much had changed since the turn of the twentieth century. The entrance was mosaic, the internal walls tiled from floor to ceiling, reflecting the Victorian obsession with hygiene. Today we'd probably call it a 'deli' since it seemed to carry every kind of foodstuff known to man. But it was more like a supermarket, in that shoppers were spoiled for choice. Unlike supermarkets, which were just beginning to establish a foothold in Britain's high streets, Greig's prided itself on personal service. There seemed to be as many staff as customers; the men in white trilbies and coats, the women in starched white pinafores and caps which made them look like nurses. Often the queues would stretch out on to the street. On one side the counters contained dried goods: tins of cling peaches, canned fruit salad; tinned soups such as mock turtle and mulligatawny; potted meats and fish paste; tins of sardines; Gentleman's Relish; jams in a variety of flavours from damson to blueberry; pickles; piccalilli; pickled onions, pickled eggs; Swiss chocolates; an assortment of fancy biscuits (not broken like Rolph's); a vast selection of teas from India and Africa; liquid Camp Coffee in bottles; liquorice sticks in glass jars; toffees; fruit cakes, coffee cakes, rum and raisin cakes.

There were strict demarcation lines. The dried goods counter was staffed exclusively by women. Across the aisle, the male assistants served the fresh food: vast York hams; smoked and green bacon, sliced to order; fresh chickens and geese, hanging from giant hooks; cheeses, including local Stilton; butter carved from giant slabs and fashioned into pound servings by a man with a pair of giant, corrugated paddles. Once the shopper nodded her approval, it would be wrapped with great ceremony in greaseproof paper. I could have stood and watched this man work all day. How did he manage every time to carve off the exact amount, not an ounce more and not an ounce less?

When you'd gathered your purchases, you would present them to a cashier in a wooden kiosk by the front door. He'd tally them up in a ledger, take payment, hand you your change and bid you 'Good day, Madam'. It was always 'madam'. The only males you ever saw in Greig's – not counting wide-eyed schoolboys – were the men who worked behind the counter.

Shoppers began to drift away from Greig's when a MacFisheries supermarket opened around the corner, offering the novelty of self-service convenience. It could never match the magic and romance of David Greig, but it did undercut the prices. Greig's failed to adapt and its demise came when several members of the family died in quick succession and a crippling bill for death duties became due. The company passed through a number of hands, Key Markets, Gateway, Somerfield and the Co-op, without conspicuous success. Greig's original store in Brixton is now a Superdrug.

I revisited Peterborough in the summer of 2013. Westgate is now a grisly, post-apocalyptic landscape, host to garish, low rent pound shops, bookies and identikit sandwich bars. Only the Bull Hotel remains intact, if not unscathed. The piano shop next door has long since closed down and the quaint covered arcade that connected Westgate with the Cathedral Square stands as a sorry reminder of its former bustling self.

The historic centre of Peterborough was destroyed, like so many other British towns and cities, when the council granted planning permission for the hideous Queensgate Shopping Mall, entailing the demolition of architectural gems which had stood for centuries and the erasure of medieval street plans. Three decades after it opened in a fanfare of modernity, the mall is irredeemably scruffy and its public spaces largely deserted for much of the week, save for a motley collection of winos and recent immigrants from Eastern Europe. Many of the units are shuttered, and shoppers have drifted away to a giant out-of-town retail park, just as they once shunned Greig's for MacFisheries. The day I was there, the local paper reported that Queensgate had been put up for sale for £200 million. Given that it cost £60 million to build thirty-odd years ago, that doesn't seem much of a mark-up.

As I got older, the weekly trips to the library gave way to the Saturday morning pictures. Long before *Tiswas* and *Noel Edmonds' Multi-Coloured Swap Shop* arrived on television in the 1970s, Saturday mornings were a TV desert, given over to the test card until *Grandstand* came on at lunchtime. The void was filled by special programmes of films, cartoons and live entertainment aimed at children, put on at practically every cinema in Britain. In Peterborough, the two biggest cinemas, the Odeon and the Embassy, competed for our custom. Our parents would drop us off while they went shopping, to keep us safely out of mischief. If that was the plan, it was an abject failure. Saturday morning pictures made the Belles of St Trinian's look like an order of Trappist monks.

Like most things in life, the Odeon's Saturday Club and the Embassy's ABC Minors began with the best of intentions. ABC Minors was launched in the 1940s, had its own badge and club song and the emphasis was as much on self-improvement as entertainment. There were the popular cowboy films, Laurel and Hardy, Mask of

Zorro movies and Loony Tunes cartoons, but also travelogues, talent contests and awards ceremonies for butter-wouldn't-melt children who had performed a valuable service to the community, such as sweeping up leaves or going shopping for pensioners. Communal singing was another big feature, with the audience invited to follow the bouncing ball, which hopped from word to word as the lyrics were projected on to the big screen. Not having been around in the 1940s, I've no idea whether the kids behaved themselves and sat obediently in their seats. But there's no doubting the popularity of our Saturday morning ritual. In the 1950s, over a million children attended 1750 cinemas every week.

By the dawn of the 1960s, audiences were in decline but those who did attend made up in sheer mayhem for what they lacked in numbers. When the doors opened, we'd rush into the foyer like modern Chinese tourists storming the Harrods New Year's sale. Admission was supposed to cost a tanner, but how many kids actually paid is anyone's guess. As the advance guard fell upon the confectionery counter like locusts, stripping it bare of Toblerones, wine gums and Swallow toffees, raiding parties would break off from the main assault force and head for the emergency exits, which they'd open from within to let their friends flood in for nothing.

Our plan of action was always to charge upstairs to establish a bridgehead in the front row of the dress circle, an elevated vantage point from which we could tip Kia-Ora Sunkist orange juice on to the heads of the kids in the orchestra seats below and hurl ice cream at the 'goody-goodies' on stage collecting their best behaviour badges. About once a fortnight the auditorium would resonate to a collective coughing fit occasioned by some boy who'd made an early recce to the joke shop, to stock up on ammunition, and had detonated a stink bomb at the back of the stalls.

When the rioting got completely out of hand, the manager would halt the feature, turn on the house lights and appear on stage to appeal for calm. He was usually met with a barrage of abuse and missiles. And that was just from the girls. At one point he became so desperate to restore order that he even offered to hand out tanners to kids who behaved themselves, an offer met with predictable derision, especially from those members of the audience who had got in for nothing – which was about half of them.

The days of the Saturday morning flicks were numbered. The management only had a couple of hours to prepare the auditorium for the Saturday afternoon matinee, made up of OAPs and courting couples with nowhere else to go other than the back row. While the debris could be collected with a concerted effort on the part of the management and the usherettes, the stench of rotten eggs caused by a stink bomb or two could linger for days: not much of an aphrodisiac for a young man taking his girlfriend to the matinee and hoping for a bit of heavy petting in the semi-darkness. A lingering aroma of rotten eggs tended to be a right turn off, even if he had plied her with a Mivvi and a box of Weekend.

The aggravation wasn't worth it and by the late sixties most cinema chains had thrown in the towel. When Saturday morning TV arrived, it really was the end of an era. Video may have killed the radio star, but television sounded the death knell for the Saturday morning pictures. I suppose it was inevitable, but I feel sorry for kids who never experienced the anarchic thrill of the Saturday morning pictures — a couple of hours when the adult world gave way to the chaos of hundreds of out-of-control kids going berserk on a grand scale in an Art Deco cinema, with the tacit approval, and in retrospect almost certain connivance, of their parents.

Peterborough boasted four cinemas when we lived there – the Odeon, the Gaumont and the Embassy, all grouped in the City Centre within a couple of hundred yards of each other. The fourth was in the northern suburb of New England. Opened in 1902, it was officially called the Imperial, but it was known to everyone as the 'Bug Hutch', on account of its unsavoury, unhygienic reputation. If this picture house had been a person, it would have been Old Man Steptoe. It closed in 1966, with a performance of

Dracula, Prince of Darkness, who was reputed to be one of its best customers. Five years later the Bug Hutch reopened as an independent 'art house' cinema, showing Asian and 'adult' movies. This incarnation limped on until 1982 when DVDs came along to sate the Asian and 'adult' markets.

The Gaumont, which opened in 1910 as the Broadway Electric Theatre, was the first to go, in 1963, converted into a bingo club, like so many cinemas in the 1960s. The only film I can ever remember seeing at the Gaumont was *Petticoat Pirates*, starring Charlie Drake, more of whom later in this book.

The Odeon arrived in 1937 and kept going until 1991. It was a splendid building, in the grand Odeon tradition, designed as an escape from everyday drudgery, with a licensed bar and restaurant upstairs. In those days movies were categorised U for Universal, meaning anyone could attend; A for Adult, which meant you had to be over sixteen, but children could be accompanied by an adult; and X for X-rated, meaning no minors. Many's the night my adolescent friends and I would stand outside the Odeon trying to persuade adults to take us in. If all else failed we'd bribe someone to let us in the emergency exit.

The first X-film I managed to blag my way in to was *The Family Way*. Released in 1966, like most new films it took a year to make its way up the Great North Road. *The Family Way* stars Hayley Mills and Hywel Bennett as a young married couple. Long story short: a series of mishaps conspires against consummation of the marriage, a fact that soon leaks out. Eventually, they do the deed and everyone lives happily ever after. Sounds mild now, but it was considered terribly risqué for its day. Which is why I was desperate to see it. Unable to find anyone to open the emergency exit, we decided to confront the problem head-on. Turning up the collar of my white gaberdine mac, I marched up to the kiosk and, in my best dark-brown voice, asked to buy a ticket. The woman behind the glass looked me up and down, winked conspiratorially and sold me a seat in the one and nines (9p).

After that, getting into an X was a doddle. The following year, aged fourteen, it was the turn of *Here We Go Round the Mulberry Bush* to excite my passions. Set in Stevenage New Town, it followed the frustrated attempts of a grocery delivery boy to lose his virginity. Played by Barry Evans, he pursues assorted girls of his dreams, including Judy Geeson, who instantly became the girl of my dreams, too.

Here We Go Round The Mulberry Bush: music by Traffic and the Spencer Davis Group; script by Hunter Davies and Larry Kramer, based on the book by Hunter Davies. Hunter became a hero of mine when he wrote *The Glory Game*, arguably the best football book ever. Bill Nicholson, the legendary Spurs manager, granted Hunter exclusive access to his successful side of the early 1970s. It had never been done before and will never be done again. The book is a unique master-piece. In 1988, Hunter Davies was writing a column for the *Evening Standard*. He went on holiday for a week and the editor, John Leese, asked me to stand in for him. John never told me to stop. That was the end of Hunter Davies as a *Standard* columnist. Hunter took it all in good part and we became friends. We've since worked on TV and radio, Hunter as a guest on several of my shows, shared meals and been to White Hart Lane together. Hunter used to have a season ticket in the West Stand just down from mine. We'd always have chips on the way home, win or lose. When I left the *Standard* for the *Sun* in 1989, my column was taken over by a young woman called Nigella Lawson. I wonder whatever happened to her?

I've already mentioned the Embassy, the grandest of Peterborough's cinemas. That's where we sneaked in to watch Eric Sutton perform in *Seven Brides for Seven Brothers*. The Art Deco Embassy, opened in 1937, was noted as much for live performances as movies. Every year when I was younger we'd go to the Christmas panto at the Embassy:

> *Oh, no you didn't.*
> *Oh, yes we did!*

Between the thirties and the sixties, the Embassy hosted everyone from Laurel and Hardy to the Beatles – who played there twice, in 1962, as a support act to the yodelling Australian Frank Ifield, and the following year, when they topped a bill which included American pop stars Chris Montez ('Let's Dance') and Tommy Roe ('Dizzy').

I have fond memories of the place, too. One of my first jobs as editor of the Young Outlook column on the *Peterborough Standard* in 1971 was to interview the American rock'n'roll legend/country and western star Jerry Lee Lewis in his dressing room at the Embassy. I was shown into the great man's presence and found him stripped to the waist, halfway through his second bottle of bourbon and with a nubile young woman sitting on his lap. Since Jerry Lee had been run out of Britain in 1958, when it was revealed that he had married his thirteen-year-old first cousin, Myra Gale Brown, I thought it politic not to ask her age. And to be honest, given that half the folk in the Fens were married to their first cousins – and in some cases their sisters – most readers of our rural editions wouldn't have thought Jerry Lee Lewis had done anything wrong.

The Embassy closed in 1989. Like so many other glorious Art Deco picture houses it was unable to compete with the giant American-style Multiplex on the ring road. In 1996, it was converted into a pub. When I saw what had become of this behemoth of cinema's golden age, I really needed a drink.

Just not there.

On the way home from town on Saturdays, we'd pick up our dinner from the fish and chip shop near Rolph's. Cod and six and a scoop of scraps – crunchy shards of batter deep-fried to a golden crisp. We always had the wireless on in the background while we ate, shows like *The Clitheroe Kid* and *Educating Archie*. *The Clitheroe Kid* was a long-running radio comedy starring Jimmy Clitheroe as a cheeky eleven-year-old schoolboy, with whom I could immediately identify. I didn't realise at the time that Clitheroe was well into his forties by the time I started listening to him. Not that it mattered. That's the magic of the wireless. And if Peter Brough and his dummy Archie Andrews could work as a ventriloquist act on radio, where no one can ever see your lips move, why shouldn't a grown man pretend to be a naughty schoolboy?

After the plates were cleared away, my time was usually my own. Which meant heading outdoors to round up a posse on the Grange to play a pick-up game of football or cricket, or seek out fresh pastures for mischief. The only rule was: get back before dark. And don't get into trouble.

As I got older, I would venture further afield in search of excitement. Behind Horrell's Dairies there was a disused

RAF wartime airfield, which is where dads took their sons to learn to drive. There were a few abandoned cars there, too, which the older boys who drove the dumper trucks soon worked out how to hotwire. We used to whizz along the runway, packed into the cracked leather passenger seats of a rusting Austin Cambridge while a boy barely into his teens attempted handbrake turns. I'm surprised we escaped unscathed.

It was a hell of a lot more fun than the push-and-run 'go-karts' we used to build: wooden chassis mounted on old pram wheels, steered by string and often without a rudimentary braking system.

These go-karts were a menace, not just to ourselves but to anyone who crossed our path. Often the only way of stopping was to crash into a wall. Building and driving a wooden go-kart was a rite of passage, dating back donkey's years. They were a common sight on every street in Britain. No one ever got seriously hurt, although a beat copper might suggest gently that you kept well out of the way of pedestrians.

That, of course, was in the days when coppers walked the beat, knew everyone in the neighbourhood and everyone in the neighbourhood knew him. Long before they came up with the concept of 'Community Policing', police officers actually used to live in the communities they served. Certainly, our local bobby would never have nicked anyone for driving a wooden go-kart without due care and attention, though he might have had a quiet word in your dad's shell-like.

There's no point in harking back to the days of *Dixon of Dock Green*, even if they really existed. These days it's all about ticking boxes and nicking miscreants for the most minor infringements of the law to keep up the arrest tally for the monthly crime statistics. Sometimes you can get nicked without actually breaking any laws. In which case, the Old Bill will simply make it up as they go along.

A few years ago, WPC Donna Gibbs was driving her panda car through the village of Codsall, in Staffordshire, when she spotted three boys riding a home-made go-kart. She stopped the car, pulled the boys up and informed them they were breaking the law because they didn't have any tax or insurance. Since when have boys had to tax and insure home-made go-karts? After giving them a strict lecture, she took their names and addresses and told them she would be taking the matter further.

The boys' parents subsequently received a letter from WPC Gibbs's boss, Inspector Nick 'Nick Nick' Baker, informing them that their sons were guilty of 'anti-social' behaviour – even though they hadn't actually committed any offence. I can remember writing in my column at the time that the bold WPC Gibbs would go far in the modern police 'service'.

Out of curiosity, when I was writing this chapter I checked the Staffordshire Police website to find out what became of WPC Gibbs. Soon after nicking the boys on the go-kart, she was promoted to sergeant. And just three days before I looked her up, in September 2013, Staffordshire Police announced that the former WPC Gibbs had been promoted to Chief Inspector at Tamworth.

Chief Inspector Gibbs declared that she wanted 'the community to tell me what matters to the people of Tamworth'. She still lives in Codsall with her fiancé Michael and is the proud mother of four young sons.

Let's hope none of her boys is ever tempted to build a go-kart, just in case some ferociously ambitious, over-zealous WPC decides to make a name for herself by nicking them for not having tax and insurance and slapping them with an 'anti-social behaviour' order.

One day at the airfield we discovered a tramp living in a concrete air raid shelter. Today we'd call him 'homeless' or a 'rough sleeper' and he'd be selling the *Big Issue* outside Tesco Metro. Back then he was just a tramp. When he heard us larking about outside the bunker, he came blinking into the light and attempted to scare us off.

It wasn't long since I'd seen Bryan Forbes' 1961 film *Whistle Down the Wind*, starring Hayley Mills, and written by Willis Hall and Keith Waterhouse; Keith was later to become a dear friend and *Daily Mail* colleague. The plot revolves around three farm children who discover a fugitive living in their barn. They mistake him for Jesus Christ, although it turns out he's a wanted murderer on the run. Our tramp reminded me of the *Whistle Down the Wind* fugitive, Blakey. (Not to be confused with Blakey from *On the Buses*.) After much discussion, we speculated that he, too, might be a murderer. Should we tell the police? Best not, just in case we got into trouble. But nor could we risk a murderer living on our 'manor'.

Someone came up with the idea of flushing him out and running him out of town, like they did in the westerns. But that was easier said than done. These air raid shelters were built to withstand German bombs. He could hole up inside there for days, provided he had enough meths to drink. Someone else remembered that he'd seen a war film in which the advancing British Tommies attack a German fortification with flame throwers, setting light to the occupants, who are forced to flee, screaming, into a nearby river. That sounded like a plan, but where could we lay our hands on a flame-thrower? We agreed to reconvene half an hour later and set off on a scavenger hunt. We younger boys were dispatched to collect as many newspapers as we could while the older boys siphoned petrol from the petrol tank of the Austin Cambridge.

We soaked the newspaper in the petrol and stuffed it into the chimney-cum-air-vent in the roof of the air raid shelter. One of the older boys lit it and pushed it down the shaft into the bunker. From the bowels of the building came coughing and cursing, followed by the rapid emergence of the suspected murderer, flames and smoke licking at his heels. We didn't want to hang around to be on the receiving end of his wrath, so we scattered to observation posts a safe distance away. The tramp made a couple of attempts to re-enter the shelter but was beaten back by the heat. Eventually he gave it up as a bad job and wandered off in search of another bed for the night. He didn't come back. It never occurred to us at the time that we could have killed him.

When I arrived home stinking of smoke, my mum asked what on earth I'd been up to. 'Nothing much,' I replied.

Returning to the air raid shelter a few days later, we ventured inside and stumbled on a stash of pornography. Well, I say 'pornography'. It consisted of a few well-thumbed editions of *Health & Efficiency* magazine. Discarded copies of *H&E* used to turn up all over the place, especially in the fields and hedgerows. You could go out conkering on a Sunday afternoon ramble and come back with more copies of *Health & Efficiency* than conkers.

H&E was a publication aimed at naturists, about the only magazine freely available to feature photographs of naked bodies. *National Geographic* did contain some nude images, but these were mainly of topless African tribes-women performing some ritual dance. There was nothing erotic about these photos, aside from the thrill of looking at bare breasts. The *H&E* 'models' were all ordinary folk pictured doing everyday stuff, except without their clothes on. Most of the women were fresh-faced girl-next-door types and for some reason always seemed to be throwing medicine balls and beach balls. Below the waist, they were as bald as the day they were born. They were like the mannequins in Dorothy Perkins' window. No naughty bits. Bottoms made the cut, front bottoms didn't. It would be years before we realised that adult women had pubic hair. The only female I'd seen naked was my kid sister on bath night. In fact, there was no indication that there was anything 'down there' at all, although we all knew that ladies had some kind of front-bottom arrangement. So why wasn't this ever visible on the women in *Health & Efficiency*? We pondered this, until one of the older boys announced he had worked it out. They obviously used papier mâché to fill the void. We were familiar with papier mâché, since we used it to make models at school. The landscape variety, that is, not the *Health & Efficiency* variety.

Nor was there anything even remotely sexual about the images in the magazine. The participants were pictured playing croquet, hiking across the moors, riding bikes. Curiously, though, not leapfrog. I never have been able to work out why anyone would want to ride a bike naked, let alone hike across the moors. Stinging nettles must pose a serious hazard. The women were photographed barefoot, but the men always seemed to be wearing socks and shoes. It has often been said that there is no more ridiculous sight than an Englishman abroad wearing shorts with socks and sandals. Believe me, there is: it's an Englishman without any shorts wearing socks and shoes – and nothing else – while playing croquet.

Health & Efficiency, which was first published in 1900, continues to this day, still serving its core audience of naturists. These days, the women are still barefoot but the men appear to have graduated to designer Birkenstock footwear and expensive trainers. They still look utterly ridiculous. The attraction of *H&E* to curious young boys has long since passed, overtaken first by 'adult' magazines such as *Playboy* and *Hustler*, which cashed in on the decision in the 1970s to lift the ban on publishing photos featuring genitalia and pubic hair, and more recently by the internet.

Today's adolescents can access explicit, hardcore porn at the click of a mouse, or via an app on their mobile phone. Nudity is so ubiquitous it's astonishing that any woman can make a living as a stripper any more. We grew up in more innocent times. Modern youngsters will never know the frisson of excitement that greeted a boy's first glimpse of naked female flesh in *Health & Efficiency*, even without the naughty bits.

One Friday, my dad turned up to collect me from West Town driving a brand new car. Nanna's Ford Popular was on its last legs and Dad had invested in the very latest Ford Anglia 105E, the 'Deluxe' model no less. The basic 'Deluxe' cost £610, but Dad had splashed out on a heater, which was an optional extra. Few cars had heaters in those days. You could buy special 'car coats' and travel rugs to keep warm on long journeys. Car coats were a cross between a jacket and a full-length trench coat and were a hangover from the days of open-top motoring. A popular Christmas present for men was a pair of string-backed driving gloves. Today the idea of wearing special clothes for driving a car seems ridiculous. But, really, is it any more absurd that the outfits modern Lycra-lout cyclists insist on wearing, complete with helmets that resemble a bunch of bananas?

The Anglia had two doors, came in two-tone light and dark blue paintwork and the 'Deluxe' trim featured a full-length chrome grille, chrome side strips, chrome rear-lamp surrounds and opening rear quarter-lights. The Anglia's unique design feature was a reverse sloping rear window. Coupled with tailfins either side of the boot, the Anglia looked like a scaled-down American car, of the type we saw on TV and at the cinema. The style was copied from the 1958 Lincoln Continental. When it came to power, though, the Anglia couldn't compete with Detroit muscle. It had a puny 997cc overhead valve, straight four-cylinder engine and went from 0 to 60mph in about three weeks. The upside of this lack of grunt was that the car did a pretty economical forty-one miles per gallon. Petrol in 1961 cost 4s. 11d. a gallon (just under 25p at today's prices.)

One revolutionary feature of the Anglia was that it had two windscreen wipers, operated by an independent electric motor. The wiper on the old Ford Pop operated on a vacuum system, which meant it worked in reverse. At idling speed the wiper would sweep backwards and forwards at an impressive lick. But once you began to accelerate it would slow down to a crawl. The faster you drove, the slower it went. Over about 30mph in heavy rain you couldn't see a thing through the windscreen.

In the Popular we would regularly have to stop to top up the radiator, along with something which looked like an Oxo cube. You popped this in the radiator to plug leaks. We always carried a tin can full of water in the boot. In those days, cars overheating at the side of the road, bonnets propped open, was a fairly common sight. The Anglia promised more reliability, especially on longer journeys. Theoretically, that meant we wouldn't have to keep pulling over every few miles to effect running repairs. That was the plan, anyway. But we'd reckoned without my reaction to the new car. While the Anglia filled me with excitement, it also filled me with nausea. Overnight I developed a serious case of carsickness. I was allergic to the Anglia. On our first trip to show off our new car to my paternal grandparents back in Ilford, we'd barely reached the Great North Road at Norman Cross, on the outskirts of

Peterborough, before Dad had to pull into the nearest layby so that I could be violently sick. I spent the rest of the journey with my head hanging out of the passenger window, puking down the pristine two-tone paintwork. This continued all the way to Vine Gardens, me retching repeatedly even though I was running on empty.

I staggered from the car, green at the gills, willing myself to curl up and die in the front bedroom with the triangular bay window. It was worse than any hangover I ever had in later life – and I've had more than my fair share of those. If I was expecting any sympathy from my grandfather, I'd come to the wrong place. He thought it was hilarious.

'Just you be careful,' he counselled. 'If you can feel a little ring on the back of your tongue, whatever you do, swallow hard. Don't try to bring it up.'

'Why not?' I asked.

'Because that'll be your bum-hole and if you spit that out you'll turn yourself inside out,' he roared.

Despite my chronic carsickness, I used to look forward to our return visits to Ilford. My grandparents always made a fuss of my sister and me. There were sticky buns and Battenberg cake for tea, and Vimto. Along from Bill Fraser's sweet shop on Ilford Lane there was a Jewish bakery, which made the best bread I have tasted to this day. It had an almost tortoise shell-hard crust, peppered with poppy and sesame seeds and a fluffy centre. My grandmother had an unusual way of carving and buttering the bread. Mum always sliced the loaf and buttered it afterwards. Nanna would remove the end crust and butter the open face of the loaf. She'd then slice it off and repeat the process. I haven't seen anyone else cut and butter bread in that fashion since, which is perhaps why it sticks in my mind.

Loxford Park was within walking distance and, as I got older, I was allowed to travel unsupervised on the bus to wander round the Pioneer Market and swim at the old Ilford Baths. The main pool was long and narrow and covered by a suspended glass-domed roof like a smaller version of the engine shed at King's Cross station. Around the sides were individual changing cubicles. Kiln-fired, shiny engineering bricks extended out of the pool itself and up the walls. If you've watched the swimming pool scene in the movie *The Long Good Friday*, which was shot in Lewisham, south London, you'll get the picture. There were pools like this in towns and cities all over Britain at one stage, built between the end of the Victorian era and the outbreak of the Second World War. Ilford Baths was a particularly fine example. In 2010 it was named as one of the ten best abandoned swimming baths in Britain.

When I was revisiting old haunts for the purposes of writing this book, I discovered that the pool had only closed in 2008, but not before the council had stuck a hideous 1970s frontage on it, in a misguided attempt at 'modernising' the building. By 2011, it had been extensively vandalised and was home to rough sleepers. I learned from the *Ilford Recorder* that the land had originally been donated in 1914 by the Baron Rowallan, a former Chief Scout and Governor of Tasmania, who entered into a covenant with Ilford Urban District Council that it would be used in perpetuity as a swimming pool. The modern-day council obviously felt under no obligation to honour that covenant. It used powers under the planning acts to appropriate the land, without paying any compensation to Rowallan's descendants. In August 2013, the bulldozers moved in and started tearing it down. Judging by photographs of the dilapidated, neglected structure taken not long before demolition began, it was a mercy killing.

It was on one of these trips to Ilford, in April 1964, that I got my first pair of proper long trousers. Grey flannel, from C&A, where else? I was ten years old. We all wore short trousers at primary school, with long socks and garters. If you look at the picture on the front cover of this book I'm wearing my West Town school uniform, complete with sandals. Clarks, or Start-Rite, I shouldn't be surprised. So it was almost certainly taken in the summer. During the winter I'd wear Clarks black lace-ups. We never scrimped on footwear. My Dad swore by good shoes.

Shopping at the Clarks shop in town was a day out in itself. The children's section was kitted out like a toy soldier's fort. The chairs and footstalls were all shaped like drums. You'd stand on a giant slide rule and the assistant would take your measurements, always recommending to your parents that they buy a size and a half bigger than you needed at that particular stage of your life because within months your feet were guaranteed to grow. When I was younger I had some kind of instep irregularity, which involved having to wear shoes with wedges, specially adapted by the cobbler next to Rolph's. Not that I was aware of having any kind of disability, but a few years earlier it might have been enough to get me excused National Service.

By the time I was about nine, I'd outgrown the children's sizes and had to graduate to the adult section, which was a great relief since the novelty of sitting on a giant Ruritanian toy drum while trying on shoes had long since worn thin. No more sandals, either, thank heaven.

The photo on the front cover of this book was probably taken at the weekend. We dressed pretty much the same on Saturdays and Sundays as we did during the week. Short trousers were the order of the day in all weathers, even in deepest mid-winter. We'd even get sent out in the snow in short trousers, long socks and wellington boots. Otherwise wrapped up to the nines, in scarves, balaclavas and gloves, somehow it was deemed acceptable to expose our kneecaps to the elements. After a day spent chucking snowballs and building snowmen, your knees would be frozen solid and blue. It would take ages to thaw them out in front of the coal fire, with a toasted tea cake or crumpet to pass the time. I wouldn't have wanted to be one of the kids with callipers in winter. They'd have to be separated from their boots with a chisel and a blowtorch.

By the time I was ten, I was growing up fast, physically and temperamentally. The older boys I knocked around with all wore long strides. Some of them even had jeans. I pestered my mother to put me out of my short-trousered misery. But there was a rule at West Town that the uniform for boys consisted of short trousers, right up until they left aged eleven.

Mum finally came round to my way of thinking when she found it impossible to source short trousers to fit me. The waist wasn't a problem, but I'd developed muscular thighs, largely as a result of playing football morning, noon and night. If you look at modern footballers on TV, their trousers all sit like ballet tights. Consequently every pair I tried on chafed round the thighs, leaving unsightly red welts. Mum must have been involved in some delicate negotiations with Eric Sutton because he agreed to give me a dispensation, on humanitarian if not medical grounds. At last, I was excused short trousers. I was obviously the thin, or thick, end of the wedge because by the time we entered the fourth and last year of junior school, half the boys were wearing long trousers.

It was during the next school holidays that we travelled to Ilford. My mum and dad took me to C&A, which was unusual in that I couldn't ever remember my father coming clothes shopping. That was exclusively women's work. I suppose this was a day he wasn't going to miss: his son's first pair of long trousers. Appropriate, too, that they were bought from C&A in Ilford, a store I was first taken to in nappies.

That day was also notable for another landmark in my life. I bought my first ever 45rpm record: 'It's Over' by Roy Orbison, which went to number one and stayed in what we used to call the 'hit parade' for eighteen weeks. The record department was at the back of a traditional musical instruments shop. The name of the shop escapes me, but the set-up was fairly typical in the 1960s. You had to walk through ranks of pianos and guitars hanging from the ceiling – the guitars, not the pianos – to reach the record racks at the back. These were divided into long players (LPs) and singles, which were always on shelves behind the counter. Before you bought a record, it was obligatory to listen to it. The assistant would pop it on a turntable behind the counter and you would be directed to a booth at one side, equipped with a tinny loudspeaker. Roy Orbison recorded for Monument Records in the US, but was released in Britain on London American. This first 45 was the start of my lifelong fascination with records and record labels, American labels in particular.

As we made our way back to Vine Gardens for tea, I couldn't have been happier. I had my first pair of long trousers and my first pop record. I had entered the adult world at last.

There was only one drawback. We didn't have a record player. Neither did my grandparents. So there I was, wearing my brand new long trousers, clutching a pristine pressing of 'It's Over' with nothing to play it on. It was the next day before I could listen to the Big O.

The following morning we set off to visit Viv's godmother, Iris Blackburn, and her husband, Alan, in Seven Kings. 'Uncle' Alan had been a bit of a Teddy Boy when he was younger. He had thick, swept-back hair and black spectacles and looked to me like Buddy Holly. He also had a Triumph motorcycle and sidecar. Every time we visited he'd take me out for a ride in the sidecar, screeching round corners, forcing me to hang on for dear life. It beat the hell out of any fairground roller coaster. Bizarrely, despite screeching round the streets of Seven Kings at what seemed to me to be 100mph – in reality probably about 25mph – and about a foot off the road, I never felt in the slightest bit queasy. While I still suffered from chronic carsickness, I was immune to any ill effects from motion sickness in a motorcycle sidecar. Maybe I was too terrified to throw up.

The good news was that Iris and Alan had a record player. A radiogram to be precise. Like the televisions of the 1950s, radiograms were solid pieces of furniture, made from heavy, polished wood. I've seen smaller, less elaborate coffins. As well as a record player, geared up to play 16, 33, 45 and 78rpm discs, they contained a radio. More sophisticated radiograms also had an automatic mechanical, multi-disc changer, which could in theory play six or seven records in succession, but after about the third disc would slip, slide and slur. Some even incorporated a TV. They could be anything up to three feet tall and six feet wide. Loudspeakers were mounted either side.

Alan was a big skiffle fan and his collection included LPs by Lonnie Donegan, of 'My Old Man's a Dustman' fame, and the Chas McDevitt Group, who had a British chart hit with their version of the American folk standard 'Freight Train'. During the 1950s skiffle boom there were estimated to be anything up to 50,000 skiffle groups in Britain. All you needed was a guitar, a washboard and an old tea chest converted into a double bass by the judicious deployment of a broom handle and a length of string. John Lennon started out in a skiffle group called the Quarrymen. But I wasn't there to listen to skiffle. I handed Alan my new Roy Orbison record and watched in anticipation as he removed it from the sleeve, taking care to hold it by the label and not smudge his fingerprints on the playing surface. Then he placed it carefully on the turntable. After a sudden initial 'pop' as the needle made contact with the vinyl and a couple of scratchy crackles, it settled into the groove. And then:

Your baby doesn't love you any more. Golden days before they end, whisper secrets to the wind . . .

I still get shivers up my spine when I hear Roy Orbison. We didn't get our own record player until Christmas of that year, an HMV. Up to then, I had to rely on friends to play my one and only record. Maybe I should have bought Orbison's earlier hit, 'Only the Lonely'.

My Christmas stocking contained a couple of record vouchers and a postal order for a pound from my grandparents. The day after Boxing Day I went out and bought two more records, the Beatles EP (extended player) *All My Loving* and the Rolling Stones' debut album, simply called *The Rolling Stones*. Of these, the Stones album was to have the most influence on my future musical tastes. Mick Jagger and Keith Richards (or Richard, as he was then) would go on to write some of the most enduring, most memorable pop songs of the sixties, as would Lennon and McCartney.

But the Stones' first LP was a collection of cover versions of American soul and blues records. They included Marvin Gaye's 'Can I Get a Witness' (written by the legendary Motown inhouse team of Holland-

Dozier-Holland); Chuck Berry's 'Route 66'; Willie Dixon's 'I Just Want to Make Love to You'; and 'Walking the Dog' by Rufus Thomas. I played it over and over again. From the moment I heard this album, I was hooked on blues and soul.

We got one other record that Christmas. As I was buying *The Rolling Stones* LP, my dad was treating himself to the single 'I (Who Have Nothing)' by Shirley Bassey. I can't say I was particularly impressed by his selection, which struck me as 'square', as we used to say. It was years later that I discovered 'I (Who Have Nothing)' was a cover of an original by Ben E. King, one of my soul heroes, and had been written by Jerry Leiber and Mike Stoller, who wrote songs for everyone from Elvis to the Drifters, including Ben E. King's marvellous 'Stand By Me'. Perhaps my dad knew something about music after all.

The only other two LPs I can recall my dad buying were comedy records. One was by the American comic Bob Newhart. It was called *The Button-Down Mind of Bob Newhart* and featured half a dozen brilliant, inventive, surreal monologues, with Newhart playing his own straight man. *Button-Down Mind* includes classic sketches such as 'The Driving Instructor', in which an increasingly panicky male instructor tries to teach a woman to drive. This would probably be damned as sexist these days, and removed from sale, but it's one of the funniest five minutes ever committed to vinyl.

'Abe Lincoln vs Madison Avenue' is a skit about the advertising industry, the sixties Mad Men from the TV series trying to advise a reluctant president how to improve his public image.

The sketch I loved most was called 'Introducing Tobacco to Civilization'. Sir Walter Raleigh is trying to sell tobacco to his investors back home during an imaginary telephone conversation from the colonies. That would probably be banned, too, to appease the militant anti-smoking lobby. They'd probably argue that you could catch 'passive smoking' simply by listening to it.

The other was by the Goons: Peter Sellers, Harry Secombe, Michael Bentine and Spike Milligan, who had made their name on radio. It was called *How to Win an Election (or Not Lose By Much)*, written by the great Leslie Bricusse and released in time for the 1964 general election. One of the two tracks on *How to Win* that stood out for me featured Michael Bentine reading the football results and becoming increasingly hysterical as it dawns on him that he might be holding the winning coupon. The other featured Spike Milligan as a working-class voter in 1945 explaining why he would be voting for Winston Churchill: 'Because I believe in the Labour Party.'

*

Later in life, I met or interviewed every one of the Goons except Sellers, who had died before I started my radio and TV career. I've also had the privilege of meeting and having lunch with Leslie Bricusse, a dear friend of my agent Deke Arlon. Leslie was kind enough to send me a signed copy of his autobiography. Parky's law proved right again.

Radio captured my imagination from an early age. As well as her TV, Nanna Sparke brought a wireless with her when she moved to Peterborough with us. It must have dated back to the war, or maybe even earlier. The wireless was almost as big as the television, weighed a ton, was mains-operated, in a heavy wooden case with a single loud-speaker and a large rotary dial featuring long, medium and short waves. There were three BBC stations, the Home Service, the Light Programme and the Third Programme, as well as a number of overseas stations broadcast from exotic sounding places such as Hilversum, Hamburg and Luxembourg.

My parents already had a wireless, so I was allowed to keep Nanna's set in my bedroom. It was the source of endless amusement. When I wasn't listening to the BBC I could pretend to be a radio ham, or an RAF air traffic controller issuing directions to fighter planes.

I must have started listening to Radio Luxembourg when I was about seven or eight. In those days, there was very little pop music on the BBC. The Light Programme was still locked into a wartime mentality, with programmes such as *Workers' Playtime* and *Two-Way Family Favourites*, which played requests for and from British servicemen and women and their families stationed overseas. Radio Luxembourg broadcast a schedule of non-stop pop from its transmitter in the Grand Duchy. Initially on long wave, Luxembourg switched to its familiar 208-metres medium-wave frequency when it resumed service after the Second World War. But because of atmospheric conditions, it could only be received in Britain after dark, so I rarely got to hear more than about half an hour of variable signal before it was time for bed. Many of the DJs who would go on to become household names in Britain cut their teeth at Luxembourg, including Alan 'Fluff' Freeman, David Jacobs and, that man again, Pete Murray. Many of the shows were taped in London and flown to Luxembourg to be broadcast. Here's a typical early evening schedule from Sunday 15 October 1961.

7.00 Jack Jackson's Juke Box. *Presenting all the latest, up-to-the-minute records. Sponsored by the Decca Record Company Ltd.*
7.30 Swoon Club. *The popular teenage weekly magazine show, with the best of the top discs and all the answers to your personal problems. Sponsored by Hilltone Hair Lightener.*
7.45 MacDonald Hobley *invites you to* Make a Tape. *Hear yourself on air and have a chance of winning an all-expenses*

paid trip to New York. Brought to you by Currys Radio and Cycle Shop.

Later that night there were shows presented by Pete Murray, Anne Shelton and Sam Costa. You will have noticed that all these shows were sponsored, something unheard of at the time in Britain. Luxembourg also carried adverts, unlike the licence fee-funded BBC. The ads were almost as exciting as the music. One jingle, for Van Heusen Slim-Fit Shirts, to the tune of Chuck Berry's 'No Particular Place to Go', sticks in my mind to this day. Luxembourg also broadcast football pools predictions, which were banned by the BBC. The best-known tipster was Horace Batchelor, with his famous Infra-Draw Method. He was based at Keynsham, in the West Country, and every week would slowly read out his address, with special emphasis on 'Keynsham, that's K-E-Y-N-S-H-A-M, Bristol'.

After a couple of years, I was given a small transistor radio for my birthday. This not only meant that I was no longer dependent on the ancient valve-operated wireless I'd inherited from my grandmother, it also let me carry on listening to Radio Luxembourg long after I was supposed to have been tucked down for the night. Luxembourg was obviously aware that much of its audience comprised relatively young people tuning in in their bedrooms. The station launched the Under The Bedclothes Club, presented – as it 'appens, guys and gals – by one

Jimmy Savile. Now then, now then, I know what you're thinking. Is Operation Yewtree aware of this connection? As I have been known to observe on occasions: you couldn't make it up.

My other favourite feature on Fabulous 208, as Luxembourg branded itself, was the Battle of the Giants, which pitted two of the top pop groups or solo artistes head-to-head. The DJ would play five records by each and listeners were invited to decide who had 'won'. One week, it would be the Beatles against the Stones; the next, the Kinks against the Hollies; or the Swinging Blue Jeans versus Billy J. Kramer and the Dakotas; or Cliff against Elvis. I always voted for the Stones over the Beatles, but when the Stones came up against the Kinks, I was torn. The Stones were ultimately more successful, but Kinks frontman Ray Davies wrote the best songs. I even preferred the mid-sixties Kinks to the Beatles in their pomp. The Kinks have always been the most quintessentially English of all those sixties groups. I can remember buying one EP early on which featured the band all wearing hunting pink. That alone would be enough to get them banned from the BBC these days.

Ray's finest compositions stand comparison with anything written by Lennon and McCartney in their prime. Many's the time I fell asleep listening to Radio Luxembourg. My mum would tell me the next morning that she'd had to creep in and remove the radio from my ear.

Outside of Radio Luxembourg, there still wasn't a great deal of popular music on mainstream radio and television. The Light Programme broadcast lunchtime shows featuring house bands like Bernard Hermann and the NDO (Northern Dance Orchestra) performing cover versions of the latest records from the hit parade. This was something to do with a Musicians' Union restriction on 'needle time' designed to limit the amount of recorded music that could be played on air because it was seen as a threat to the jobs of 'real' musicians.

By the time I was nine or ten, I'd graduated from *Five o'Clock Club* and *Rendezvous* to 'grown-up' rock and roll shows such as *Ready Steady Go* and *Thank Your Lucky Stars*. For some reason, *Ready Steady Go* wasn't available in the Anglia TV region. If you wanted to watch it you had to redirect your aerial towards the ATV transmitter in the Midlands. After my dad's earlier fun and games with TV reception, I never did pluck up the courage to ask him if we could get another aerial, so I had to watch the show at a friend's house. *Thank Your Lucky Stars* featured a panel of teenagers who were asked each week to vote on the hit potential of new releases, rating them one to five. One regular panellist was an office clerk from Birmingham called Janice Nicholls, who had a rich, distinctive Brummie accent. Her catchphrase was: *'Oi'll bouy it, and oi'll give it foive.'*

Most of the top acts of the day appeared on the two programmes at some stage, everyone from The Who to the Beach Boys. *Ready Steady Go* in particular featured many American artistes, who had rarely, if ever, appeared on British TV. I can still remember being blown away the first time I saw Otis Redding. Redding sang live, which was fairly unusual since most of the acts mimed to their records. Miming was to be both shows' eventually downfall. They were taken off the air in 1966 following a campaign by the Musicians' Union, which, as I've suggested, had a stranglehold on the music business back then. We tend to think of stroppy shop stewards calling wildcat strikes in car factories and steel works in the sixties but the Musicians' Union, which was affiliated to the TUC, could be just as militant and unreasonable as any of their counterparts in heavy industry. The unions didn't only kill British Leyland, they also killed *Ready Steady Go*.

The BBC had launched *Top of the Pops*, but it was a more staid, family-oriented show than its commercial rivals. You were as likely to see Englebert Humperdink and Acker Bilk as Otis Redding and Jimi Hendrix. The BBC's answer to *Thank Your Lucky Stars* was *Juke Box Jury*, presented by David Jacobs, which used 'celebrities' instead of the teenagers who sat in judgement on new releases on ITV. *Juke Box Jury* had some bizarre panellists, including the Earl of Arran and Pinky and Perky, the two pig puppets who had their own TV show and released novelty cover versions of pop hits.

*

In 1964 came a radio revolution that would eventually shake the BBC from its complacent cultural stupor and challenge Luxembourg's commercial dominance. A young Irishman, Ronan O'Rahilly, manager of the singer Georgie Fame, bought a 763-ton passenger ferry, equipped it with a broadcast studio and sailed it outside British territorial waters and beyond the jurisdiction of the British government. On Sunday 29 March, Radio Caroline started transmitting non-stop pop, the first of many offshore pirate stations. From just off the Essex coast, Caroline's signal could be picked up across the Home Counties and East Anglia and as far away as the Midlands. A second ship in the Irish Sea became Radio Caroline North. O'Rahilly had covered the waterfront. Caroline was soon joined by other pirates, including Radio London, Radio City and Radio 390.

Within two years there were twenty-one pirate stations broadcasting from ships and wartime forts off Britain's coast to audiences of up to fifteen million. My transistor radio was my passport to this wonderful world of wireless. Whereas a couple of years earlier I could have twiddled the rotary knob on my grandmother's radio without stumbling across any station playing pop music, now the slightest adjustment of the dial on my tranny brought access to almost two dozen.

Everywhere you went, especially in summer, you could hear the pirate stations through kitchen windows, in shops and garages, from open car windows. The Anglia didn't have its own radio, but my dad would let me listen to the tranny suspended by a strap from the rear-view mirror. I think that's what cured my carsickness.

Transistor radios meant you had music on the move, in the street, on the bus. In the summer, the parks and back gardens were a cacophonous collision of competing pirate radio stations. Schools banned transistor radios because pupils were listening to pop music in class via discreet earpieces, the prototype for today's miniature iPhone headphones.

We all had our favourite station. Although Caroline was the original, I was a big fan of Radio London. Wonderful Big L was anchored three and a half miles off Frinton, on the Essex coast, and was bankrolled by a Texan businessman who wanted to bring American Top 40 radio to Britain. He imported and adapted US advertising and continuity jingles, some of which turned up on The Who's album *The Who Sell Out*. Big L's DJs included many who would go on to enjoy great success on the BBC and on ITV, including Tony Blackburn, Ed Stewart, Kenny Everett and John Peel.

On one of our trips back to Essex, my dad agreed to drive me to Frinton so that we could park on the seafront and flash our lights at Radio London as darkness fell. It was something the disc jockeys encouraged their listeners to do. I suppose it was my first proper political act.

I was aware of politics reasonably early through the weekly current affairs quizzes Eric Sutton would set us. In 1964, we even had a debate in class about the relative merits of the Conservative and Labour manifestos. At West Town we'd be taught about Parliament, the British Empire and the European Coal and Steel Community. Even though we were only ten, we were encouraged to read the newspapers and discuss the issues of the day.

The Profumo Affair even managed to impinge on our young consciousness. I can remember a playground song, to the tune of 'On Top of Old Smokey':

> On top of Profumo, where nobody goes,
> Lies Miss Christine Keeler, without any clothes.

I don't imagine any of us had the faintest idea what the Profumo Affair was about, but the notion of a woman without any clothes on was irresistibly hilarious.

The wild popularity of the pirate stations clearly spooked the politicians and undermined the BBC's radio monopoly. Labour's Postmaster General Tony Benn introduced the Marine Offences Act, designed to drive the pirates off air. On 14 August 1967, Radio London ceased transmitting. I can remember sitting at the foot of the stairs with my tranny, listening to the final broadcast. I wanted to go to Frinton, but wasn't old enough. My friend Chris later told me that he'd joined the farewell party, as carloads of Big L fans assembled on the front, hormones akimbo, flitting from vehicle to vehicle for a quick fumble with the opposite sex. Chris says that was the night dogging was invented.

By then most of the pirates had already thrown in the towel, but Radio Caroline announced that it would defy the government and carry on broadcasting. It moved its base to the Netherlands, where marine broadcasting had not yet been banned. But in March 1968, both Caroline vessels were boarded and seized by officials and towed to Amsterdam.

Most of the pirate DJs found a billet at the BBC's new Radio 1, which had been created to assuage public anger at the pirates being forced off air. Although it gained a ready audience, Radio 1 was a pale imitation of the pirates. The number of records it could play was limited by the same rigid Musicians' Union restrictions on airtime that killed *Ready Steady Go*.

Looking back, I can appreciate that the death of the pirate radio stations taught me a valuable political lesson: governments exist to find out what people like and then stop them doing it. My attitude towards big government, free speech and broadcasting plurality was formed between the ages of ten and thirteen, thanks largely to the treatment of the pirate stations.

It was also while I was listening to Radio London, which had replaced Radio Luxembourg as my under-the-bedclothes entertainment, that I decided I didn't want to be an engine driver after all. I wanted to be a radio disc jockey. Twenty-five years after the pirates were killed off, I finally got my own radio programme, a talkshow on LBC. But it would be another few years before I realised my ambition of being a radio disc jockey. I was invited to sit in for Jimmy Young on his Radio 2 lunchtime show for a few weeks in the late nineties. A couple of days into the gig, I happened to look up and through the control-room window, grinning and giving me the thumbs-up, was Alan 'Fluff' Freeman, to whom I'd listened as a boy with my ear glued to Radio Luxembourg.

Not 'arf!

Part 3

*I*n the years after the Second World War, more than a million British subjects emigrated to Australia under the Assisted Migration Scheme. Australians believed they had only narrowly avoided invasion and occupation by the Japanese and so must implement a 'populate or perish' policy. The Australian government decided to subsidise the fares of those who chose to migrate from Britain. The new immigrants became known as 'Ten Pound Poms', a tenner being the price of their passage. In exchange they had to agree to stay in Australia for a minimum of two years. In 1958, my Uncle Ken, Dad's younger brother, came to the conclusion there was little future for him in Britain. With his wife and young daughter, Ken signed up for the Ten Pound Pom scheme and departed for a new life on the other side of the world, settling first in Melbourne and later in the Sydney suburb Dee Why.

Nanna Littlejohn didn't want them to go. She hadn't been all that thrilled when we moved to Shenfield, a handful of stops away on the overground. Now that her youngest son was relocating thousands of miles away, it felt as if the close-knit family was falling apart. For generations the Littlejohns and the Frenches had all lived in tight proximity, within a few miles of each other. It would be a wrench. This kind of drama was being played out in homes across the country as young men and women, ground down by post-war austerity and shortages, were seduced by the promise of sunshine and opportunity Down Under. There was, of course, no guarantee that their new adventure would be successful. Ken had the offer of a job in a market garden in Australia, run by a sister of Nanna and Grandad's next-door neighbour Mrs Osband – not his chosen career, but it was a start. He was able to reassure his mother that if things didn't work out they'd be back in two short years. In the event he never looked back. When we moved to Peterborough the following year, Nanna must have felt as if she'd been abandoned.

Global communications were in their infancy. The first satellite had yet to be launched and telephone calls were ludicrously expensive. Not that we had a telephone. Ken would write home with his news crammed into a flimsy, self-sealing air mail letter, deliberately light to keep the weight down and reduce the costs. These blue letter-cum-envelopes, with their 'Par Avion' logos, fascinated me. We'd also receive regular postcards with typical Australian scenes – kangaroos, koalas, Aborigines and the Sydney Harbour Bridge.

One Christmas, probably 1961, we got a parcel from Ken containing presents – a cuddly koala for Viv and a boomerang for me. Boomerangs were all the rage that year, thanks to the novelty record by the comedian Charlie Drake, 'My Boomerang Won't Come Back'.

The record sold well, despite the BBC's refusal to play it in its original version. Although the modern cult of 'diversity' was decades away from establishing its suffocating grip, the BBC's taste police decided that the lyrics were offensive because they contained the line 'Practised till I was black in the face, I'm a big disgrace to the Aborigine race'.

Not that there were many Aborigines to be offended in Britain in 1961. But the line 'Practised till I was black in the face' was ruled to be inappropriate. The BBC's ban was eventually lifted after Drake went back into the studio and changed the offending line to 'blue in the face'.

Drake was one of Britain's highest paid performers in the fifties and sixties. Standing just an inch and a half over five feet tall, he was apparently irresistible to women and was regularly pictured with tall, willowy models. Although he amassed a fortune during his career, he was reported to have blown over £5 million on women, fast cars, yachts and gambling. By the time I met him, in the mid 1990s when he was a guest on one of my TV shows, Drake was already on his uppers. When his name came up on the autocue as featuring among the following night's guests, it was the first I knew of it. As the closing credits started to roll, I blurted out: 'Charlie Drake? I thought he was dead!'

Another Australian-themed pop song, however, released four years earlier, eluded the censors. 'Tie Me Kangaroo Down, Sport', by Rolf Harris, slipped under the radar. Eventually, it was banned in Singapore – a ban that spread to Britain – when someone spotted the words of one verse which went: 'Let me Abos go loose, Lou'.

To be honest, I'd have thought 'Let me Abos go loose, Bruce' would have been a better rhyme. But what do I know? Harris eventually deleted the verse in 1964. Curiously, neither song was banned in Australia, which until the late sixties would only accept white European migrants like my Uncle Ken and came late to the embrace of multi-culturalism.

Rolf Harris also turned up on the same TV series that featured Charlie Drake. After a brief interview I was persuaded to join him in a live performance of his version of Led Zeppelin's 'Stairway to Heaven', with Rolf playing his trademark wobble board. It wasn't my finest hour.

My boomerang was lying under the Christmas tree. I didn't have much trouble guessing what it was or where it had come from. There are only so many ways of wrapping a boomerang and no attempt had been made to disguise it. The following morning, Boxing Day, I rushed over to the Grange to try it out. I'd enjoyed limited success with a cardboard boomerang, which had been given away with one of my weekly comics. Once or twice I'd succeeded in getting it to spin back in my direction, but nine times out of ten it would simply go straight on before crashing to earth. Now that I had the genuine article, I was convinced I'd become more proficient. The boomerang came with detailed diagrammatic instructions. You're supposed to give it a flick just as you release it, to impart spin so that the boomerang would change direction in mid-air and return to you like a homing pigeon. All I can report is that it's easier said than done. Try as I might, I couldn't get the damn thing to vere from an arrow-straight flight path. After about an hour, I gave it up as a bad job, convinced I was a big disgrace to the Littlejohn race. My boomerang wouldn't come back.

After a couple of years, it was apparent that Ken and Joan wouldn't be returning to Britain. They were settling in Australia for good. When Grandad retired from the docks, Ken persuaded his parents that they should visit him and his family Down Under. Australia was a long way to go for a holiday, and the regular fares were prohibitive, so he suggested they apply for the Assisted Migration Scheme. Although Grandad was past retirement age, they were accepted. The plan was that they'd stay in Australia for two years. Nanna's sister, Emily French, 'Auntie Em', had recently retired herself from her job running a clothing factory in Northern Ireland and it was agreed that she would move into Vine Gardens while they were away, to look after the house.

On the day my grandparents became Ten Pound Poms, we travelled down to wave them off on the boat train to Southampton from Waterloo. It must have been an emotional day for my father, but I don't recall him showing it. His generation never did. My grandmother was in floods of tears. That, however, is not my abiding memory of the day.

As we were making our way down the platform to see Nanna and Grandad to their carriage, I noticed something flutter to the ground from the general direction of a couple walking a few yards in front of us. I ran ahead and picked it up. It was a pristine £10 note. I'd never seen one before, which was hardly surprising since £10 notes had been withdrawn during the war and were not reintroduced until February 1964. There can't have been all that many in circulation. Ten pounds was a great deal of money then. It could get you all the way to Australia. My dad thought it must have been dropped by the couple in front. He told me run after them and ask if they'd dropped anything.

The man took out his wallet and went ashen. Yes, he said, he had dropped something, a £10 note. Was this it? A look of sheer relief came over his face. He'd been checking their tickets and the note must have fallen out then. I gave it back to him and he reached into his pocket and handed me a silver half-crown. I hesitated and looked back at my dad. 'Go on, son, take it,' the man said. 'You've earned it. You're a life-saver.' My dad nodded and I pocketed the shiny coin. 'You should hang on to that,' he told me. Naturally, I ignored him. It kept me in comics and sherbert lemons for a fortnight.

The best-laid plans of my grandparents soon began to unravel. Not long after they landed in Australia, Auntie Em had a stroke and was taken into hospital. Even though she recovered, she was not fit enough to run Vine Gardens on her own. Her doctor had said that he couldn't rule out her having another stroke, so she shouldn't be left alone. Nanna and Grandad weren't able to return to Britain to care for her, since they were locked into Australia for at least two years under the Ten Pound Pom deal. Em had never married, like a lot of young women who suffered from a shortage of eligible men after the First World War, so had no children to look after her. There was only one solution: Em would have to move in with us in Peterborough.

This can't have been an easy decision for my parents to make, but there was no alternative. Nor would any alternative have been considered. Dad wouldn't put his aunt into a nursing home, even if she could have afforded it. Today, people dump their elderly relatives in hideous, and often abusive, granny warehouses without a second thought. Back then, extended families always looked after their own. Having three generations living under the same roof was far from uncommon. Dad was the eldest son and considered his aunt's welfare his responsibility. We already had Nanna Sparke living with us, so we'd just have to make room for Em, too.

Our house in Ledbury Road had four bedrooms, which were already taken, so our sleeping arrangements would have to be reshuffled. Em would need her own room, so would Nanna. It was decided that I could keep my room and Viv would sleep with my parents. This wouldn't be a full-time arrangement, since Nanna was already dividing her time between Ledbury Road and Ingatestone, where Mum's sister Olive lived with her husband, Tom, and their two young sons. It meant Nanna could also spend time with her four grandchildren.

This was all about to change, too. Tom Millar, Olive's husband, was being transferred by his employer, Ford Tractors, to America, and would have to relocate to Detroit, the company's world headquarters. It was agreed that Nanna Sparke would alternate, spending a year with us in England, and a year with Olive in the US. Once, moving to Shenfield, let alone Peterborough, was considered the end of the world. Now the family was going to be spread out over three continents. Dad's brother and parents would be in Australia, Mum's sister and mother would be in America. We, meanwhile, would keep the home fires burning.

When Nanna Sparke moved in with Olive in Michigan, Auntie Em took over her room and Viv went back into hers. Emily French was a tall, independent woman, with a shock of white hair, who had held down a responsible managerial job in Ireland. I don't suppose she was much older than her early sixties, though she seemed ancient. To my young mind, she wasn't short of a few bob, either. Once a week she'd slip me a pound note and send me to the shops to buy her favourite brand of cigarettes, Olivier. My cut was a tanner (2p approx). I can't swear to it, but I think that a quid was enough for half a dozen packets of twenty. Olivier was a 'luxury' brand from Benson & Hedges, launched in 1956 and promoted by the actor Laurence Olivier. I've managed to find an old advert for Olivier, priced at 3s. 3d. (16p) for twenty and 1s. 7½d. (roughly 8p) for a pack of ten. The black and white advert features a framed photo of dear, dear Larry, in blazer, collar and tie and cufflinks, looking pensive and clutching a lit cigarette in his left hand. Advertised as 'Specially Blended for Laurence Olivier', the copy reads:

You'll enjoy this successful cigarette. Blended from fine tobaccos and specially tipped for coolness and flavour, Olivier cigarettes maintain the Benson and Hedges tradition for quality at an economical price.

Em was also a woman of robust opinions, which she was eager to share. She was no great lover of popular music, which I'd have on most of the time. About the only group in the Top 20 that she could tolerate was the Bachelors, a clean-cut Irish folk trio, brothers Con and Dec Cluskey and John Stokes. They had hits across the globe with ballads like 'Ramona', 'I Believe' and 'Charmaine'. In the early sixties, they were regulars on *Top of the Pops*. Just as Em adored her delightful Dublin boys, so she loathed the Rolling Stones – especially Mick Jagger. Whenever Jagger appeared on TV, she couldn't disguise her contempt.

'Look at him, he's disgusting. Dirty suzer.' At least, I think that's how you spell it. Could be 'dirty soozer' or 'dirty soosah'. I've tried looking it up but can't find any spelling or definition of 'suzer', 'soozer' or 'soosah' in any dictionary or anywhere online. Maybe it's a word she picked up in Ireland. It might have been old East End slang. My mum thought it might have been Yiddish in origin; she said she thought she'd heard it before when she worked in Stratford. Or perhaps Em invented it herself. People who never swore in the conventional sense often made up suitable substitute expletives of their own.

Wherever the word came from, fifty years later I still can't look at Mick Jagger without hearing Auntie Em's voice: 'Dirty suzer!'

★

Most of Auntie Em's weekly tanner went over the sweet counter at Rolph's, or the NSS newsagents which had opened in the brand new shopping arcade at the end of Ledbury Road. All these sweets were already beginning to take their toll on my teeth, which necessitated regular visits to the school dentist in the Town Hall, appointments I used to dread. My early experience of home dental care hadn't been a bundle of laughs. When I was teething, and subsequently when I had a toothache, my grandmothers would soak a piece of cotton wool in whisky and make me bite down on it until the anaesthetic effect of the alcohol numbed the pain. Although I grew up to like a drink, on the odd occasion someone gives me a scotch I still associate it with having toothache. Probably why I stick to vodka these days.

When my milk teeth were hanging by a gossamer thread, my mum would tie a length of cotton round them and attempt to yank them out. Brute force didn't always do the trick. In which case she'd declare that the tooth wasn't quite ready and we'd try again the following day. On at least one occasion, we borrowed an idea from a cartoon strip – *Tom and Jerry*, probably. This entailed attaching the cotton to the partially dislodged molar and tying the other end to a door handle. While I stood there, braced with my mouth wide open, my mum, on the count of three, slammed the door – wrenching the tooth from its roots. Crude, but effective. And since it had worked for Tom and Jerry, it helped overcome my terror. The upside was that if you put your lost tooth in a piece of tissue under your pillow, in the morning there would be a shiny sixpence in its place, put there, we were assured, by the tooth fairy. Yeah, right. I would pretend to be asleep until my mum or dad had made the swap. But I never once let on, for fear that if I broke the spell I wouldn't get the sixpence and the bloody tooth would still be there in the morning.

Once my milk teeth were gone for ever, I was constantly reminded that my new set were the only teeth I was ever going to have. Brushing after meals was a supervised routine. We were a Colgate household. Others swore by Gibbs SR, which was the first product ever to be advertised on ITV when it began transmission in 1955. Everyone had their own favourite brand. There was a great stir when Signal was introduced in 1961. It was the first toothpaste to feature red and white stripes, like a stick of seaside rock, and was obviously aimed at children. I tried pestering Mum to buy a tube of Signal, but toothpaste was toothpaste as far as she was concerned and Colgate was a few pence cheaper. I'm sure she was right. The amount of sugar I was shovelling into my mouth, I might just as well have brushed my teeth with a stick of rock.

On the way home from West Town, if I had any money I'd call into Rolph's for Black Jacks, Fruit Salads, all four for a penny, a hangover from the days when you could buy a single sweet for a farthing – a quarter of an old penny.

Farthings, which were first minted in 1714 were withdrawn on 4 December 1960, but still had a notional value. Retailers could easily have set a minimum price of a halfpenny for all their goods, which would effectively have been a price increase of 100 per cent. But they resisted the temptation to revise their prices when the farthing ceased to be legal tender, unlike the rampant greed and inflation that followed the introduction of decimalisation in the Heath government in 1971, a giant con-trick that saw many prices double overnight as plenty of people, especially the elderly, struggled to come to terms with the new coinage.

In 1961, the spivvery and cynicism that would become the standard operating procedure of large chunks of the retail trade in later years had yet to manifest itself. You can no more imagine Mrs Rolph trying to rip off her customers than envisage her entering a glamorous granny competition wearing an itsy-bitsy, teeny-weeny, yellow polka-dot bikini.

My downfall was Maynards wine gums, Rowntree's fruit pastilles, aniseed balls, crystallised jellies, Everlasting Strips of toffee, which lasted about five minutes, and Traffic Lights.

Traffic Lights were giant gobstoppers which filled your mouth and could give you lockjaw if you attempted to chew them. They would change colour as you sucked them and, unlike Everlasting Strips, seemed to last for ever. We'd take them out every few minutes to inspect them for signs of erosion. Half-eaten gobstoppers would be stored in your blazer pocket, wrapped in a hanky or a piece of tissue paper, to be retrieved later and popped back in your mouth, covered in lint and other unmentionable bits and bobs of flotsam and jetsam.

Then there was the great delicacy of the age: Jubblies. Most people today associate the expression 'Lovely Jubbly' with Del Boy Trotter in the late John Sullivan's brilliant BBC comedy classic *Only Fools and Horses*. Its origins actually go back to the 1950s. 'Lubbly Jubbly' was an advertising slogan for Jubbly, a brand of orange soft drink which came in a pyramid-shaped wax carton. The idea was that you tore off one corner of the carton and drank from it. But the design of the packaging inevitably meant that most of the contents squirted out before you could get it to your lips.

Someone – some unsung, nameless genius – must one day have come up with a solution. By the 1960s, sweet shops and newsagents had started storing Jubblies in their ice-cream freezers. Suitably frozen, Jubblies could then be tackled without fear of spillage, like an ice lolly without a stick. Better still, three children could 'drink' a frozen

Jubbly simultaneously, sucking on a corner apiece. We used to have Jubbly-sucking competitions. The aim was to see who could extract all the orange colouring from the Jubbly before it melted. Lovely Jubbly, indeed.

So popular did frozen Jubblies become in the early sixties that the established lollipop manufacturers, such as Wall's and Lyons Maid, became seriously worried. They'd send their sales reps to newsagents and sweet shops to put the frighteners on the owners. Deep freezes were expensive and were supplied free of charge by the ice-cream manu-facturers. I can remember Tony Saunders, who ran the NSS, telling us that he'd been handed an ultimatum: dump the Jubblies or lose the deep freeze.

No surprise, though, that my prodigious consumption of confectionery started to wear away at the enamel on my teeth. When evidence of cavities or discoloration appeared, my mother would march me off to the school dentist based in Peterborough. This wasn't exactly a modern, touchy-feely experience, complete with soothing mood music, aromatherapy candles and overhead TV monitors. It was more like being committed to a Victorian mental institution and subjected to a frontal lobotomy, as a basis for negotiation.

The Town Hall itself was intimidating enough: a serious, soaring, Gothic-columned, between-the-wars edifice that dominated the main drag, dwarfed only by the adjacent cathedral.

From what I recall, the dentist was in the basement at the back of the building, down some stairs and a long corridor. It was like being led away to jail, or the gallows. The surgery stunk of floor polish, Jeyes Fluid and naked fear. The Town Hall only dated back to 1930, but the school dentist's place of work seemed to belong to another century.

The dentist's chair was an intimidating piece of equipment, which looked a bit like the barber's chair in *Sweeney Todd*. I shouldn't have been surprised if it had a trapdoor which dispatched naughty children with tooth decay into a dark pit below, whence they would be butchered and turned into game pies for sale in David Greig's. The tools of his trade looked like medieval instruments of torture. It was absolutely bloody terrifying. I'd like to describe the dentist's appearance, but all I can recall is his evil eyes peering over the mask he wore, like a diabolical mad scientist from the silent movies. He only had two types of therapy – drilling and extraction. And he figured that, while you were there with a specific complaint, he might as well drill and fill a few more teeth at the same time, as a precaution.

You had the option of local or general anaesthetic. Or no anaesthetic at all, unless your mother asked for it. The dentist favoured option three: 'Be over in no time, you won't feel a thing.' Presumably the sooner he could relieve you of the offending tooth, or drill a quick hole and bung in a bit of molten mercury, the sooner he could get back to the important business of carrying out some hideous medical experiment on a local virgin, or injecting himself with monkey glands. Or propping up the back bar of the boozer on Cathedral Square, for a light lunch of eight pints and a cheese and pickle sandwich, before returning suitably refreshed to his torture chamber to disfigure another press-ganged procession of schoolchildren.

He did have a dental nurse, of sorts, but we're not talking Barbara Windsor in immaculate starched whites, with a winning smile and a tantalising glimpse of cleavage. This one was built like a prop forward, more Hattie Jacques's ugly sister than Babs Windsor. The nurse's job was not to reassure, or to soothe fevered brows. It was to hold down the dentist's victims by force while he did his worst and to mop up the blood. It was rumoured she had a second job, swabbing the floors of the Co-op abbatoir.

On my first visit, my mum recommended that I opt for the local anaesthetic, so that I didn't lose consciousness and would know exactly what was going on. Clearly she didn't appreciate that I *wanted* to lose consciousness, to be completely oblivious to this entire ordeal and wake up in my own bed the next morning when this bad dream was all over. It didn't help when I realised that the local anaesthetic was to be administered with a contraption which looked as if it had in a previous incarnation been used for the artificial insemination of farm animals. This was no surgical strike, it was a thousand-bomber raid on my jaw. Christ, it was excruciating. Maybe the injection wouldn't have been so bad if it had actually worked. But the mad scientist was so eager to get stuck into this irritating schoolboy, who was standing in the way of him disembowelling a drugged virgin or downing a gallon of strong ale in the Bell and Oak, that he set about his task before the anaesthetic had taken hold. Fortunately, the noise of the drill drowned my screams, otherwise the local nick would have scrambled the murder squad.

My mouth was wedged open with one of those devices they use in maternity hospitals for forceps births. The drill itself was about the same size as the one used to tunnel out the Jubilee Line extension under London. In the event, I should have opted for the general anaesthetic since I passed out anyway. The anaesthetic didn't start to kick in until it was all over and I was bundled out of the surgery, biting down hard on a swab of cotton wool to staunch the flow of blood. By now, the side of my face was frozen solid. It felt as if someone had surgically inserted a coconut in my lower jaw. The terrified looks on the faces of the children next in line, sitting petrified in the waiting room anxiously clutching the hands of their mothers, is etched in my memory.

Next time – and there was a next time, since the

experience clearly didn't deter me from stuffing my face with sweets – I was allowed to opt for the general anaesthetic. This, too, was a mistake. A giant cylinder of gas was wheeled into the studio by a man in a rubber apron, face mask and wellington boots. I assumed he worked in the same slaughter house as the dental nurse. While the anaesthetist adjusted the levels of the gas, the dentist readied a mask with an expandable hose which looked just like those worn by the pilots in Bomber Command during the Second World War. I was familiar with these masks from Sunday afternoon war films on TV, such as *The Dambusters*, so was marginally reassured. If it was good enough for Guy Gibson, it was good enough for me. Frankly, I was horribly misguided. I'd have felt safer flying solo into the teeth of German flak on the approach to the Eder dam. As the dentist forced the mask over my mouth, I was overcome with waves of nausea and blind panic. As I lost consciousness, it seemed as if I was spiralling downwards into a bottomless well of death and despair, from which I would never emerge. There were flashing, swirling lights in front of my eyes, like a kaleidoscope designed by Satan himself, before I blacked out completely. When I came round, I was puking violently into a bucket at the side of the dentist's chair. The only good news was that my face wasn't frozen numb, as it had been when I'd opted for the local jab. The bad news was that I felt as if I'd been fifteen rounds with Cassius Clay and blood was running down the back of my throat. I was helped from the chair, barely able to place one foot in front of the other. As I was dragged away through the waiting room, I must have looked like Albert RN, the prison-camp dummy used to fool the guards in another of those wartime films.

By the time I left school, my mouth resembled a war zone, entire neighbourhoods destroyed by enemy shelling. There were gaps top and bottom, left and right, although my front teeth somehow survived unscathed. There was no bridgework or ceramic implants back then, at least not on the NHS. What molars remained at the back of my mouth were reinforced with enough toxic mercury-based amalgam to contaminate every fish in the South China Sea.

But so traumatised was I by my mauling at the hands of the sadistic school dentist, it would be the mid-eighties before I finally plucked up the courage to get my teeth fixed – and then only after falling victim to an abscess over a Bank Holiday. Otherwise, the school dentist would have left me scarred for life.

Once a year the school doctor would arrive at West Town to give us a full physical inspection. Two rooms above the kitchens were set aside for the purpose. Boys to the left, girls to the right. In class order, girls first, then boys, we'd strip down to our undies and stand shivering in the assembly hall until it was our turn to ascend the stairs to the makeshift consulting room, which reeked of boiled cabbage and resonated to the timpani of clashing sauce-pans and the crone-like cackling of the cooks from the kitchens below. From a distance the school dinner ladies sounded like Macbeth's witches on a hen night. First the doctor would comb through our heads for nits, which were fairly common. He'd take our blood pressure, check our pulse, listen to our hearts and then make us drop our pants while he grabbed our privates and told us to cough. I can remember briefing my sister about what to expect before her first school medical. She came home disap-pointed, wondering why the doctor had forgotten to ask her to cough.

I escaped nits, but I did have a tapeworm. When I first heard, I was quite proud. Other kids had rabbits and hamsters, but I was the first to get a tapeworm. Perhaps we could keep him a tank in the living room, where others kept their goldfish, or make him a nest in a shoe box and feed him lettuce. I soon discovered that tapeworms don't make great pets. This was when I was bent over the bath with my mother trying to entice the tapeworm to leave my body voluntarily. Boiling water was supposed to draw them to the surface, so I was told to squat over a bowl while my mum topped it up from a kettle. After a while, my new friend and lodger made an appearance, popping his head out into the daylight sufficiently far, thus allowing my mum to grab him by the neck and pull him free, while I clung on to the taps. The tapeworm had obviously become quite attached to me. He really didn't want to play, wrapping himself round my lower intestine in a nautical knot, so this tug of war went on for an eternity. Eventually, something snapped. Or, rather, the tapeworm snapped. Much to my relief my triumphant mother was able to remove a good four feet of tapeworm and uncoil it on to the bathroom floor. What was left of him followed naturally over the next few days after I was fed a three-meals-a-day diet of stewed rhubarb and my Nanna's All Bran. Next time, I'd settle for a rabbit.

We were never a religious family, but in the years after we moved to Peterborough the Church played an important role in our lives, in a social if not a spiritual sense. The nearest church to Ledbury Road was St Botolph's, in the village of Longthorpe, a couple of miles away. The church is a simple thirteenth-century structure, built from rubble left over from the construction of the Bishop's Palace at Peterborough Cathedral. There was rumoured to be a tunnel connecting the cathedral with St Botolph's, said to have been used by monks from the Abbey of Burgh to gain access to a holy bathing pool on the estate of the Fitzwilliam family, the local aristocracy. Certainly when we used to play in the grounds of the Fitzwilliams' ancestral seat, there was a partially concealed tunnel entrance, guarded by a metal grille. We always planned to investigate further, but never plucked up the courage.

It was the church hall, rather than the church itself, which was the focal point of much of our social activity. Sunday school, whist drives, barn dances, bring and buy sales, harvest festivals, flower arranging, exercise classes, music lessons, ballet classes, amateur dramatics, concerts. Never a dull moment and all good, clean family fun.

I've found a picture in a scrapbook of a pop group formed with my West Town school friends, which we put together for a Christmas concert at Longthorpe village hall. It must have been Christmas 1964, because we're all wearing long charcoal-grey trousers, with matching white shirts and ties. Twin brothers Kevin and Steve Richman are on guitar. Kev was known to everyone as 'Lank' because he was about six inches taller than the rest of us, including his twin brother – who, if I remember correctly, was the elder. The Richmans were like a prototype of the Trotter brothers – Lank towering over Steve, just as Rodney towered over Del. Also on guitar is Steven 'Skip' Skipper, with his kid brother David – known as 'Butch', after the dog in *Tom and Jerry* – on piano. I'm playing the maracas, about the only musical instrument I ever managed to master, and doing my best Mick Jagger impersonation. We didn't have a drummer, probably because we couldn't lay our hands on a drum kit, except for a model drum kit made for Sooty. Otherwise I might have had a crack on the drums, given it the full Dave Clark. We performed a version of 'Not Fade Away' – singing along to a record playing in the background – largely because it involved little more than three chords and, having managed to get hold of some maracas, I knew some of the lyrics, which weren't difficult, mainly consisting of 'Well love is love and not fade away'.

Words and music by Buddy Holly; taken to number three in the UK charts by the Rolling Stones in February 1964; laid to rest at Longthorpe village hall, by a bunch of tone-deaf schoolboys, Christmas that same year.

There's also another boy with a guitar in the photograph. He looks familiar but for the life of me I can't put a name to his face. He's stuck out to one side on his own, a bit like those pictures of Pete Best, 'the forgotten Beatle', in Hamburg.

Before 'aerobics' there was keep fit. Mum and Nanna used to go to keep fit once a week, armed with fearsome looking medicine balls, which they would swing like dervishes. They both had exercise tunics with little pleated skirts, which reminded me of the outfits worn by Robin Hood and his Merry Men in the ITV series. Jane Fonda leg warmers, sweat bands and Lycra 'bodies' were still half a century away in the future.

Jumble sales were the sixties version of car boot sales,

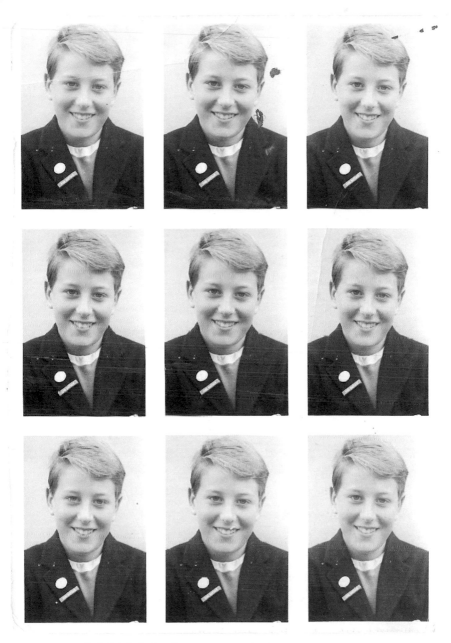

Andy Warhol takes the West Town School photographs, 1964.

Viv and me in our
new school uniforms,
Ledbury Road, 1965.

(*Facing page*) Alf Tupper,
the Tough of the Track.

Ten Pound Poms. Bill and Min off to Australia. Catching the Boat Train
to Southampton Waterloo Station, 1964.

West Town School's triumphant football team, 1964
That's me, front and centre.

Not Fade Away.
Front and centre again, Longthorpe Village Hall, Christmas, 1965.

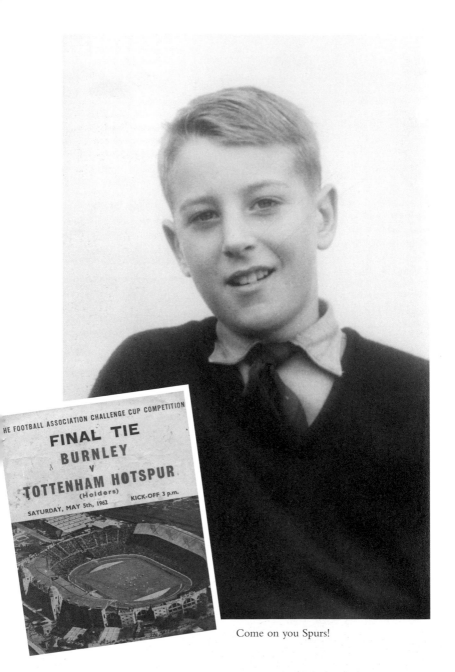

THE FOOTBALL ASSOCIATION CHALLENGE CUP COMPETITION

FINAL TIE

BURNLEY

v

TOTTENHAM HOTSPUR

(Holders)   KICK-OFF 3 p.m.

SATURDAY, MAY 5th, 1962

Come on you Spurs!

School's cup triumph (1)...

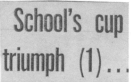

The Kursaal, Southend.

When West Town School beat Fulbridge School yesterday to win the final of the cricket knockout competition, hero of the day was West Town bowler Richard Littlejohn (above) who took nine wickets for 22 runs.

Fulbridge were all out for 38 and West Town scored 50 for three, N. Edmundson hitting 29 not out. The trophy was presented to West Town by Mrs. Rickaby.

RADIO LUXEMBOURG
The Station of the Stars

☆

☆

☆

208 METRES MEDIUM WAVE
WEEKDAYS 6.30 PM—2 AM SUNDAYS 6 PM—2 AM
AND ON 49.26 METRES SHORT WAVE
RADIO LUXEMBOURG (LONDON) LIMITED
38 HERTFORD STREET LONDON W1

The Littlejohns, 1967.

Spector's back
Mama's should go

RICHARD LITTLEJOHN

Reviewing records for the *Peterborough Evening Telegraph* as a 15-year-old DJ at the Spinning Wheel, 1969.

A FIFTH former at School, Richard Littlejohn for himself on the local di

Richard is one of five D. discotheque in Bridge St Road Show which travels taking music to the dancer

With the Road Show, Ric bit — a few weeks ago he Louth, then at Wisbech C the show goes to Peterbor

But he still found time to listen to six of the latest releases and here he comments on them:

"And When I Die"—Blood Sweat and and Tears (CBS)

"This is from their latest album and I think it's the best track. Blood, Sweat and Tears are probably one of the best groups to emerge from America in a long time. Unfortunately, their album did not sell and I think this may be too clever for the British charts."

"Proud Mary" — Checkmates Ltd featuring Sonny Charles (A & M)

"Spector's back with a bang, and it shows. The production makes the record and because of this it could easily outsell the original Creedence Clearwater version."

"Yester Me, Yester You, Yesterday"—Stevie Wonder (Tamla Motown)

"This is very reminiscent of 'Place in the Sun'. But Stevie Wonder hasn't lived up to the expectations of his youth. This aside is still a good record and should make the lower part of the thirty."

"Like Uncle Charlie" — Climax Chicago Blues and Band (Parlephone)

"On the whole the record is very like Crosby, Stills and Nash on their LP. Unfortunately, a very thirdrate version of them, though. Can't really see it

nd

well

ıgh's Deacon's
g quite a name
scene.

Spinning Wheel
helps run the
ut East Anglia

around quite a
youth centre in
ıb and tonight
h Centre.

TOP TWENTY

1 (1) **Sugar Sugar** — Archies (RCA)
2 (2) **Oh Well** — Fleetwood Mac (Reprise)
3 (5) **Return of Django** — Upsetters (Upsetter)
4 (3) **He Ain't Heavy . . . He's My Brother** — Hollies Parlophone
5 (12) **Wonderful World, Beautiful People** — Jimmy Cliff (Trojan)
6 (4) **I'm Gonna Make You Mine** — Lou Christie (Buddah)
7 (7) **Delta Lady** — Joe Cocker (Regal Zonophone)
8 (11) **Love's Been Good to Me**—Frank Sinatra (Reprise)
9 (-) **Call Me Number One** — Tremeloes (CBS)
10 (9) **Nobody's Child** — Karen Young (Major Minor)
11 (6) **Space Oddity** — David Bowie (Philips)
12 (16) **What Does it Take** — Junior Walker (Tamla Motown)
13 (-) **Something** — Beatles (Apple)
14 (10) **A Boy Named Sue** — Johnny Cash (CBS)
15 (8) **I'll Never Fall in Love Again** — Bobby Gentry (Capitol)
16 (15) **Do What You Gotta Do** — Four Tops (Tamla Motown)
17 (-) **Sweet Dream** — Jethro Tull (Chrysalis)
18 (18) **Long Shot (Kick the Bucket)** — Pioneers (Trojan)
19 (-) **Cold Turkey** — Plastic Ono Band (Apple)
20 (-) **Liquidator** — Harry J and the All Stars (Trojan)

Westwood Park Road, with two-tone Ford Corsair 2000E in the drive, 1969.

The first record I ever bought. *It's Over* by Roy Orbison.

Deacon's in 'Top of Form' contest

A TEAM from Deacon's stede Road, and captain Introducing the Peter- Footnote: The result of school, Peterborough took Martin Chambers, aged 16, borough school John Ellison the contest cannot be an-

On Top of the Form, 1967. We went out in the first round on away goals.

Black Sabbath played the Spinning Wheel in 1970. I managed to upset Ozzy Osbourne (second left).

Deacon's Grammar School First XI, 1970. Skip (second right back row) and me (centre back row) already sporting our shaggy Isle of Wight pop festival haircuts.

only without the stolen property. I loved the second-hand book stalls, where you could pick up musty, dusty copies of the classics for a few pence. Leather-bound, hardback editions of everything from Dickens to Richmal Crompton, well-thumbed, dog-eared paperbacks by Ian Fleming and Neville Shute. In a couple of years I managed to build up a pretty decent library for less than ten shillings.

Mum played an active role in the Young Wives Club, which gave her regular contact with women of her own age. No doubt modern 'liberals' would sneer contemptuously at the very concept of a 'young wives' club as patronising and demeaning and an instrument of male chauvinist suppression, just as Tony Blair viewed the Women's Institute as one of the 'forces of conservatism'. But these kind of voluntary organisations, best described by the philosopher Edmund Burke as the 'small battalions', were the glue which bound the community together. For instance, my mother and the other women would always give up their time to arrange the flowers in church for harvest festivals, Easter and Christmas, and help out at Sunday school and other events in the church hall. Today, these young mums would all be considered potential paedophiles.

In July 2013, the Archbishop of Canterbury, Justin Welby, announced that all church volunteers likely to come into contact with children will be required to submit to a full Criminal Records Bureau check. This would include bell-ringers, sidesmen, refreshment stall volunteers. And, yes, flower arrangers. Guilty, unless you can prove yourself innocent. Centuries of British justice has been turned on its head. Welby said that if volunteers were not prepared to submit themselvs to CRB scrutiny: 'Don't come to church.' And the C of E wonders why congregations are disappearing faster than lead off a hot church roof.

Fortunately, the church hall still has a central role to play in country life today, although the world has moved on from the Young Wives Club and nativity plays. The church hall has adapted to the requirements of our progressive, secular society. In September 2013, it was revealed that the village hall in Trumpington, Cambridgeshire, had been playing host to secret bondage sessions. For a £10 admission fee, punters were offered flogging, caning and spanking, as well as tuition in the erotic application of hot candle wax and the deployment of 'violent wand devices'. When the trustees found out the true nature of what they had been told was a 'relationship support group' they called an immediate halt.

I can't imagine Longthorpe village hall in the sixties serving up synchronised sado-masochism along with the stewed tea and bourbons. But, then again, you never know what they got up to with those medicine balls . . .

Friday night was swimming club at the 1930s open-air lido, built in classic Art Deco style, with immaculate gardens in front. The lido opened its gates at Easter and closed at the end of September, whatever the weather. Some years, Easter fell at the end of March and the temperature could still be in the 30°s F, but that was no impediment. We'd be herded into the changing rooms and forced to walk through the icy blast of a cold shower and a six-inch-deep foot-bath even before we got to the pool. Risk aversion isn't entirely a modern obsession. In the sixties, they were worried that we might pick up all manner of infections if swimmers weren't properly de-loused and disinfected before diving in. Just in case the school doctor had missed something contagious.

One year there was a plague of verrucas, a nasty strain of plantar warts which attach themselves to the feet, to which I was not immune. I was convinced that I'd contracted verrucas from the foot-bath designed to stop us transmitting verrucas. It was like a stagnant swamp. Heaven knows what diseases lurked within. That summer, verrucas were my constant companion. This particular strain was especially resistant, both to prevention and cure. The lido management pumped so much chlorine into the pool that it could have stripped paint. Maybe they'd put Dr Crippen in charge. It would have been safer swimming in an acid bath. A couple of dips and your brand new navy blue bathing trunks were virgin-white.

By the end of April we all had bleached blond hair and looked like poster children for an Aryan master race. That's if you overlooked the bright red eyes. As a result of the management's attempt to eradicate verrucas with industrial quantities of chlorine, I managed to contract conjunctivitis. While my streaming eyes could be treated with drops and cream, the verrucas stubbornly refused to disappear. It wasn't just me, either. Every other kid at the pool seemed to be wearing socks with their swimming trunks. Mum tried cutting them out and burning them off, applying an assortment of lotions and malt vinegar, all to no avail. That was until we went to the seaside, sunny Hunstanton on the North Norfolk coast, for a brief holiday. After a couple of days paddling and swimming in the salt waters of the Wash, the verrucas had vanished completely.

If there was a verruca epidemic today, no doubt the local council would close the lido, drain the pool and send in an 'environmental rescue' team in *Doomwatch*-style haz-chem space suits to carry out a clean-up, which would inevitably last until the end of September. Back then, we just got on with it.

Much of the school summer holidays was spent at the lido. It had two pools: a full Olympic-sized main pool with high-diving boards and a learner pool for mums and toddlers. There was also a generous grassed area for picnics and sunbathing. While Mum would take Viv paddling or teach her to swim at the shallow end, I'd amuse myself doing cannonballs from whichever diving board I felt brave enough to jump off. There were allegedly rules forbidding running, jumping and 'horseplay' but these were enforced mostly in the breach. The lifeguards were primarily interested in impressing the older girls, who never seemed to get wet and spent most of their time, when they weren't giggling, adjusting their swimming costumes and playing with their hair.

A second-tier balcony ran around the perimeter of the pool. This was where the older boys (and the lifeguards) would slope off for a cigarette, or a quick snog and a grope with the girls. We younger boys would be granted a sly drag in exchange for not blowing the whistle on their light petting. The balcony also had a couple of vending machines, which dispensed chicken soup, Bovril and Vimto in paper cups for a couple of pence. It didn't matter which button you pressed, it all tasted the same. What you got was a perfectly disgusting, tepid chicken/Bovril/Vimto mix. The machines also sold Smith's crisps. One flavour: plain, with a little blue bag of salt. In our new age of infinite choice, you can buy every flavour of crisp under the sun from pickled onion to chicken vindaloo, crinkle-cut, ultra thick, ultra-thin. But if you want a plain potato crisp which comes anywhere near the quality of those old Smith's crisps, it'll cost you a fiver for a packet of designer 'Kettle Chips', bring your own salt.

The lido also had its own resident nonce, who would stand in the shallow end on club nights and encourage children to swim between his legs. He was well known for it. Parents would warn their kids not to go anywhere near him. The clue was in the name: he was called Frank the Bummer. Frank never pushed it too far, to the best of my knowledge. If he'd ever acted on his urges, he'd have been lynched from the top diving board. Years later, I mentioned Frankie B in my *Daily Mail* column, in relation to a story about paedophiles being given Viagra on the NHS. I had heard from his former probation officer. Turned out Frank did have a bit of form, after all. Nothing serious, but enough to warrant the authorities keeping an eye on him. Given the 'paedo' mania of recent years, Frank would today have been burned out of his home by an angry mob before he got anywere near the Lido, just to be on the safe side. After one bout of *News of the World*-inspired anti-'peed-io-file' hysteria in the early noughties, a lynch mob on the south coast attacked an innocent paediatrician.

Friday nights weren't just about fun, they had a serious purpose. We were taught life-saving techniques and learned to become stronger swimmers: a skill which was to save my own life years later when I ventured too far from shore in the swirling currents of a river in the Ardèche. Theoretically, I suppose, I could still save someone from drowning after being drilled Friday night after Friday night in how to tow a flailing figure to the side of the pool. In practice, who knows? I've also got a certificate somewhere which proves that I can pick up a brick from the bottom of a six-feet-deep pool. It's one of the few qualifications I *have* got.

In my early teens, I'd take out a season ticket to the lido every year. It was one of *the* meeting places during the summer holidays, prized as much for posing and picking up the opposite sex as swimming: somewhere to show off new fashions and listen to transistor radios, which were strictly against the rules but openly tolerated. Most of my sex education came from the lido: especially the diagrams carved into the cubicle doors, some of them complete with helpful orifices, which were far more explicit than anything we were ever taught in biology classes.

By the late sixties, the lido was becoming increasingly shabby and it seemed destined to share the fate of hundreds of others around Britain that were closing with depressing regularity. The City Council drew up plans for a shiny new leisure centre to replace the lido. This would be called 'Wirrina' – an Aborigine word for 'meeting place'. Maybe they were hoping that Rolf Harris would agree to open it. Do you know what it is, yet?

(I shouldn't have thought there were many Aborigines in Peterborough back then. Today? There's probably a thriving community. Aborigine may well be one of the twenty-plus languages they 'celebrate' at West Town.)

Like the lido, Wirrina was to feature an Olympic-sized

pool to attract prestigious international competitions. Unfortunately, due to a planning cock-up, the pool was built one metre short and the titans of the Olympic swimming community never dipped so much as a pinkie in the waters of the Wirrina. Result: the pool never turned a profit and by the 1990s was being subsidised to the tune of £5 a head for everyone in the city. So the council voted to shut it. Even then, it cost taxpayers £85,000 a year to keep it closed.

Somehow, the lido struggled on. In 1989, the council wanted to flatten it, but it was saved when a seven-year-old boy drowned in the River Nene. The coroner ruled that children needed somewhere safe to swim in the summer. Two years later, the lido was damaged by fire and was only reprieved from demolition when a local councillor, to his enormous credit, dipped into his own pocket to pay for repairs.

In 2002, the lido was refurbished and granted Grade II Listed status. It is still thriving today, one of the few surviving lidos in Britain, and a poignant reminder of a different age of innocent fun, fresh air and civic pride. And verrucas.

When Olive and Tom moved to Detroit, we inherited two of their prized possessions: a fridge and Tom's company car, a Ford Consul 365. This was the first fridge we'd ever had. Until then, Mum kept everything in the pantry. Our 'new' fridge had been manufactured in the 1950s, looked like, and was built like, a Chevrolet, with curved bodywork and chrome trim. It occupied pride of place in the kitchen at Ledbury Road, humming away like a nuclear reactor. Its enormous exterior bulk belied a relatively small interior. The walls were about six inches thick, to provide insulation. This meant that available space for groceries was somewhat limited. There was no egg tray, for instance, which wasn't any great hardship since my mother's generation believed, with good reason, that eggs should be kept at room temperature. Anyway, in our house eggs never hung around long enough to go off. They were a daily part of our staple diet. The double yoke jobs from the Egg Man would probably have been too big for any standard size rack.

Cold milk was a bonus, though. In the summer, Mum had previously kept the milk in a jug of water in the pantry to stop it curdling. Milk from the fridge now tasted as Alpine fresh as the cartons from the machine outside Horrell's Dairies. When it came to butter, however, the fridge was a mixed blessing. Yes, it prevented the butter from going rancid. But you had to remember to take out the butter well in advance of using it, otherwise it was a bugger to spread – something my father remarked upon on more than one occasion. In the winter, it had to be taken frozen from the fridge and placed on top of the boiler until it was soft enough to be used.

The real bonus, as far as Viv and I were concerned, was that we could now make our own ice lollies. The ice compartment wasn't huge, but there was room to fill a tray with orange squash, with a toothpick propped up in each individual cube. We're not talking commercially produced Mivvis or space rockets here, but lollies on tap were a great leap forward. In the fullness of time, you could buy proper lolly-making kits from Woolworth's, complete with specialist moulds and genuine lolly sticks. Thinking back, I can't help wondering if home refrigeration and lolly kits helped hasten the demise of the Jubbly.

Dad didn't exactly 'inherit' the Consul. He sold the Anglia and paid Tom the difference. But it was still a great deal, since Tom was entitled to full employees' discount. I was thrilled, as by then I'd pretty much overcome my chronic carsickness. The Consul was a step up from the Anglia, even though its design pre-dated its smaller cousin. The 375 model seated six on two bench seats and had an enormous 1.7-litre engine. Enormous for an ordinary family saloon in those days, that is. It had a three-speed gearshift mounted on the steering column, just like the American cars we saw in the movies, and a linear speedo which went up to 100mph.

On one visit to Ingatestone, not long after Tom got the car, he decided to take Dad and me for a 'spin', as he called it, to put the Consul through its paces. We headed for the Southend Arterial Road, the A127, between Gallows Corner and the Fortune of War roundabout, named for the pub and a local landmark. This was a stretch of dual carriageway popular with boy racers and bikers, all determined to do the 'ton', the elusive 100mph. The 70mph speed limit on Britain's roads wasn't introduced until 1965. So trying to break the three-figure barrier was still perfectly legal. I was sitting in the middle of the front bench, between Tom and my dad. There were no seat belts, so if Tom was compelled to execute an emergency stop or accidentally left the road and crashed into a lamp post, I'd have been thrown straight through the front windscreen. This particular section of the 127 was notorious for its body count. My old man didn't seem too bothered. I suppose if you've been on the Russian convoys, sunk in the Irish Sea, and shelled by your own side in Marseilles, the Southend Arterial Road doesn't hold too many horrors.

We set off slowly. According to specs I looked up recently, the Ford Consul 375 did 0–60mph in twenty-nine seconds. Gradually gathering pace, we moved into the outside lane and began to overtake lines of Sunday drivers, old men in string gloves and wives in their best hats, making their way sedately to the seaside at sunny Sarfend. Occasionally, a biker in leathers on a Norton or a Triumph, one of the famous 'ton-up' boys would flash past us, head and torso bent forward over the handlebars. I gripped my dad's hand and hoped for the best, with my eyes fixed on the speedometer panel. Faster and faster went the Consul, the speedo needle dancing backwards and forwards, making it impossible to tell exactly what speed we were doing. By now, the whole car was rattling and shaking and bouncing along like one of Barnes Wallis's bombs. Tom was gripping the steering wheel like grim death. As we approached the Fortune of War roundabout, he let out a triumphant shout of 'ONE HUNDRED miles per hour!' – like a darts referee's 'One-hundred-and-EIGHTY!' – and slammed on the anchors. I had no way of telling if we'd done the 'ton' or not. It certainly seemed we had. My insides felt as if they had been rearranged. Wait until I told my friends I'd done the magic ton. Even though the speedo was worse than useless over about 55mph, careering from 0 to 100mph and back again like a deranged pinball, I had no reason to doubt Tom's word that we'd broken the 100mph barrier. It was only when I was researching the Consul for this book that I discovered that the top speed of the 375 model, flat out, downhill and with a fair wind, was 79.3mph.

After Dad took possession of the Consul, the world, in the words of the great Arthur Daley, was our lobster. Or, rather, our Cornish crab. The greater luggage and passenger capacity of our new car meant we could travel further afield on holiday. It was therefore decided that we should explore the Cornish coast. Today, the easiest way would be to hit the A1 (M), take the M25 orbital to the M4 West and join the M5 south-west as far as it goes before picking up the local dual carriageways. In the early to mid-1960s, motorways to the West Country weren't an option. Work didn't start on the M4 until 1965. The only way to get from Peterborough to Cornwall was cross-country. But during the day, that simply wasn't a runner. It would take for ever, through ancient market towns still without by-passes and along single carriageway roads where the likelihood of getting stuck behind a combine harvester was a very real possibility.

We would drive all night until we reached our destination, the fishing village of Port Isaac. This is where the bench seats in the Consul came into their own. Dad filled in the gap between the front and back seats to create a double bed where Viv and me could sleep top to tail. Mum and Dad would share the driving and take it in turns to nap in the passenger seat. This way we'd avoid the daytime traffic and arrive in Port Isaac for breakfast.

Rolling into the Cornish fishing village for the first time as dawn broke was a magical experience. As we couldn't check in to our boarding house until after lunch, we parked and found a fisherman's café for breakfast. Cornwall was still unspoiled in the early sixties. The holiday resorts all had working harbours before Britain's fishermen were sold out by Grocer Heath's decision in the 1970s to surrender Britain's traditional fishing grounds in exchange for the poison chalice of membership of what was then called the European Economic Community. I imagine that the Port Isaac that I first encountered was a bit like Padstow before celebrity chef Rick Stein turned it into a congested foodie Disneyland. I've no beef with Stein, who is one of the finest TV chefs and a shrewd businessman to boot. But modern Padstow, or Padstein as it's more commonly known today, is a classic example of Oscar Wilde's dictum that each man kills the thing he loves.

Every morning, we'd take breakfast in the boarding house before setting off for our day's adventure. The landlady would pack us up with home-baked Cornish pasties – piping hot from her oven and filled with meat, potatoes and vegetables in a thick pastry crust – wrapped in cloth. They bore no relationship to the mass-produced muck you can buy in chain-store bakeries today.

Pasties were orginally created for Cornish tin miners to eat underground. One end contained meat and potatoes, sometimes swede, the other a sweet mix of apples and sugar. Its crimped edge was designed to be used as a handle and then discarded. The thick crust insulated the contents and kept them hot, something I was surprised to discover when we first cut into our pasties three or four hours after they'd come out of the oven. We'd eat ours on the beach, after a morning exploring the rock pools or climbing the cliffs. This was a great deal more agreeable than eating a pasty hundreds of feet below ground, although sand could intrude, proving a little extra, unwanted, crunch.

In the sixties there were still working tin mines in Cornwall and Devon. The last mine in Cornwall, South Crofty, soldiered on until 1998, when it finally closed. A number of plans aimed at reviving the mine have been put forward, as the world price of tin has fluctuated. It's estimated there are 7.95 million tonnes of tin still in the mine, potentially worth £1.5 billion. But none of the plans have reached fruition. In 2006 South Crofty was declared a World Heritage Site and in 2013 the company still interested in reopening South Crofty went into administration. On the walls outside South Crofty someone has daubed graffiti, said to date from 1999:

Cornish lads are fishermen and Cornish lads are miners, too. But when the fish and tin are gone, what are the Cornish boys to do?

What indeed? What jobs there are today are largely seasonal, pandering to wealthy tourists. Cornwall is an inequitable mixture of economic basket case and rich man's playground. It also rivals Edinburgh as the heroin capital of Britain. In the summer of 2013 three generations of a Bodmin family were sentenced to seventy years in prison for their part in running a trafficking ring which supplies the ever-growing demand for heroin in the Cornish peninsula.

When we first visited Cornwall it had changed little since the turn of the twentieth century. Most of the locals would have thought heroin was the main female character in a Daphne du Maurier novel.

The glorious beach at Polzeath is one of the great treasures of the English coastline. It's where I learned to surf – or, at least, to fall off a surf board and swallow half a gallon of sea water. Polzeath was a favourite haunt of Sir John Betjeman and is mentioned in some of his verse. In the first of Enid Blyton's Famous Five stories, written in 1942, the children express disappointment that they will not, as usual, be spending their holidays at Polzeath.

Julian, Dick, George, Anne and Timmy the dog would not have been disappointed had they returned to Polzeath two decades later. They wouldn't have noticed much difference. The beach was still pretty deserted and, from what I recall, the only building was a shack selling the usual seaside selection of buckets and spades, shrimping nets, rubber rings, plastic footballs, beach cricket sets, rock, tea and ice cream.

Picture-postcard Polzeath is still like that: endless, pristine sand stretching into the sea against the seductive backdrop of a setting sun, with barely a soul in sight. The reality is somewhat removed from the tourist board fantasy. Cornwall in recent years has become a favoured destination for the spoilt sons and daughters of the rich: trustafarians from Kensington; Sloane Rangers; Hooray Henries; Notting Hillbillies; the Chipping Norton set. Even the young royals have been known to put in an appearance. As far as the locals are concerned, this hasn't been entirely beneficial. According to a report in the *North Cornwall Focus and Forum*, summer 2013 edition:

> Police and traders have confiscated more than 400 fake ID cards from under age drinkers in a holiday resort in less than a month. The seizures came as hundreds of public schools students descended on Polzeath for an early summer holiday before the state school term ended. Locals have complained of rowdy beach parties, noise, drunkenness, and vandalism involving up to 500 people.
>
> Polzeath resident Tess Smith said that the problem was worse than last year. 'There were a thousand kids on the beach on one night, screaming, chanting and urinating. There was an horrendous amount of noise until three in the morning. It was total anarchy.
>
> 'They could do exactly what they wanted because there were only four policemen there.' One under-age youngster, among a group drinking and smoking cannabis on the beach, said alcohol was easy to get. 'Some serve you under age. If you have fake ID they will serve you anything.'

It must have seemed as if the Famous Five Hundred had landed, with 'lashings' of cheap beer, champagne and cannabis. The kind of place, indeed, that a well-brought-up Conservative Prime Minister, an Old Etonian to boot, with a public image to maintain might go out of his way to avoid. But in August 2013, who should stroll on to a crowded Polzeath beach? None other than the Prime Minister David Cameron, Call Me Dave himself, stripped to the waist, sunburned and wrapped in a Mickey Mouse beach towel while he changed his wet swimming trunks. The pictures were splashed across the front pages of most national newspapers.

Of course, Dave is entitled to take his holidays where he likes. And given the demographic of the modern Polzeath tourist crowd, he's among his own. In a way, the only surprise was that it wasn't any surprise. But can you imagine in 1964 walking on to the sands at Polzeath and stumbling across one of Dave's Conservative prime ministerial predecessors and fellow Old Etonian Sir Alec Douglas-Home changing out of his bathing costume beneath a Mickey Mouse beach towel?

If Douglas-Home had been there, I think my mum and dad might have noticed him.

Another prized posession we got from Tom was a barbecue set, which he'd brought back from a trip to Detroit before he was transferred permanently to the States. This was still in its box, since Tom had never got round to using it. Unlike today, when any self-respecting garden centre will sell you an elaborate open-air kitchen, complete with instant-on gas burners and built-in rotisserie, barbecues were a rarity in the 1960s, if not unheard of. The only chargrilled food we ever ate were baked potatoes cooked in the embers of the bonfire on Guy Fawkes Night.

One summer's day, my dad unpacked the barbecue and put it together. It was little more than a dustbin lid on an aluminium tripod, but to us it was impossibly exotic. We'd only ever seen anything like it on American TV shows, with grinning All American men like Darrin from *Bewitched* sipping Coke and grilling vast T-bone steaks, juicy hamburgers and hot dogs.

There was only one problem. In mid-1960s Britain you couldn't get the special charcoal briquettes for love nor money. Certainly not in Peterborough. Dad asked the coalman, but he'd never heard of them. B&Q hadn't been invented yet. After a bit of research he was reliably informed that you could definitely buy charcoal in Harrods, which boasted it would sell you anything known to man, from an elephant to a Rolls-Royce.

As luck would have it, the following week I was due to go on a school coach trip to the Natural History Museum in London's Kensington, a stone's throw from Harrods. My dad slipped me a ten bob note (50p) and said that if I had half a chance, could I peel off from the main party and investigate. When the day came around, I managed to slope off unnoticed while the rest of the class was being treated to a lecture on the mating habits of the stegosaurus, or similar. Hopping on a bus, I covered the three-quarters of a mile from the museum to Harrods in about five minutes and headed straight for the Home and Gardens section, where, just as promised, there were a few bags of imported barbecue charcoal on display. I bought one for five bob (25p) and lugged it back to the museum, where I managed to locate our coach driver and persuaded him to stash it in the luggage compartment for me until we got home. I'd have bought two if I could have carried them. I rejoined the class as it wended its way past the Tyrannosaurus Rex. One or two of the kids had noticed I was missing, but no one was any the wiser.

When we got back to Peterborough late that night, my dad was there to pick me up. The teacher who'd accompanied us on the trip was somewhat puzzled to see my old man slipping the coach driver half-a-crown as he loaded a sack of barbecue charcoal into the boot of the Consul.

At the weekend, the sun was shining and the barbecue was set up on the patio in the back garden. Dad arranged the charcoal over fire-lighters, as per the instructions, lit the metaphorical blue touchpaper and stood back. Nothing much happened. 'Wait until the coals glow grey before cooking' the instruction book commanded. My old man wasn't best known for his patience – a characteristic I have inherited – and after a few minutes decided to give the fire a helping hand by dousing the charcoal briquettes in paraffin. Even though he almost took off his eyebrows in the process, it seemed to do the trick.

Just as Mum brought out the chicken legs and sausages from the kitchen, a dark cloud descended over the garden. Within a minute of my dad slapping them on the grill, the heavens opened. The barbecue was too damned hot to be manhandled into the garage, so the food was removed and finished off in the oven. It would be years before we attempted another barbecue.

As the Netherton Estate expanded to provide homes for the increasing numbers of newcomers arriving in Peterborough, the cornfields disappeared. Within a couple of years, there were no fields left between the Grange and Horrell's Dairies. An adventure playground was lost for ever. I barely noticed. By then, I was growing up fast and the novelty of recreating the Alamo in a cornfield in the East of England had faded.

When 1965 came around my mind was already on the next leap forward. That was the year I took the 11-plus. Success or failure, we were told, would determine the path you took for the rest of your life. The 1944 Education Act had for the first time established a tripartite system of fully funded state secondary education. Schools were divided into three categories: grammar; secondary technical; and secondary modern. In Peterborough, there were just two, grammar and secondary modern, which also catered for those who elsewhere would have gone to technical school. Grammar schools were designed to cater for the 'top' 25 per cent adjudged to be the most intellectually able. This 'elite' 25 per cent was weeded out by a one-off exam at the end of your primary/junior education called the 11-plus. Eric Sutton made it abundantly clear that he expected a better than 25 per cent pass rate. West Town had consistently topped the charts of primaries in the city sending pupils on to grammars.

He always set his sights high, in the classroom as on the playing field. I've uncovered a faded cutting from the local rag, recording Eric's supremacy in the sporting area. It is a photograph and accompanying report of:

> The West Town School Team which beat Fulbridge School in the final of the primary schools knock-out cricket competition. Fulbridge were all out for 13 (Littlejohn four for five, Melanson four for six) and in reply West Town scored 15 for three.
>
> West Town now hold, or share, all the primary sporting trophies, the cricket cup, the football league cup, the football knock-out cup, which they share with Dogsthorpe, and the Whittlesey tournament trophy, which they share with St Marks.

We'd beaten Dogsthorpe the previous year, too. The *Peterborough Citizen and Advertiser* recorded that:

> *Hero of the day was Richard Littlejohn, who took nine wickets for 22 runs.*

Aged ten, I fancied myself as 'Fiery' Fred Trueman, opening bowler for England and Yorkshire. I'd practise my bowling action in front of the mirror and in the back garden with a tennis ball, with an apple tree as stumps. On the Grange we'd play cricket in summer until it got dark. I could bowl a bit, but couldn't bat to save my life. Sadly, nine for twenty-two, aged ten, was as good as it got. A lifetime best. Although I had a trial with the Northamptonshire Colts when I was about fourteen, under the watchful eye of the Northants and England batsman Colin Milburn, I was destined never to trouble the professional game. 'Watchful eye' is probably an unfortunate turn of phrase in the circumstances, since the following year 'Ollie' Milburn lost the sight of his left eye in a motoring accident, which was to cut short his flourishing career.

Perhaps the highlight of my cricketing career came in the mid-nineties, when I stepped out at the Oval to open the bowling from the pavilion end against the late David Frost in a charity game, organised by LBC and Capital Radio.

Frostie, who had played cricket at Cambridge, promptly put me to the sword and I was taken off after the first over. On another occasion, during Michael Parkinson's annual cricket match at Bray, I had Gary Lineker caught at long leg off my sixth delivery. Not as impressive as if sounds, unfortunately. Gary hit the first five balls to the boundary, three fours and two sixes. He was caught on the boundary attempting to smash me for a third six.

Mind you, I did clean bowl George Best in the very next over. It would have been a memorable achievement had Bestie not been so pissed he brought a drink to the crease, handed it to the umpire (who I think was Jimmy Tarbuck), took guard somewhere between middle stump and square leg and fell flat on his arse as soon as I released the ball.

There's also a report of the schools football cup final, in which I appear to have played a small but influential part.

West Town centre forward Richard Littlejohn was the most dangerous attacker on view, however, leading his line with drive and confidence far above his years. It was Littlejohn who snapped up a half chance to put West Town into the lead after the Dogsthorpe keeper failed to hold a centre from left winger Raymond Crawford, son of Posh player Ian Crawford.

Melanson had really started the move, switching the ball effectively away from the middle, and Littlejohn might have

made it 2-0 a couple of minutes later with a tremendous effort
that dropped just over the bar.

Don't ask me why, but I can still remember that effort
– an overhead bicycle kick which I'd seen Jimmy Greaves
execute brilliantly on *Match of the Day*. The difference is,
Greavesie actually scored, instead of landing on his backside in the mud while his shot sailed over the bar.

'The Posh' was, as I mentioned earlier, the nick-
name of the local Football League side, Peterborough
United, which had a reputation for FA Cup giant-
killings. It was a measure of Eric Sutton's success as a
coach that West Town provided half a dozen of the
Peterborough schoolboys' side, me included. The
expectation was that at least a couple of us would go
on to play at a higher level. In my case, that never
happened, mainly because of an absence of the requi-
site talent but partly for educational reasons, which I
will explain in due course.

On the morning of 30 January 1965, I scored for
Peterborough Boys in a 2-1 cup victory over Corby Boys,
a team mostly made up of kids who'd learned their
football on the cobbles in Glasgow. They'd moved to
Corby when their fathers had been recruited to work in
the steelworks. Corby was essentially a Scottish industrial
town transplanted to the middle of Northamptonshire.
The authentic accents of the West of Scotland were

entirely unaffected by the local Northants dialect, me duck.

Corby away was a hostile fixture, with the partisan allegiances and tribal aggression of Ibrox and Celtic Park having been transported wholesale to the playing fields of Middle England. Quite a few of the home side's supporters were drinking from whisky bottles, even though we kicked off at 10.30 a.m. It was as if Rab C. Nesbitt and Jamesie Cotter had turned up to cheer the lads on. From what I remember it was a bit of a kicking match and my shin-pads took a battering. We were glad to get out of there alive.

Our famous victory and my part in it wasn't the best bit of the day, which had only just begun in earnest. All the schoolboy team had been given free tickets to the main attraction of the afternoon: the fourth round FA Cup tie between Third Division Peterborough United and the mighty Arsenal of the First Division at Peterborough's London Road ground. Although the Posh had a distinguished giant-killing tradition in their non-league days, this was expected to be a walkover for the aristocrats of the Arsenal.

Our coach back from Corby arrived at London Road about half an hour before kick-off. The stadium was already packed and queues were still snaking back hundreds of yards, fans decked out in the red and white of Arsenal and the blue and white of the Posh. They all wore scarves, bobble hats and rosettes, not the ghastly replica shirts which infest the game today. My nanna had made me a blue and white Posh rosette with a tinfoil FA Cup in the middle. She'd also bought me a wooden rattle. Anyone attempting to get into a football ground with a rattle today would be arrested for carrying an offensive weapon. But this was before the era of widespread football hooliganism. On my other lapel I wore a Spurs pin, which I'd sent away for a couple of years earlier. Arsenal are, of course, Spurs' deadly rivals. This was the next best thing to a north London derby as far as I was concerned.

I'd only ever been to London Road once before, when my Uncle Ron and cousin Russell came to visit in 1962 and took me to a Third Division game between Posh and Reading. Peterborough United versus Arsenal was a whole different dimension. The official attendance was recorded as 30,056, although there must have been several thousand more squeezed inside the ground. Looking back, it was a Hillsborough waiting to happen. There was no way we were going to make it through the turnstiles in time, so a blazered club official escorted us through the main direc- tors' entrance, along the players' tunnel and we took our places crouched down on the cinder track in front of the standing enclosure in the lower tier of the main stand, just to the right of the home dugout. The roar was deaf- ening as we emerged from the tunnel. Now I had some idea what the pros went through. The ground was a cauldron. I've been to some big games in my lifetime, FA Cup finals, European finals, but I've never experienced anything like it.

The Arsenal side was packed with full internationals, big-namestars like Frank McLintock, Don Howe, John Radford, Joe Baker, George Armstrong and George Eastham.

Every player in the Arsenal line-up that afternoon came from the British Isles. Almost exactly forty years later to the day, Valentine's Day 2005, Arsenal, once the most English of clubs, named sixteen players of assorted nationalities for the match against Crystal Palace – a starting line up of eleven and five substitutes – none of whom was English, Scottish, Welsh or Irish. I know we live in a global economy, but what a sad indictment of the English game. By the time of England's World Cup qualifiers in 2013, the manager Roy Hodgson had a severely diminished pool from which to choose. Only 37 per cent of all players in the English Premier League were qualified to play for England.

Although a Third Division side, which had only been elected to the Football League in 1960, the Posh could boast a few internationals of their own, including Vic Crowe who played sixteen times for Wales, and Ollie Conmy, capped five times for the Republic of Ireland.

They also had a not-so-secret weapon in the Northern Ireland international Derek Dougan, who had come to my attention when he played for Blackburn Rovers in the very first FA Cup Final I ever watched on TV. Dougan was a volatile character, with a great sense of his own worth, who had a habit of falling out with his managers. He would go on to become an accomplished television presenter, who could rival Brian Clough when it came to expressing incendiary opinions. Dougan had actually demanded a transfer from Blackburn on the morning of the 1960 final. He signed for Peterborough in 1963 after a spectacular bust-up with Aston Villa, even though it meant dropping down a couple of divisions. He was the only player in the Posh team who could have walked into the Arsenal side. That afternoon the stage was set for Dougan.

Arsenal took the lead, but it didn't suck the wind out of the sails of the fanatical home crowd. The equaliser came, inevitably, from 'The Doog', who scored with what seemed like consummate ease after waltzing imperiously past Arsenal's Scottish international centre-half Ian Ure. Before I knew it, I was in the vanguard of a pitch invasion as thousands of fans spilled on to the pitch to embrace their hero. Because I was already sitting on the touchline, I had a head start. Even the local cops on crowd control duty were going berserk.

In the second half, the Scottish winger Peter McNamee,

a long-time servant of the club who had played for the Posh in the club's non-league days, slotted a winner into an empty net after Ron Barnes had left Don Howe for dead and crossed from the right. It was McNamee's finest hour but the headlines belonged to Dougan, who was a class apart. In ninety appearances for the Posh, Dougan scored forty-six goals, better than one every two games. He would leave the following year for First Division Leicester City. The fee? £35,000, a club record for Peterborough United. Today the bidding would start at £20 million. I was sad to see him go, but that afternoon against Arsenal Derek Dougan sealed his place alongside Jimmy Greaves as one of my all-time footballing heroes.

Believe it or not, neither the Littlejohn goal against Corby, nor the Dougan goal against Arsenal was the biggest event of the day, as far as the rest of the world was concerned. I'd completely forgotten, but 30 January 1965 was also the day of Sir Winston Churchill's funeral. We're all familiar with the cortège making its stately way on a barge along the Thames, the cranes at London Docks dipping their heads respectfully. The impression is that the nation came to a complete standstill. That's not how I remember it. I'm not even sure there was a minute's silence before kick-off at London Road.

I was only reminded of this when I was writing a football column for the *Daily Mail* in the immediate aftermath of the death of Lady Di in 1997. All sporting fixtures in England were cancelled on the Saturday of her funeral as a mark of 'respect'. There was all hell to pay when the Scottish FA decided to go ahead with a World Cup qualifier against Belarus a few hours after the funeral was due to end. The SFA's chief executive Jim Farry was vilified for saying: 'I have been to family funerals and what I can say is the natural rhythm of life should be resumed as quickly as possible after that.'

Farry escaped lightly, as a wave of hysteria, fuelled by an inexplicable epidemic of vicarious grief, engulfed the nation. In Hendon, north-west London, a man innocently washing his car on the morning of the funeral was subjected to a vicious kicking by an angry mob of 'mourners' for failing to show the proper 'respect'. The streets were awash with floral tributes and teddy bears. It was utterly bewildering and deeply disturbing. A nation once known for its stiff upper lip, which had withstood the Blitz with fortitude, had succumbed to a disgusting bout of emotional incontinence.

On 30 January 1965, thousands of Arsenal fans had attended the Churchill funeral procession in the City of London in the morning before making their way to the mainline stations to catch football specials to Peterborough. Life went on, as I imagine Churchill would have expected.

After the abuse to which Jim Farry was subjected, I decided to check out exactly how sport had responded on the day of Churchill's funeral. In the afternoon there was a full football programme. As well as the Posh versus Arsenal, there were other ties played in the fourth round of the FA Cup. At White Hart Lane 43,992 saw Tottenham thrash Ipswich 5-0. Jimmy Greaves scored a hat-trick. Alan Gilzean got the other two. Elsewhere, 50,051 watched Leeds and Everton draw 1-1 at Elland Road, and another 51,857 were at Anfield, where Liverpool, the eventual cup winners that season, were being held at home by a similar scoreline by Stockport County.

It wasn't just football: rugby matches and race meetings all went ahead as scheduled. None of those who attended racetracks and rugby grounds were accused of lacking respect. There was no vilification of those who ran the sports and organised the games.

The idea that Lady Di, a dopey Sloane Ranger famous for marrying the heir to the throne, should warrant more 'respect' than Britain's greatest ever Prime Minister, who led the nation to survival during our darkest hour would be as abhorrent as it would be incomprehensible to the generation who stood in the stands at London Road that Saturday afternoon in January 1965. Many of those present will have fought in the war, will have known genuine loss. Most of those holding candlelit vigils for Lady Di and depositing flowers and teddy bears by the container-load in every available open space couldn't even begin to comprehend the sorrow and pain endured by their forebears. Many of them were too young even to have lost a close relative. Perhaps that might explain their exaggerated sense of despair over Diana.

We have to accept that Britain is a different country, more trembling lower lip than stiff upper lip. But we don't have to approve. It's not enough to grieve; what matters is being seen to grieve, to show the world you *care*. Professional football is the worst offender, like a sociopathic gangster who has to wallow in sentimentality to demonstrate his sensitive side. Supporters are forced to stand for a minute's silence before just about every match. At Spurs, we even had to observe a minute's silence for Glenn Hoddle's dad.

This cult of vicarious grief reached its nadir in March 2012, when football went into a prolonged period of mourning for someone who was still *alive*. I was at White Hart Lane for the game against Bolton Wanderers, when the Bolton player Fabrice Muamba fell to the ground, as if he'd been poleaxed. Pretty soon it became obvious that there was something seriously wrong. We are used to cynical footballers feigning injury by rolling around theatrically, clutching their heads. But the figure on the ground wasn't moving.

As the medical teams rushed on to the pitch, the anguished reaction of the other players told us that the man down wasn't faking it. The deployment of a defibrillator confirmed that this was a life-threatening incident.

Around the stadium, 35,000 supporters fell into an eerie silence, still unsure of what had occured. Most of us weren't even certain who was receiving treatment. It was only when the Bolton fans started to chant 'Fabrice Muamba' that we were able to put a name to him. To cut a long story short, Muamba had suffered a massive cardiac arrest. Thanks to the intervention of a heart specialist who was in the crowd, he was revived and taken to intensive care.

But while Muamba was in hospital, the world of football went into Lady Di overdrive. That Sunday, Manchester United and Wolves staged a pre-match display of synchronised applause for Muamba. In Spain, Real Madrid wore 'get well soon' messages on their shirts, even though I doubt many of the players have ever heard of Muamba. The English disease had gone global.

At Stamford Bridge, the Chelsea defender Gary Cahill, a former Bolton team-mate, 'dedicated' his goal to Muamba and unveiled a tee-shirt bearing the slogan 'Pray 4 Muamba' for the benefit of the TV cameras. He couldn't even be bothered to spell out the word 'for'.

One of the most absurd manifestations of this lachrymose carnival was at Shepway District Council, which covers Folkestone, Hythe and Romney Marsh, in Kent. Before the start of the meeting, the vicar led prayers for Muamba, even though the footballer had absolutely no connection with the area.

There is a fine line between a tasteful show of solidarity and exhibitionism. And in this case, as in so many other instances, football yet again trampled across it.

Of course, football doesn't exist in a vacuum. It reflects the values of our modern society, particularly when it comes to wallowing in the kind of self-indulgent weeping and wailing which first manifested itself over the death of Lady Di and reached its gruesome nadir with the demise of Michael Jackson.

For instance, the death of Wales manager Gary Speed, who hanged himself, was a tragedy for his family and friends. But the aftermath was a carefully choreo graphed travelling circus of remembrance, which made its way around the country and went on for weeks. If it's Wednesday, this must be Manchester City. Quiet, please.

Miraculously, Fabrice Muamba made a full recovery. But not before he'd received a minute's applause at every football stadium in Britain and fans of Bolton Wanderers had created a full-blown shrine to him outside their Reebok Stadium – the first recorded example of a shrine to someone who isn't actually dead.

We live in an increasingly godless society, virtually unrecognisable to my parents' generation, where Christians are marginalised, sacked and even prosecuted for upholding their beliefs, yet we are urged to 'Pray 4 Muamba'.

With a dwindling number of people attending

church, millions have taken to worshipping footballers and celebrities instead.

In the words of G. K. Chesterton: 'When people stop believing in God, they don't believe in nothing – they believe in anything.'

Meanwhile, back in 1965, we were being prepared for the 11-plus. This wasn't so much a test of knowledge as an exercise designed to assess intelligence, comprehension, verbal and numerical dexterity. You couldn't cheat. On the appointed day of the examination we were seated in regulation rows of chairs and desks in the main assembly hall. Eric Sutton presided magisterially from his vantage point on the stage. Teachers patrolled the aisles to prevent conferring. Absolute silence was demanded. Papers were distributed with the reverence of hymn sheets being handed out at a memorial service. The acrid aroma of fear and flatulence permeated the air.

At 9 a.m. sharp, Mr Sutton blew a whistle, pressed his stopwatch and battle commenced. The exam came in three parts and I think we had an hour to complete each one. One element was an IQ test, which could have been written by Edward Lear. It involved solving the kind of riddles my dad was fond of posing, such as: 'If it takes a man a week to walk a fortnight, how long will it take him to skin an elephant down to a whippet?'

The time seemed to pass in a blur. When the final

whistle went, the papers were snatched from our desks, put in sealed envelopes and sent off to be marked.

Honestly, I had no idea how I'd performed, although I knew I'd done pretty well in the 'mocks' we'd been given in the run-up to the exam proper. Despite the pressure, and even though maths was never my strong point, I was fairly confident I'd pass. I'd always been good at busking it. If the exam had been based on coursework, I'd have gone straight to secondary modern, without passing Go.

When the results were announced, I hadn't only passed, I'd achieved the second highest marks in the whole city. Heaven knows how that happened. My parents were thrilled, but I was horrified. The top two 11-plus passes each year were entitled automatically to a scholarship at one of two minor public schools: Oundle and Bishops Stortford. The last place on earth I wanted to be sent was to public school. And a boarding school, to boot. I'd assumed that in the event of my passing the 11-plus, I'd go to my first choice grammar school, Deacon's, along with most of my mates.

Everything I knew about public school came from *Tom Brown's Schooldays* and the 1948 movie *The Guinea Pig*, starring Richard Attenborough. This was one of those black and white films that turned up regularly on TV, on those wet Sundays when *The Dambusters* or *The Cruel Sea* wasn't being shown for the umpteenth time. Attenborough plays a tobacconist's son from Walthamstow who, as part of a social experiment, is given a scholarship to public school where he is subjected to a life of sadistic bullying, fagging and abject misery. Gradually, in order to survive, he is forced to adapt to this new world of privilege, but when he goes home for the holidays he discovers he no longer has anything in common with his old friends. I wasn't exactly a tobacconist's son from Walthamstow; I was a railwayman's son from Peterborough, and I'd won my place on merit rather than been handed it as part of some ghastly 'enlightened' experiment. But Walthamstow was close enough to Ilford, which I still considered my spiritual home, and I could identify with the Attenborough character. I had absolutely no intention of suffering the same fate, or being thrashed by some public schoolboy like Flashman in *Tom Brown's Schooldays*.

There ensued an awkward stand-off. I was well aware that my parents were hugely proud of their son's achievement. They'd both left school at fifteen. No one in our family had ever dreamed of going to public school, let alone – at risk of sounding like Neil Kinnock – gone to university, which was the glittering prize that awaited me if I caved in and accepted a place at Oundle.

I didn't want to let them down, but I was buggered if I was going to go to boarding school. Actually, I probably would have been buggered if I'd gone to boarding school, from arsehole to breakfast time on a regular basis. While I could understand that they thought this was a great opportuntity, all I could see were the petrified faces of Richard Attenborough in *The Guinea Pig*, and John Howard Davies in the 1951 version of *Tom Brown*. I tried moral blackmail: if they loved me so much, why the hell did they want to send me away?

Mum and Dad cajoled, bribed, enlisted the help of Eric Sutton, who was equally proud that one of his snot-nosed charges had made it to public school. I was persuaded to look round Oundle and Bishops Stortford schools. Once I'd absorbed the tradition, the facilities, the extensive manicured playing fields, I was bound to change my mind, they reasoned. My mum and dad drove me to Oundle, about twelve miles south-west of Peterborough, while Viv stayed at home with my nanna and Auntie Em. We were given a guided tour of the place by a house master and a prefect, who seemed to me to be about thirty-five. If they thought this was going to convince me, they couldn't have been more misguided. Oundle was worse than I'd imagined. Established in 1465, it was a dead ringer for Tom Brown's Rugby. I saw Flashman lurking round every corner. The following weekend I was driven to Bishops Stortford, my chronic carsickness returning before we'd even reached the A1. I took one look at the place and refused point-blank to go in.

In a final, desperate roll of the dice, I was taken to meet the boy who had won the scholarship to Oundle the previous year. They obviously figured that once I'd heard what fantastic fun he was having as a boarder, learned about all the wonderful new friends he'd made, my resistance would melt. Things didn't quite work out like that.

We were shown into the parlour of a large house in one of the more exclusive roads in town, where the boy and his parents were waiting for us with tea and petits four. His name was David Beaney; he was wearing his school uniform and a pair of NHS circular spectacles. I vaguely remembered Beaney as a notorious swot from the year above me. He looked like Harry Potter, or a schoolboy version of the *Guardian*'s editor, Alan Rusbridger. Pleasantries were exchanged, and Mr and Mrs Beaney extolled the virtues of Oundle. I remained unmoved. Did we know, for instance, that the school was famous for its music facilities, its one-on-one tuition?

If this was supposed to impress me, it was a mistake. My musical horizons extended to playing the first few bars of 'Telstar', by the Tornadoes, on the recorder and shaking the maracas to 'Not Fade Away'. In the middle of the room there was a highly polished grand piano. Why didn't David play us something, to show us how far he'd come under the excellent tutelage at Oundle? David stepped up to the joanna, lifted the lid over the keyboard and carefully placed his sheet music in his eyeline. Somehow, I didn't think he was going to play 'Roll Over Beethoven'.

A pregnant hush settled on the room, as David announced he was going to perform Mendelssohn's

Hebrides Overture, also known as Fingal's Cave. If you're not familiar with the piece, here's Classic FM's idiot's guide:

> How do you conjure up the sounds and sights of Scotland in a single piece of music? That was the challenge facing Mendelssohn when, in 1829, he travelled home from a memorable trip to the Scottish island of Staffa and its famous Fingal's Cave.
>
> The journey had evidently made an immediate impression on the German composer: just hours later, he had written the first few bars of this piece and sent them off to his sister, Fanny, along with a note that described 'How extraordinarily the Hebrides affected me'.
>
> His travels to Scotland were part of a wider tour of Europe for Mendelssohn during his early twenties, and it's not hard to see why he was particularly captivated by what he encountered on Staffa. Fingal's Cave is over sixty metres deep and in stormy tides the cacophonous sounds of the waves inside it rumble out for miles. The intense and rolling melodies within the music perfectly capture this sense of both drama and awe; calmer passages, meanwhile, convey stiller waters and more tranquil surroundings. But it's never long before the return of that stormy scene . . .

You get the general idea. The Fingal's Cave overture lasts anywhere between ten and twelve minutes, depending on how long you allow for the silences. David Beaney treated us to the full half-hour. I think somewhere between the 'cacophonous sounds of the waves' and the 'stiller waters' the scales fell from my old man's eyes.

We drove home in silence. When we got into the house, my dad poured himself a large gin and tonic and said to my mum: 'Right, that settles it. I'm not having my son turn out like that little ponce.' The next day, we went out and bought my Deacon's grammar school uniform.

Trollope's was the official schools' outfitter in Peterborough. It had opened on the corner of Westgate and Queen Street in 1911 and had altered little since the First World War. Trollope's was a typical Edwardian store, decorated in the same style, and with similar grandeur, as David Greig's grocery shop a few hundred yards away. Black, marbled front, large display windows, elaborate gilt lettering above the door. It was a riot of polished wood and brass – if such a sedate establishment can ever be described as a 'riot' – with all the goods stored in gleaming glass display cases. Trollope's was a sort of scaled-down Grace Brothers, from the BBC sitcom *Are You Being Served?*. In 1965, old Mr Trollope still worked the counters, even though he was pushing ninety, Peterborough's answer to Young Mr Grace.

I was fascinated by the Heath Robinson system of vacuum-propelled tubes which were used to send orders to the stockroom and payment to the accounts department. The assistant would seal your order or your money in a cylindrical container, load it into one of the tubes and 'whoosh!' it vanished in a rush of air, like a torpedo from a submarine. A few minutes later an Arthur English look-alike in a brown warehouse coat would appear from the bowels of the building bearing whatever it was you had ordered. If you required change it would be sent back to the counter, along with your receipt, in another cylinder.

Quite a few shops still used this system in the 1960s, but it died out with the introduction of mechanised and electronic cash registers. I didn't see its like again until I started work on London's *Evening Standard* in 1979. The *Standard*'s old Shoe Lane building, off Farringdon Road in the City of London, was the last in London to use DC current. It was also the last newspaper in Fleet Street to utilise a vacuum tube system for sending reporters' copy from the newsroom to the print works below. It was like filing a page lead from the knitwear section at Trollope's. Nothing much had changed at the *Standard* since the First World War, either. Incredible to think that only seven short years later Rupert Murdoch would move his titles to Wapping and usher in the age of the electronic newsroom.

Trollope's began as a haberdashery before expanding into ladies' and gentlemen's clothing. My mum used to buy fabric from there to make dresses for my sister. The cloth was stored on huge rolls, taken off the shelves with great ceremony and presented for the customer's approval by assistants in white gloves. Once madam had made her selection, it was measured with a yardstick – which was chained to the counter, like a giant bookie's biro, as if anyone was going to nick it – and cut to length with enormous scissors that looked as if they had been designed to castrate cattle. They also sold frock patterns with tissue-paper templates, which mum would lay out on the kitchen table, carefully cutting around the perimeter with a pair of sawtooth pinking shears.

At some stage, Trollope's had cornered the market in official school uniforms. This must have been a lucrative monopoly. The grammar schools, in particular, were extremely fussy about regulation clothes and footwear. School uniforms were expensive, too. According to a survey published by John Lewis in time for the start of the autumn term in 2013, adjusted for inflation the average school uniform cost £116.50 a year. And with the speed at which kids of that age grow in their pre- and post-pubescent years, that meant *every* year. Non-branded gear was frowned upon, so there was little point in buying a cut-price C&A alternative. Some schools subsidised uniforms for children of families on lower incomes.

The Deacon's uniform consisted of navy-blue blazer, cap, striped school tie, grey or white shirts, grey or navy jumper, charcoal-grey trousers and black shoes. Blazer and cap badges cost extra and had to be sewn on by hand.

Trollope's also sold Cash's name tapes. If your family could afford it, you could have your name embroidered on to the name tapes, otherwise they would be handwritten and sewn into the inside collar of your blazer and shirts. After I'd been at Deacon's for a while, we'd test the regulations to the limit – wearing tab-collar or button-down collar shirts, introducing wing-tip brogues and elasticated slip-ons in place of the regulation Clarks. As I became more fashion-conscious, my school uniform came to represent a struggle with the authoritarian forces of repression and presented a daily challenge to stretch the rules to breaking point.

That would come later. Once I'd been fitted out for my formal uniform, it was on to the sports' shop down the road from the Co-op to buy my rugby, cricket and gym kit. The official stockist's was run by a bloke called Busky Wright, who was rumoured to be the brother of the former Wolverhampton Wanderers wing-half Billy Wright, one of the most famous footballers of his generation. Born the same year as my dad, Billy Wright captained England and was the first player to win one hundred international caps. He was also married to Joy Beverley, one of the popular Beverley Sisters singing trio. Billy Wright and Joy Beverley were the Posh and Becks of their day, without Beckham's tattoos, Posh's permanent pout and the £100 million fortune. Joy and her sisters, twins Teddie and Babs, had hits in the fifties with, appropriately, 'Sisters', 'I Saw Mummy Kissing Santa Claus' and 'Little Drummer Boy'.

At Christmas Mum and Olive's party piece was to get on their hind legs after a few sweet sherries and sing 'Sisters'. Written by Irving Berlin in 1954, the year I was born, it begins:

Sisters, sisters, There were never such devoted sisters . . .

There were other verses, but that's about as far as Mum and Olive ever got, before collapsing in a fit of giggles.

Billy Wright went on to become head of sport at ATV, the Midlands independent television franchise. Busky Wright had a tin leg, which was the main reason many people believed he had been unable to emulate his more famous brother's achievements and had instead decided to open a sports shop in Park Road, Peterborough. That was the story, anyway. Unfortunately, though he did nothing to discourage the rumours, Busky Wright was absolutely no relation of Billy Wright.

My grammar school career began in the first week of September 1965. I'd chosen Deacon's for a number of reasons. Firstly, I preferred the navy-blue and white sports kit, Spurs' colours, to the maroon of the rival King's

School. Although Arsenal played in red shirts with white sleeves, their original strip was maroon – technically 'redcurrant' – a colour to which they reverted for a year before they moved out of Highbury to the new Emirates Stadium down the road. King's was also the establishment school. It was founded by Henry VIII in 1541 to educate cathedral choristers, a function it still performs today. King's also had a reputation, however deserved or otherwise, as a hotbed of homosexuality. My friend Geoff Allen, who went to King's, assures me it wasn't just *Catholic* priests who had an insatiable appetite for young boys.

Deacon's was a relative newcomer, opened as recently as 1721 by a wealthy wool merchant, Thomas Deacon, as a charity school for twenty poor boys. Having always seen myself as an outsider, Deacon's fitted the bill. It also had the added advantage that it only operated a five-day week. King's had lessons on a Saturday morning.

One of my principal objections to Oundle was that it didn't play football – association football, that is – to which public school types refer condescendingly as 'footie', just like the dopey birds who fastened on to football in the Beckham years. Deacon's didn't play football, either, only rugby. But your free weekend allowed you to play all the football you wanted. I'd recently joined West Town Boys Club, turning out for the under-13s, who played on the Grange on Saturday mornings.

Originally in the city centre, Deacon's had moved to

the outskirts in 1960. By the time I shipped up, Deacon's consisted of a brand new sixties main block and a series of Nissen-style prefab huts arranged around a parade ground – laughably referred to as 'The Quad' – a bit like Stalag 13. It was a cross between a prisoner-of-war camp and a minor public school, towards which it had pretensions. The swanky new building housed the headmaster's study, staff room, the administrative offices, the main assembly hall and gymnasium, and the prefects' quarters. We lowly first-formers were billeted in Stalag 13. It would be five years before my name came up on the escape committee.

Upon arrival, we were divided up into two 'forms' – we had classes at West Town, not 'forms' – selected in alphabetical order. L for Littlejohn failed to make the first cut and I went into 1B. They didn't start streaming by results and ability until the third year. We were also allocated a 'house'. There were four: Normans, Saxons, Britons and Danes. I was to be a Saxon.

In twenty-first-century Britain, the idea of houses called Normans, Saxons, Britons and Danes would be vilified as 'hideously white' and offensive to ethnic minorities. In order to be properly inclusive and represent our new demographic, they'd have to be called 'Hezbollah, Hamas, Taliban and Al-Qaeda'.

*

Each 'house' had a number of masters assigned to it and an officer class of prefects. One of our housemasters, let's call him Mr Clelland, had been head boy at Deacon's a few years earlier, before going off to university and teacher training college, then returning as a master, aged about twenty-five. Truth was, he'd never really left Deacon's. Pupil, head of Saxons, head prefect and now housemaster. His life in education had gone full circle: a vicious circle. And I mean vicious. He didn't seem much older than the prefects, and he didn't act it, either.

Clelland taught geography, but his natural habitat was in the gym and on the sports field. He'd been captain of everything during his time as a pupil. And didn't we know it. He'd flatten small boys he was supposed to be teaching rugby. He'd always want to open the batting and the bowling at cricket practice.

One winter's afternoon – it was in the first year so we could only have been eleven or twelve – we were playing rugby and Clelland was refereeing. I was second row, behind the prop forward Richard Klazowiecz (I think that's how you spelt his name, apologies if I've got it wrong), son of a Polish brickworker who lived in a close at the end of Ledbury Road. As the ball was put into the scrum, I heard a sickening crack and Richard – we'll call him Richard for the sake of simplicity – let out a blood-curdling scream and fell to the ground, collapsing the scrum.

Clelland went berserk, blowing his whistle until he

was blue in the face, yelling at Richard to get up, telling him he was a disgrace. Richard was clearly in agony, but Clelland dragged him to his feet by the neck. I protested, telling Clelland that I'd heard a crack and perhaps Richard should see the nurse. Clelland turned on me: another word and I'd spend the afternoon running round the outside of the playing fields before reporting to him for a caning. He'd already caned me once, for some imagined infringement in geography class, and I wasn't going to give him the satisfaction of a repeat performance.

Despite Richard's obvious distress, Clelland forced him to play on, until he passed out from the excruciating pain and had to be carried to the medical room. Richard was taken to hospital, where he was X-rayed and diagnosed with a broken collarbone. I hated Clelland from that day on. Richard was off school for weeks. I can remember visiting him at his home. He sat there, encased in plaster from the chest up, like a First World War Tommy who had copped a 'Blighty' and been sent home from the trenches. These days, Mr and Mrs Klazowiecz would have been within their rights to sue the pants off the school. Clelland would be subject to a full inquiry and would probably be brought up on child cruelty charges.

I'm not usually in favour of knee-jerk litigation against teachers, who are usually as much sinned against as sinning, but in this case it might have stopped Clelland in his tracks. Nothing else was going to.

Clelland had obviously modelled himself on Flashman. After he'd taken us for gym, we'd hose down in a communal shower. Clelland would amuse himself by turning the water thermostat to freezing and then, as we were running out, he'd flick our shrivelled genitals and raw backsides with a wet towel. The man was a grade-one sadist. In class, he specialised in grabbing boys by the short hairs next to their ears and yanking them from their chairs.

There was no point complaining. No boy who lodged a complaint against a teacher would ever be taken seriously and would probably have been caned to make sure he didn't do it again. I consoled myself that if this is what it was like at grammar school, how much worse would it have been at a public school like Oundle? At Deacon's, at least you got to go home of an evening and at weekends.

I've never kept in touch with anyone from Deacon's, apart from my old friend and neighbour 'Skip' Skipper, with whom I shared an assortment of adventures. And I haven't heard from him for about ten years. So I thought I'd check out the internet to see if anyone else agrees with my memories of the bold Clelland. Then again, I may have misjudged him. The first ex-pupil I came across on the Deacon's reunion website was someone called Tim Cullis. He, too, remembered Clelland.

He had a very nasty habit of pulling boys up and down by the hair just at the top of the ear. A nasty piece of work if ever

there was one. These days, organisations like Child Line would
take a great interest in specimens like him.

That's just the way it was. There was no point in complaining to your parents, either, since they would have sided with the teachers. I don't blame them; it's how they were brought up to respect authority without question or dissent. I was to have another major run-in with Clelland later, which almost cost me my place at Deacon's. But that can wait, for now.

My reward for passing the 11-plus was a brand new Raleigh racing bike, with ten-speed Derailleur drop gears, attached by cable to a lever on the handlebars. It was my pride and joy. A few weeks later I parked it outside the lido, chained to the railings with a special combination lock. When I came back, it had been stolen, the chain severed in half by bolt cutters. I never saw the bike again.

I wasn't the only 'new boy' in our house. When he turned forty, my dad decided it was time for a career change. His kid brother was carving out a new life in Australia and his brother-in-law had been transferred to America, the land of opportunity. Dad was in a rut, something of which he was reminded daily as he went to his offices next to Peterborough's slipper baths. In the days when few people had an indoor bathroom, communal public slipper baths were quite common. In the 1960s, Peterborough's slipper baths were still fully operational, twenty-four individual cubicles charging 6d. a bath, a penny for soap and another 6d. for the use of a towel. They were sandwiched between British Railways' purchasing and supplies division and the city museum. Here was my old man in the middle of Harold Wilson's 'white heat of technology' generation and he was stuck in the age of steam, working next door to a grimy Victorian building offering baths for a tanner. It must have felt like East Ham in the 1920s. With the railways reeling from the Beeching closures, and trains rapidly being relegated to transport for those who couldn't afford a car, Bill must have concluded he might as well be working in the museum. Professionally, he was living in a time warp.

He'd worked for British Railways for seventeen years and had recently been offered a promotion, but this would have involved uprooting still further north to York or Doncaster. If he'd been promoted back to King's Cross or Liverpool Street, he'd probably have bitten their hands off, since Mum still hankered for the Smoke – or at least Essex – and behaved as if she was running a family in exile. I'm not sure she was ever fully reconciled to Peterborough, though she made her brilliant best of it.

Dad would have gone back south in a heartbeat, but Viv and I were both settled in school and he figured we didn't need the upheaval. If he'd asked me, I'd have walked out of Deacon's at the drop of a school cap. I wouldn't have described myself as 'settled'. But Dad decided he should seek a solution closer to home. He applied for, and got, a new job working in purchasing at Perkins Engines, the local diesel engine factory. Perkins wasn't particularly glamorous but it paid well. It may not have seemed like a great leap forward at the time, but it would come to transform his life.

When Dad went to Perkins we finally got our own telephone. I still remember the number: Peterborough 67918. Up until then it was public call boxes only; put your pennies in the slot, dial the number, press button A to connect, press button B for your money back in the event of no one answering, or the even more unlikely event of the number being engaged. We rarely used the phone, other than to call my grandparents in Ilford, before they moved to Australia. They had an old Bakelite model in the hallway and shared their connection, their 'party line', with another subscriber down the road. Before you made a call you had to press a button to make sure the other party wasn't talking on the line. In the days before STD (subscriber trunk dialling, not sexually transmitted diseases) and automated exchanges crossed lines were common.

After we'd had the phone installed, it meant that Mum and Nanna could keep in touch with Olive in her new home 3700 miles away in Detroit. But these calls were kept to a minimum, mostly birthdays and Christmas, since overseas calls had to be booked with the GPO weeks in advance and cost, from what I recall, the exorbitant sum of £1 a minute. This meant that transatlantic chat was kept to a minimum.

'Say hello to your auntie. Come on, hurry up.'

'Hello, Auntie Olive . . .'

'That's enough, give me the phone back. We're not made of money.'

Funny how you remember things. 'We're not made of money' was a fairly common expression. I was never conscious of ever going without, although I was aware that some of the other kids always seemed to have the latest toys and gadgets as soon as they came on to the market. Viv and I had to wait until Christmas or birthdays – which, to be honest, was no real hardship. I came to realise that my parents had different priorities from some of their neighbours. They believed absolutely in putting their money into property and spending it on what 'mattered'. Both had been brought up to invest in bricks and mortar, a lesson they passed on to me. Sometimes this meant going without life's little luxuries. There were no credit cards back then, and even if there had been I can't imagine my dad running up a hefty debt, which might take for ever to pay back. There was no credit-fuelled culture of instant gratification, although

HP (hire purchase) was an increasingly popular way of paying for cars, furniture and domestic appliances. The only borrowing my parents really found morally acceptable was the mortgage.

(And that wasn't really debt, it was an 'investment' – the glib phrase Gordon Brown cynically appropriated and distorted to excuse his own drunken sailor spending spree at the Treasury which brought Britain to the brink of bankruptcy in the early twenty-first century. Difference was, Gordon believed in spending *other people's* money and letting *other people* live with the consequences of his politically motivated profligacy.)

Live within your means: that was my parents' motto. Mum adhered to the 'make-do-and-mend' mentality she'd learned out of necessity during the war. She threw nothing away. She improvised to stay within her household budget.

Here's a little vignette which has stayed with me all my life. One summer evening, I'd been playing on the Grange with my friends from the neighbourhood. The other boys announced they were going for chips. I'd spent all my pocket money, as usual, and asked my mum to let me have a tanner to go with them. She explained that she simply didn't have a tanner to give me. I was disappointed, but had to accept it. I went back outside, made some excuse and told my mates I'd see them later. I can remember sitting on the garden wall watching them jealously as they headed off to the chippie.

Ten minutes later, my mum emerged carrying a bag of chips. She'd fried them up herself from some leftover potatoes and even wrapped them in newspaper, just like those you got from the fish and chip shop, so that I wouldn't feel as if I was missing out. They were the best chips I've ever tasted in my life.

That summer, when my dad was away on business, I decided to test out his golf clubs, which he kept in the garage. Mum told me not to hit balls in the garden, but to take the clubs on to the Grange. The quickest way to the Grange, I reckoned, was to drive the ball over the fence. Teeing up on the lawn in front of the crazy paving patio, I swung the club and struck the ball sweetly. Gary Player couldn't have hit it any harder. The ball ricocheted off an apple tree, which Dad had planted a couple of summers previously, and rebounded, causing me to duck evasively. This was followed by the sound of breaking glass as the ball smashed through the closed French doors. Let's just say that my mother wasn't best pleased. I was dispatched to find Peter the Plumber, a workman who did odd jobs for people on the Netherton. With putty and glass, he made the repair, which my mum insisted would come out of my pocket money. As a further punishment I would be 'grounded' for a week, banned from playing out with my friends. To amuse myself, I borrowed Mum's old Imperial typewriter, set up a chair and tressel table in the garden and decided to produce my own newspaper, a digest of local gossip and imaginary sports reports. And that's how I got into journalism.

Around the same time I started at Deacon's, Dad began his new career at Perkins. To celebrate this new departure, he decided to treat himself to a new suit. I went with him to Shelton's, the local family-owned department store, which carried a range of gentleman's clothing a cut above common-or-garden chain stores such as John Collier 'The Window to Watch' (originally 'The Fifty Shilling Tailor') and (Montague) Burton's. There have been a number of theories as to where the expression 'The Full Monty' came from. I am persuaded by the explanation that it referred to the fact that there was a time when you could get suited and booted at Montague Burton's for fifty bob (£2.50 today) – shirt, tie, jacket, trousers and waistcoat. The Full Monty.

Shelton's prices were a little more steep, but on a Perkins salary my old man was newly minted, as never before. Shelton's aimed to give you a West End service, even if it cost a few bob extra. This wasn't Never Mind The Quality, Feel The Width. It was Never Mind The Width, Feel The Quality. Dad chose a suit by Saxon Hawk, an upscale brand often associated with Savile Row, but actually made in Leeds, in the sixties still the centre of the rag trade. He looked a million dollars, as they said in all the best Hollywood movies. Dad went on to buy a few more Saxon Hawk suits over the years, navy-blue pinstripe, charcoal-grey with a chalk stripe. He even bought a blazer with brass buttons and a pair of 'slacks' by Daks, made from a mysterious material called cavalry twill, which to my untrained eye appeared to have been made from horse blankets.

Watching him standing there in front of the mirror that day, trying on his first Saxon Hawk, admiring his reflection, I couldn't wait until I got my own suit. I was already beginning to take an interest in fashion and was attracted by the smart Mod look, which I'd seen on *Ready Steady Go*. In those days, fashions were slow to spread. Even though this was the age of Swinging London, Peterborough still had a long way to go to catch up. England might be swinging like a pendulum do, but Peterborough's grandfather clock was running slow.

Some of the older boys at Deacon's had adopted the Mod style, made popular by The Who and the Small Faces. A couple of them even had scooters, Lambrettas and Vespas and parkas with an image of World Cup Willie – England's 1966 World Cup mascot – plastered on the back. That was the look I wanted to copy.

I didn't have to wait long. Before he left the railways, Dad had brought home a length of suit cloth which had been hanging around in the stores unclaimed. I was thrilled when he produced it on my birthday and announced he was going to have it made up into a suit for me.

That Saturday, we went back to the men's tailoring department at a local gents' outfitters called Harry Nobbs, which was run by a neighbour who lived further down Ledbury Road. Wilf Smith was a dapper little man, a tailor by trade, who had worked at Harry Nobbs as long as anyone could remember. He was quite a bit older than my dad, but I couldn't tell by how much. He certainly wasn't as old as my grandfather. Wilf was married to Myrtle – 'Auntie' Myrtle to all the kids in the street – a kindly woman, neat as a hat-pin, who loved children but didn't have any of her own, which I gathered from Mum was a matter of some considerable sadness. Wilf kept budgies. Plural. He didn't keep a budgie like most people, in a cage in the living room with a bell and a little bowl of water, a piece of cuttle bone and a mineral block. Wilf collected budgies like philatelists collect stamps. He had an aviary in his back garden, packed with the buggers. Wilf was the Bird Man of Ledbury Road. He'd invite us to inspect his feathered treasures. We could hardly refuse. The place stank of bird shit, which carpeted the floor like the snows of Kilimanjaro. The distinctive aroma of budgie guano attached itself to Wilf and never really left him, which was a bit of a disadvantage in a man who made his living in a close-proximity customer service industry.

We arrived at Harry Nobbs bearing the length of suit

cloth, a rich, dark green Tonik mohair. My dad obviously wasn't quite as oblivious to modern trends as I always imagined. Tonik mohair, with its distinctive sheen, was *the* Mod suit material of choice.

I inspected Wilf's shoes and shoulders for tell-tale signs of birdshit. He was rumoured to kiss them all goodbye before he left for work every morning. Who's a pretty boy then? Today, he was spotless, which was just as well since he would be measuring me up, though he whiffed a bit of budgie. Wilf ran the tape measure up hill and down dale, across my shoulders, round my chest and waist, along my inside leg measurement. I hadn't been this intimate with a strange man since the school doctor at West Town had grabbed my tackle and asked me to cough.

Which way did I dress? Wilf asked. Well, I normally put my shirt on first, then my trousers . . .

No, no, that wasn't what he meant. That wasn't what he meant at all. My dad whispered in my ear. Oh, I see, I blushed. Never really thought about until now. To the left, I suppose, but not as far as I'd have liked.

Finally it was time to give him my specifications. What I wanted was an Italian-cut jacket, narrow lapel, three-button front, three slant pockets, two on the right, with fifteen-inch side vents. Trousers, one pleat, front ticket pocket, tapered legs. After some debate, we compromised on nine-inch vents, since fifteens would have almost gone up to my armpits. This was obviously the first time Wilf had been asked to make a Mod suit. He was accustomed to gentlemen of more conservative taste.

Wilf jotted down what seemed like two hundred different sets of numbers, measurements and instructions to the cutters, relieved us of the mohair and informed us that the first fitting would be in three weeks' time. Three *weeks*? I had expected to go home wearing my suit that day. Dad's Saxon Hawks were ready-to-wear: any alterations, like half an inch off the leg or a quick tuck at the waist, were performed on the spot while we went off for a cup of tea in Shelton's cafeteria. Bespoke tailoring operated in a whole different time continuum. It proceeded at its own, leisurely, pace.

Three weeks later, we reported back to Harry Nobbs for the fitting. The suit seemed to be taking shape, but it was half finished. The seams and lining were exposed. Wilf helped me on with the jacket, then proceded to fuss over me with his tape measure and chalk, a dab here, a slash there. Then, to my surprise, he ripped off one of the sleeves with one violent tug. The last time I'd seen anyone do that was a clown at the circus. I hoped he didn't have a custard pie handy.

I had two more fittings before the suit was finally ready. When I tried on the finished article it fitted as if it had been custom made for me, which of course it had, and made me look five years older and three inches taller. I thought back to the day not so long before when I'd got my first pair of long trousers in Ilford. I'd come a million miles from C&A.

I may have had the Mod suit, but there was one other item of clothing I hankered after: a pair of original Levi's 501 jeans. They cost 47s. 6d. (£2.37 today) and I knew that if I wanted a pair I'd have to save up for them. This wasn't impossible, because I already had a job. I've always been an early riser. My parents would come downstairs at Ledbury Road to find me sprawled in the hall devouring the old broadsheet *Daily Express*, sports pages first, which we had delivered. My old man figured that since I was up anyway, and seeing as I was already obsessed with reading the newspapers, I might as well get a paper round. He fixed me up with a job at the NSS newsagents, which had recently opened in the new parade at the end of the street. I'd already had a little experience of delivering papers, having put in a few shifts at Rolph's during the school holidays.

The NSS was run by a young bloke called Tony Saunders, young compared to my dad anyway, probably only in his early twenties. He'd moved to Peterborough from, I think, Portsmouth, and lived with his wife and baby in a flat above the shop. Tony's task was to break the Rolph's traditional monopoly on newspaper delivery in the area. With the Netherton expanding rapidly and the all-new Westwood Estate taking shape on the site of the former airfield north of Horrell's Dairies, there were plenty of customers for all.

Tony's system had one major advantage over Mrs Rolph's. She would hand you a bundle of unsorted papers and a scruffy old exercise book containing the addresses and chosen papers of her regular orders and leave you to sort out for yourself who had what on the hoof. Mistakes were not infrequent. Tony had the papers all marked up before you arrived, which meant you could hit the streets straight away.

In the early days, the NSS had a few customers but they were widely scattered. My initial round must have covered five miles, from the village of Longthorpe in the west, almost to the main railway lines in the east, taking in the Netherton Estate on the way: from thatched cottages to sixties semis and thirties villas. I aimed to do it in about an hour, so I could get home in time to change for school. In those days, the local factories would sound hooters fifteen minutes before clocking-on time to alert employees living nearby to get their skates on. The first from the nearby Baker Perkins works, which built equipment for the bread and confectionery trade, would go off at 7.15 a.m. on the dot. That was also the signal to me to get a move on. If I was still on my round by the time the second hooter sounded, I knew I was running late.

When I was behind schedule, I had only myself to blame. I couldn't help reading the papers I was delivering.

Many's the time a customer emerged from his front door to deliver an early morning bollocking, after looking out of his window and finding me poring over what was supposed be his pristine morning newspaper. Today, I understand why they would get so agitated. I hate opening a paper which someone else has already read. It spoils the sensation of discovery, the pure joy of turning a page, to go where no man has gone before. Even though most news is posted on the internet the night before, I still look forward to opening the *Daily Mail* when I come down in the morning and can get pretty grumpy if a house guest has beaten me to it. About the only source of friction with my beloved late father-in-law Jim, a master baker by trade who was used to early starts, was coming down to find him with his head buried in my *Daily Mail*.

I knew every house on that round, every vicious dog, every stiff letter box. You could tell a great deal about a person by their choice of daily newspaper. Most people took the *Daily Express*, the *Daily Mail*, or, in the case of the doctors and solicitors, the *Daily Telegraph*. It was fair to assume all these people were of a small-c if not large-C conservative persuasion. One chap, a shop steward at a local engineering works, took the *Daily Worker*, the official newspaper of the Communist Party of Great Britain, later to become the *Morning Star*. This was a sad apology for a newspaper, consisting of no more than four pages of humourless Red propaganda. It didn't even carry the football results. No wonder Communism never caught on in Britain. The rest took the *Daily Mirror*, like the bloke known locally as Foreman Bovril, newly promoted from the shop floor at Baker Perkins, as I came to learn.

Foreman Bovril was a precise, pedantic individual, with a cloth cap and a bog-brush moustache. He thought he knew everything and, if he didn't, it clearly wasn't worth knowing. He fancied himself as a landscape gardener, the Incapability Brown of Ledbury Road. One morning on my paper round I noticed a brand new pyramid of cement in his front garden, with a wheelbarrow sticking out of it, and wondered where it had come from. Turned out Foreman Bovril had decided to build himself a new driveway and had told the cement company to prepare the mix to his own specifications. Readymix had warned him that his formula could prove tricky since it would dry rather quickly. That was the whole point, the foreman explained. He knew what he was doing. On the day the cement was being delivered he positioned himself beneath the chute at the back of the lorry and instructed them to pour away. Pour away, they did. The mix dried almost immediately it came into contact with the air. Foreman Bovril's barrow was frozen solid, like a petrified body from Pompeii. He screamed at them to stop pouring but they pretended not to hear him. Sorry, mate, you'll have to speak up, they yelled back, through tears of uncontrollable laughter. This was one for the lads back at the depot after work, light ales all round. Foreman Bovril had to hire a pneumatic drill and spend the whole weekend breaking it up. I believe he built himself a rockery in the back garden from the rubble.

Undeterred, a few months later he decided to construct a water feature in the front garden, complete with fountain. This time, he obviously took professional advice since it went without a hitch. It became something of a tourist attraction. Passers-by would stop to admire the Netherton Estate's answer to the Trevi Fountain, which Bovril had stocked with a selection of exotic fish.

One afternoon, I was cycling along the road when I noticed a crowd gathered outside Bovril Towers, all staring at the foreman's famous fountain. Forcing my way to the front, I discovered that the object of their fascination was two dogs copulating furiously. The bitch had her front legs up on the side of the ornamental pond and her canine suitor was giving it all he was worth from behind. Doggy fashion is, I believe, the correct expression.

As a horrified Foreman Bovril rushed out of the house, the crowd started cheering the dogs on. Bovril managed to separate the animals, the bitch yelping free and making her escape through the bubbling waters. Sadly, the rutting male was in the throes of passion and was already on the vinegar strokes. He had a maniacal rictus grin on his snout, like Muttley from *Wacky Races*, and had reached the point of no return. Bovril grabbed him by the collar but to no avail.

The dog carried on as if the bitch was still there, eventually completing the deed with a shuddering flourish, directly into the pond. The cheers reached a crescendo, before the crowd moved away, laughing uproariously. Foreman Bovril spent the rest of the afternoon trying to fish the evidence out of the pond with one of his wife's serving spoons.

Tony Saunders paid 12s. 6d. (62p) for a six-day week, Monday to Saturday, and an extra five bob for a Sunday round. Most people took more than one Sunday paper, commonly the five-million-selling *News of the World* wrapped inside the *Sunday Times* or the *Sunday Telegraph*, so that their delivery looked outwardly respectable. The now defunct *News of the World* – the major casualty of the recent phone hacking scandal – was a digest of dirty vicars, adulterers, celebrity confessions and brothels in suburbia. Mind you, if you really wanted the gory, salacious details, the place to go was page three of the *Telegraph*, which carried forensic, every cough and spit, court reports of sensational sex cases, designed to titillate the matrons of Middle England.

Earning the princely sum of 17s. 6d. a week, you'd have thought I'd have saved enough for a pair of Levi's 501s in little over a month. It didn't quite work like that. The NSS was the equivalent of the company store, an American concept that press-ganged workers into spending their hard-earned in a shop owned by their employers. Their wages were simply recycled. Tony Saunders was obviously a student of the company store, since he extended unlimited credit to his staff. Never has the expression 'like a kid in a sweet shop' been more apt. Tony would advance us cigarettes, sweets and comics against our wages. Every paper boy had a packet of Park Drive tipped with his name on in Biro behind the counter. On darker mornings you'd see schoolboys setting off on their rounds with the ends of their fags glowing from their lips. When we got back to the shop, we'd need some mint imperials to remove the smell from our breath before we went home for breakfast and set off for school. Park Drive tipped cost 9d. for a packet of five. Tony would charge us 2d. for each cigarette, a handsome mark-up. The more we smoked, the greater his profit. I took full advantage of my credit arrangement, stocking up on American hard gums on the way to school; buying magazines like *Melody Maker*, *Record Mirror* and *Charles Buchan's Football Monthly*. We were also encouraged to put money into a Christmas Club, so we could afford presents for our families at Christmas, a box of Milk Tray for Mum, a packet of Liquorice Allsorts for Dad. Some weeks, by the time pay day came around, I owed Tony Saunders money.

I started delivering papers when I was eleven. Even though the minimum legal age was supposed to be thirteen, no one seemed to care. Certainly there were no checks. Society may have moved on from sending kids up chimneys, but children were expected to work for their pocket money.

These days you rarely see a paper boy, certainly not in my neck of the woods. Stricter enforcement of 'child protection' rules is only partly to blame. According to figures from the newsagents' trade federation a couple of years ago, a third of all newsagents have given up on home deliveries altogether. A BBC report quoted a newsagent in Liverpool as saying:

> We just couldn't get the paperboys. We used to have a book full of names. We used to do 10 paperboys but it was gradually dropping off. Basically, they seem to have got too much cash. The majority seem to have unlimited funds from mum and dad.

The same report also quoted a fifteen-year-old from Orpington, in Kent, who had tried a paper round for a few weeks but had given it up as a bad job:

> It was horrible. The papers were heavy, it rained every day, it was cold and I wanted to sleep but couldn't because I had to get up at 6.15. My hands were really cold. If it was raining you couldn't have an umbrella – you needed your hands to do the papers.

Words fail me.

Eventually, I did manage to save up 47s. 6d. for a pair of Levi's and trotted off to Millets, the outdoor clothing store, then the only stockist in town. The original 501s were imported from the Levi Strauss factory in San Francisco, California. 501s dated from the 1890s, featured metal rivets on the pockets, a steel button fly, and the design had changed little over the years.

Unlike today's pre-shrunk, pre-washed denims, 501s were sold as 'shrink-to-fit'. The idea was that you bought bigger jeans than you needed – typically, two inches in the waist and four inches in the leg. When washed they would shrink to your exact size. In those days I was a 28-inch waist and a 30-inch inside leg. Which meant I should buy a 30-inch waist and 34-inch leg. The only trouble was Levi's didn't do a 34-inch leg. Not in Peterborough, anyway. They came in one-size-fits-all 36-inch. There was no point trying them on. And in any case, Millets didn't have changing rooms. Most of their customers came in to buy camping equipment. No one ever wanted to try on a tent. So I held them against me, just to get a rough idea of what they would look like. They practically came up to my neck. They were stiff as an ironing board.

The accepted way of shrinking them to fit was immersing yourself in a bath full of warm water. When I put this to my mother, she wasn't thrilled, but agreed reluctantly to go along with it. I struggled into my new jeans and lowered myself into the bath. Within a couple of minutes, the water had turned bright blue, as the indigo dye from the unwashed denim started to bleed.

After about five minutes, my mum had had enough and ordered me to get out. She wasn't going to spend the rest of the day scrubbing the bath to get rid of the stain. She'd rinse them out in the twin tub and hang them on the washing line. When it came to Levi's, we weren't talking drip-dri. They were still wringing wet come nightfall. I finally pulled them on the next morning, even though they remained damp to the touch. Obviously I hadn't spent long enough in the water. They still had plenty of slack in the waist and the legs concertinaed round my ankles. They fitted about as snugly as the bomb disposal suits in *The Hurt Locker*. Despite my pleading, Mum refused to let me have a second go in the bath, which she had only managed to get clean with copious quantities of Ajax scouring powder and plenty of elbow grease.

I was determined to wear them, though, to show them off to the other kids in the street. Unfortunately, as well as being slightly damp they were still somewhat stiff. I left the house walking like Douglas Bader.

This wasn't the stylish, ultra-cool look I was aiming for. My Levi's still needed more work. Since I couldn't shrink them in the bath, I'd have to find another way. I hit on a plan. Every summer we'd go swimming in the River Nene, at a lock known as Orton Staunch. That was it. I'd soak in the river until my jeans shrank to the required size and shape. So I made my way to the Staunch, stripped to the waist and jumped in. Soon I found myself pinned against the lock wall, hanging on to keep my head above water. The jeans were a dead weight, dragging me down. I might just as well have tied a block of concrete around my waist. This could have been the first case of suicide by Levi's. An inquest jury would have had to record a misadventure verdict. After about twenty minutes, my mates helped fish me out and pulled me to shore. Despite dicing with death, I was jubilant. The jeans had shrunk. They fitted perfectly in the waist, even though they were still far too long in the leg. This probably explains why in every picture you see of someone wearing jeans in the fifties and sixties, they've all got turn-ups.

I waddled home, clambered out of my Levi's with some difficulty and hung them on the line. Mum refused point-blank to put them in the twin tub, even though she relented later when she could no longer stand the smell of stale river water in the house. The other unwelcome side effect was that the indigo dye from the denim had stained my legs blue. Whenever I pulled on my football shorts for the next couple of weeks, I must have looked like a jolly hockey sticks 'bluestocking' female undergraduate from Girton College, Cambridge.

Levi's 501s fell out of fashion as the sixties wore on, overtaken by the fad for bell-bottoms and ludicrous 'loon pants'. In the 1980s, there was a revival sparked by an advert starring the impossibly handsome male model Nick Kamen. This featured Kamen wandering into a laundrette, stripping off his Levi's and loading them into a washing machine, in front of an admiring pair of dopey birds, while the soundtrack played Marvin Gaye's 'I Heard It Through the Grapevine'.

If it was historical accuracy they were after, they should have had a schoolboy jumping into a river in a pair of 'shrink-to-fit' 501s, while the Supremes sang 'Going Down For the Third Time'.

Part 4

I discovered my Nanna Sparke had died when I was summoned to the headmaster's study one morning to find my dad sitting there. He'd come to collect me. Dad explained what had happened and then drove me home. Well, not quite home: to our next-door neighbour's house. Vivienne was already there, eating Dairylea sandwiches, not quite grasping what had happened. We couldn't go to our own house, because the coroner's officer was still fussing round, as they have to do in the case of a sudden death.

I couldn't quite grasp that Nanna was dead. I'd only seen her at breakfast. She always ate the same thing: a small bowl of All-Bran and a piece of fruit. I'd said cheerio, as usual, and expected her to be there when I got home from school. I'd have described my nanna as old – everyone over thirty was 'old' in my world – but in rude health. She was slim as a whip, active: still going to keep fit with Mum every week. Nanna hadn't been ill, to the best of my knowledge. She didn't drink, except for the odd sherry at Christmas, and ate sparingly. For lunch every day she'd have an apple and a piece of cheese.

That morning Mum had gone upstairs to help Nanna make the bed and found her lying flat out on the floor. The doctor said Nanna had suffered a massive stroke and died instantly. She would have known nothing about it, which my dad said was a mercy.

Here's the strange thing. If you'd have asked me which of the old ladies living in our house would have gone first, I'd have put money on Auntie Em. She was a couple of years older than Nanna, had a history of heart trouble, had already suffered one stroke and smoked like a chimney. Mum told me later than when the neighbours heard there'd been a death in the family, they all assumed it was Auntie Em, too.

It was the first time I'd been aware of anyone close to me dying. I was too young to understand when my Grandad Sparke died. Nanna had shown no sign of ill heath and was excited about flying back to America to stay with Olive and Tom and the boys. The previous week, she'd been out with Mum buying new clothes for the trip. She was only sixty-five, just five years older than I am now.

C'est la vie, said the old folks. It goes to show you never can tell.

I knew people died young, because I'd been with my Nanna Sparke watching TV the night John F. Kennedy was assassinated. Mum and Dad were out for the night and Nanna was baby-sitting. I was sitting in front of the fire and she was brushing my hair. She did that every night, fifty times back and fifty times forward. She said it kept your hair healthy and made it grow, something to do with releasing your natural oils. I don't remember what we were watching – Z Cars, probably – when programmes were interrupted, the test card came on screen and a special announcement was made, that President Kennedy had been killed in Dallas, Texas. Nanna paused briefly, absorbed the news, then carried on brushing my hair. They say everyone remembers where they were when JFK died. In my case, it's true, even though I was only nine.

Despite the horrible Clelland, Deacon's wasn't a complete nightmare. There were some quite brilliant teachers, older men who had seen military service. Word was that this or that master had had a 'good' war. There could be no higher praise, even though what constituted a 'good' war remained unspoken. But we got the general idea. They were quietly heroic and if anyone had ever made the movie, they'd have been played by John Mills or Jack Hawkins.

I was fond, in particular, of the two English teachers – Johnny Hynam and Mike 'Spud' Taylor. Maybe it's because I loved English, language and literature. But, unlike the savage brute Clelland, these struck me as civilised men, with a love of learning and passing on knowledge. Their lessons were never boring. Hynam was a squat, agricultural chap, with a demeanour which belied a fierce intellect. He had enjoyed some success as a playwright. A science fiction series he had written, called *Sword From the Stars*, had been recorded and broadcast on the BBC. He played it proudly to us during lessons, on an old reel-to-reel tape machine. Hynam was a carrot man, not a stick man. Every week he'd reward the best essay with a Mars Bar from the tuck shop.

Spud Taylor was another master who could captivate a classroom of pubescent boys without recourse to violence, though he wasn't averse to aiming a board rubber in the direction of any pupil he thought was not paying full attention. He rarely missed. Spud was also the school cricket coach, and played for Peterborough Town First XI, decent bat, useful fielder and expert left-arm spin bowler. The fact that English was about the only subject I was interested in, apart from history, and that I was a fairly accomplished quick bowler by the time I arrived at Deacon's probably explains why I had a pretty good relationship with Spud. Under the expert tutelage of Taylor and Hynam, I was entered for both English language and literature GCE a year early, when I was still in the fourth form, and passed both with flying colours.

More than a quarter of a century after I left Deacon's, I heard from Spud. I was working at the *Daily Mail* and had been named Columnist of the Year in the annual Press Awards. He sent me a congratulatory note. By then, Spud had retired and was living in a flat at the back of the cathedral, if memory serves. If he liked to think that he'd played some small part in my future success in Fleet Street, he was damn right. So did Johnny Hynam.

Spud went on to become headmaster of a brand new secondary school which opened to serve the expanding population of the Netherton and Westwood estates. My sister Viv was one of his pupils.

Thinking back, I can't really remember any pupil having a bad word to say about him. It's a pity he had to move to further his career and secure a headship of his own. He'd have made a brilliant head of Deacon's, certainly better than the pompous oaf who had the job, one W. R. Upcott-Gill, a comedy headmaster from central casting. I couldn't stand him either. We'll come back to Upcott-Gill in due course.

Before the school broke up for the 1967 summer holidays, it was announced in morning assembly that Deacon's had been invited to enter a team in the BBC schools' quiz show *Top of the Form*. The programme began in 1948 and ran until 1986, first on radio and later on television. Its theme tune, 'This Is Marching Strings', by Ray Martin and his Concert Orchestra, was as familiar as the theme from *Grandstand*, the Saturday sports magazine programme on the BBC.

There was a great buzz of excitement around the hall when Upcott-Gill told the school we were going to take part in the programme, only slightly dampened by the realisation that we were going to be on the wireless, not the TV version. The show would be recorded at the start of the new term in September and broadcast in the October. The Deacon's team would be picked on the strength of the marks we had achieved in our weekly general knowledge tests. Since these tests were largely based on what had been in the news that week, I always had a head start on the rest of the class thanks to the spread of information gleaned during my daily paper round. Which is how I came to be selected. As the local paper reported:

A team from Deacon's grammar school, Peterborough, took part in a round of the BBC's Top of the Form radio programme yesterday afternoon. The team, pictured above from left, are Michael Conning, aged 12, of 15 Marholm Road; Richard Littlejohn, aged 13, of 32 Ledbury Road; Martin Bradshaw, aged 15, of 54 Caverstede Road; and captain Martin Chambers, aged 16, of 28 Grimshaw Road.

They played a team of schoolgirls from King's Norton Grammar School for Girls, Birmingham. Deacon's team were

asked questions by John Ellison and the rest of the school packed
the assembly hall and cheered their team on. He asked the team
questions on various subjects, including well-known people,
commentaries, fact and fiction, and sport.

A few days before we broke up for the summer, researchers from the BBC came to the school to interview the team members. What we were reading, what subjects we were studying, what kind of music we liked, and so on. This would allow them to tailor the questions to individual competitors to at least give us a fighting chance. They didn't want anyone scoring a humiliating Eurovision Song Contest-style 'nul points'.

On the day, I have to admit that I felt pretty self-conscious. Not because I didn't think I could handle the heat of competition or would struggle with my answers, but because my voice was breaking. One minute I sounded like a full baritone, the next like Frankie Valli, the falsetto lead singer of the Four Seasons. When it was my turn to say 'hello' to my opposite number in Birmingham as we were introduced at the start of the show, it sounded as if I'd been castrated mid-sentence.

Round one came and went in a blur. I can't remember what my question was, but I do remember I managed to get it right. Round two was the musical round. I was mightily relieved to be asked to identify 'In the Hall of the Mountain King' and name its composer, Edvard Grieg.

I would have preferred to have been asked what was on the B-side of 'Reach Out (I'll Be There)' by the Four Tops, but fortunately we'd studied Grieg's Peer Gynt Suite, from which 'Mountain King' is taken, so I was able to provide the correct answers.

All went well in the early exchanges. We were running neck and neck with the girls from King's Norton and feeling quietly confident. There was one problem, however. Our team captain, Martin Chambers, was a late replacement. Our original captain had left school over the summer, so Martin had been drafted in, having come second in his year in the general knowledge test. Martin was, I think, a Sixth Form (Arts) student, as opposed to his predecessor who was Sixth Form (Science). The *Top of the Form* researchers had naturally tailored their questions to the boy they'd interviewed, not his replacement, so they were all geared towards his interests and areas of expertise, not Martin's.

Which is how our clever new captain, exceptionally well versed in literature and the arts, came to be asked questions about potassium permanganate and nuclear physics. Needless to say, he hadn't a clue and ended up with an individual 'nul points', which was enough to swing the contest in favour of our opponents. It wasn't Martin's fault and we couldn't help feeling sorry for him, especially when he had to perform his captain's duty at the end of the programme and call for three cheers for the girls of King's Norton Grammar School.

Still, as I went home that night I consoled myself that, although we may have lost, there was a bright side. It wasn't Radio Caroline, but at least I'd made my radio debut.

The last *Top of the Form* on the radio was broadcast in December 1986. The TV version ended in 1975. The demise of the show coincided with the phasing out of the grammar schools, which began under the Wilson governments of 1964–70. *Top of the Form* had largely featured grammar schools, like Deacon's, but by 1975 their numbers were dwindling. The show staggered on for another eleven years and increasingly featured fee-paying independent schools in place of the grammars. In 1986 the BBC decided to kill it off altogether in keeping with the 'anti-elitist' policies of the educational establishment. The producer, Graham Frost, was reported to have said that the competitive nature of the programme jarred with 'progressive' philosophy. He claimed there were plans to replace *Top of the Form* with a 'non-competitive' schools quiz where there was no 'right' or 'wrong' answer. The BBC denied this, but it rings true. In the event the show was never replaced.

Tony Crosland, Wilson's education secretary at the time a government bill creating the comprehensive system was passed in 1965, is reported by his wife, Susan, to have boasted: 'If it's the last thing I ever do, I'm going to kill off every fucking grammar school in England. And Wales and Northern Ireland.' When the Tories, under grammar school boy Ted Heath, came to power, they lacked the political will to save the grammars – probably because most Tory MPs of that vintage sent their children to fee-paying private schools and so didn't give a damn.

Crosland, it almost goes without saying, was educated privately at Highgate School in north London and Oxford University. He was a prime example of privileged politicians pulling up the ladder behind them. Grammar schools gave clever children from modest backgrounds the chance to escape their humble beginnings and go on to university. The 1997 Labour government, under Fettes-educated Tony Blair, attempted to close down the last handful of remaining grammars. By 2010, social mobility in Britain had gone into reverse.

In October 2013, a study by Glasgow University's School of Education found that there had been a significant collapse in educational standards since the grammars were scrapped. School leavers had poorer literacy, numeracy and problem-solving skills than their grandparents. A survey of twenty-four developed nations showed that, in Britain alone, the over-fifty-fives outperformed not only their grandchildren but also their counterparts in other countries. Researchers put this down to the fact that the over-fifty-fives were the last generation to benefit from a grammar school education.

Here was damning, conclusive evidence – as if any

were needed – that Tony 'fucking' Crosland's callous act of educational vandalism was one of the most wicked policies ever implemented by a modern British government.

By the summer of 1967, I was already being given quite a lot of independence by my parents, just so long as I was on the last bus home. Even though I was still only thirteen, I could pass for a couple of years older. This meant I could blag my way into discos. Once a month, a local DJ called Steve Allen would take over the Town Hall for a soul night. One summer's evening I can recall climbing the marble stairs to the suite next to the council chamber where the disco was being held. Out of nowhere, I was assailed by a barrage of extraordinary extra-terrestrial noise. It sounded as if Dr Who was landing in the Peterborough City Council chamber. This was the first time I ever heard 'Reflections', by Diana Ross and the Supremes, an electronically enhanced single that marked a major departure for Motown and was heavily influenced by the psychedelic pop music being produced by the Beatles and others. It was a land-mark record, an early precursor of the future direction of a label which rose to prominence as 'The Sound of Young America' and would go on to produce much of the soundtrack of the sixties and early seventies protest movements. One of these Motown protest songs would later have a profound influence on the direction of my own life.

The summer of 1967 was the Summer of Love. Not that you'd have really known it in Peterborough, apart from a few wannabe hippies wearing floral shirts and starting to grow their hair over their ears. They always say that if you can remember the Swinging Sixties, you probably weren't there. The fact of the matter is that most people who claim to remember the Swinging Sixties weren't there, either.

The Summer of Love, the Swinging Sixties, the Permissive Society seemed to be the exclusive preserve of a handful of pop stars and privileged young people living in a couple of postcodes in central and west London. None of it had much purchase in the provinces.

My friend Skip and I decided that if Swinging London wasn't going to come to us, we would have to go to Swinging London, even if by the time we got there we were a couple of years late. Skip was a year older than me, and his parents also gave him plenty of rope. My mum had no objection to me catching the train up to London. Why would she? When she was the same age, she'd regularly take the overground into town – and that was during the war. So Skip and I would catch the first off-peak train to King's Cross, with the usual 'last-bus home' proviso ringing in our ears. Although we wanted the world to think of us as five years older than we were, we paid the child's fare, which I seem to recall was 12s. 6d. return (62p). This caused the occasional run-in with the conductor, who wanted to know why, if we were travelling on a children's ticket, we were sitting in a smoking compartment puffing our way through a packet of Park Drive tipped.

The journey took around an hour, pretty much as it does today, about the same time it takes to get into central London on the Undergound from the outer suburbs. In the sixties going up to Town, as I'd learned to call London, was still a big event. Today, so many people from Peterborough commute into London to work every morning that the city, like most of south-eastern England, is effectively another suburb. Greater London now stretches from the south coast to the East Midlands, from Bristol to Southend.

The moment we arrived at King's Cross, we'd head for the nearest Golden Egg to fuel up for the day. In the sixties, the Golden Egg chain of restaurants was an institution, famous for their jazzed-up decor. They were a colourful cross between a coffee bar and a greasy spoon, offering cheap and cheerful meals – many, as the name makes clear, but not exclusively, egg-based. No two Golden Eggs in London were the same. One would have an Italian theme, others Pop Art or pure Hollywood, although as they expanded across Britain they became increasingly homogenised and soulless.

To us, the central London Golden Eggs seemed impossibly exotic. The Wimpy Bar was about as funky as it got in Peterborough in 1967, although there was a local hangout called Purdy's on Cathedral Square, which had a bakery at the front and sold shrivelled-up burgers and minuscule milk shakes from counters out the back.

The Wimpy Bar brand was owned by J. Lyons and Co., of Corner House and knickerbocker glory fame. Named after a character from Popeye, J. Wellington Wimpy, they were designed as a British incarnation of an imaginary American diner, offering hamburgers and chips and a peculiar sliced frankfurter in a bap with the unfortunate name 'Bender'. Like most home-grown attempts to ape American culture, they were poorly executed, as I was to discover for myself a couple of years later. Wimpy Bars had about as much in common with your average American diner as a Berni Inn had with Peter Luger's world-famous steakhouse in New York.

A 'Bender' cost 1s. 10p. (9p), a pineapple burger 3s. (15p), a basic Wimpy 2s. (10p) and a King-Size Wimpy 3s. 9d. (18p). You could also buy, were you so inclined, a 'Shanty the Golden Fish Burger', a deep-fried slab of frozen fish served in a bun with tartare sauce. We're not talking *American Graffiti* here.

From the Golden Egg it was off to Carnaby Street, a compulsory port of call. By 1967, Carnaby Street was already completely commercialised, or so it seemed. Boutiques were crammed cheek-by-jowl, most of them owned by the same handful of fashion pioneers who by then were already prosperous rag-trade moguls well on their way to multi-million-pound fortunes. The big names were all established, including Lord John, John Stephen and Irvine Sellars, who went on to enjoy a second successful career as a property developer and is best-known today as the man responsible for the Shard, London's tallest building.

It was in one of these boutiques, I forget which, that I bought a pair of salmon-pink hipsters, with a thick exposed zip. I have no idea what possessed me, but I remember my old man hitting the roof the first time I wore them.

That summer, my grandparents had returned from Australia and Auntie Em had moved back to Ilford. The day we took Em home, I was wearing my Levi's 501s and a brand new pair of Hush Puppies suede slip-ons, with black elasticated gussets. Grandad, who had always associated suede shoes with homosexuals, took one look at my footwear and said to my old man: 'What the hell are those, then? Is he turning into a brown-hatter?'

(I assumed this had something to do with my brown suede shoes, until my grandfather enlighted me in graphic detail. Without elaborating too crudely, brown-hatter is Cockney slang for a homosexual. Mind you, few people did know what brown-hatter meant, or where it came from. It even managed to slip under the radar at the BBC, which then still had a formidable list of expressions banned on the grounds of taste and decency. There's a fabulous episode of *Steptoe and Son* in which Harold takes his dad, Albert, to a gentlemen's outfitter to buy a new suit. As the assistant attempts to take Albert's inside leg measurement, old man Steptoe recoils and says: 'Oi, what's your game?' An embarrassed Harold, who fancies himself as a bit of a sophisticate, puts on his best posh accent and explains: 'I'm so terribly sorry. My father wasn't trying to imply that you was a brown-hatter.')

The shock of hearing his son described as a brown-hatter by his own father caused my dad to wince with embarrassment. He clearly took it to heart. There'd been a battle royal over the Hush Puppies before my mum finally gave in while Dad was working away. So you can imagine how the salmon-pink hipsters went down. My old man finally snapped a couple of months later. I'd decided to get my hair cut like Stevie Marriott, the lead singer of the Mod band the Small Faces. This was a layered look, centre parting, with the crown back-combed to make it stand up and held in place with lashings of hair lacquer.

Dad came home from work to find me sitting in front of the TV looking like a pompadoured poodle. With my grandad's 'brown-hatter' remarks still fresh in his mind, he went berserk. Grabbing me by the scruff of my neck, he dragged me upstairs to the bathroom, bent me over the bath, pushed the nozzles of the rubber bath-hose on to the taps and, using the shower-head, washed my hair until all traces of back comb and hair-spray had disappeared for ever. I hadn't had a more uncomfortable experience in the bathroom since the extraction of my pet tapeworm. The following day he drove me to his own traditional Italian barber, Franco, and told him to give me a proper man's haircut. It would be another couple of years before I plucked up the courage to grow my hair back over my collar.

Ray Davies of the Kinks had already lampooned the whole Carnaby Street scene the year before in his brilliant hit record 'Dedicated Follower of Fashion', with its dig at the fickle 'Carnabetion Army'. Although Davies was one of the biggest pop stars in Britain at the time, he had a healthy contempt for those obsessed with the 'latest fads and trends'. Davies is a born and bred Londoner, who wrote the ethereal anthem 'Waterloo Sunset', a love song to sixties London. But I've always seen him as a quintessential outsider, a sceptical suburbanite, looking down with suspicion on fashionable, neophiliac London from the serene northern heights of Muswell Hill. Perhaps that's why I've always identifed with his music, especially his beautiful social mockumentaries from the mid-sixties. Years later, I was presenting my own TV series, *Littlejohn*

Live and Uncut, for London Weekend Television. One of my first musical guests was Ray Davies. Yet another instance of Parky's law about getting paid to meet your heroes. We had a long chat in the green-room (hospitality suite) after the show, but I thought it best not to mention the salmon-pink hipsters.

After Carnaby Street, we'd explore Soho, stopping for a banana sandwich in one of the many Italian cafés in the area's narrow streets. Apart from the Carnaby Street fashion ghetto, Soho hadn't changed much since the early fifties. It was still a warren of delis, cafés, dive bars and knocking shops. When I started going back to Soho in the late seventies, after I joined the *Evening Standard*, it was much the same. Independent businesses still predominated. The gay scene was well established, but not as visible as it is today. Ray Davies wrote 'Lola' about picking up a transvestite in 'a club in old Soho' as long ago as 1970. Soho has always been the spiritual home of homosexuals, bisexuals, transexuals and every other kind of sexuals. Long may it continue.

What was absent in the sixties were the ubiquitous chainstores and restaurants which have bought up the leases and moved into the area, as rapacious property owners have hiked rents to unaffordable levels for small enterprises. The old Italian caffs have fallen to Starbucks and Costa Coffee. If you could find a banana sandwich in

Soho today, it would be ethically sourced, served on wholewheat ciabatta with organic arugula and home-made paprika mayonnaise and it would cost you at least a tenner. My banana sandwich cost a shilling. This transformation has turned a louche, once mysterious part of London into just another tourist destination.

Then it was off to the HMV store at 363 Oxford Street to while away a couple of hours browsing the record racks, before it was time to take the rattler back to Peterborough. The flagship HMV store was the Harrods of the music industry and boasted 'The World's Largest Record Selection' above its doors. You could buy practically every record available from HMV: LPs, EPs, singles, rare 78s, American imports. Number 363 Oxford Street was opened in 1921 by the composer Sir Edward Elgar. It's where the Beatles cut the 1962 demo which Brian Epstein took to EMI and secured their first deal. HMV went on to open 140 stores around the United Kingdom. By the end of the first decade of the twenty first century, the company was on its knees because of the digital download revolution. The store closed in 2000, taken over by a Footlocker. In January 2013, HMV went into administration and that seemed to be that. But it was rescued, restructured and, happily, in October 2013, HMV moved back into 363 Oxford Street. The store was, appropriately, reopened by Paul McCartney to the strains of Elgar's 'Land of Hope and Glory'.

In the sixties, the Oxford Street HMV store was a revelation, a treasure trove. Back in Peterborough, records could only be purchased from a few outlets, mostly Boots the Chemist and W. H. Smith, as well as traditional musical instruments shops like the one in Ilford where I bought 'It's Over' by Roy Orbison, the same day as I got my first pair of long trousers.

Woolworth's also sold records under its own label, Embassy, next to the pick'n'mix sweets counter. These were cut-price cover versions of current hits performed by an assortment of big band and session singers familiar from the BBC lunchtime shows. An outfit called the Typhoons would record a double A-side of Beatles hits, which Woolworth's knocked out for 4s. (20p) instead of the regular price for a genuine single of 6s. 3d. (31p). Embassy compilation LPs came in at about 15s. (75p) and were half the price of a normal album, which retailed at 32s. 6d. (£1.62). Incredibly, these pale imitations shifted by the lorry-load. But no discerning music fan would be seen dead with an Embassy record under his arm.

As the sixties progressed, some of the women's fashion stores opened record departments. The biggest of these in Peterborough was Noel West One, which aimed to bring a bit of the glamour of London's West End to Cathedral Square. To get to the records, you had to walk through racks of mini skirts, floral blouses and underwear. For a teenage boy, this presented something of a challenge, since in order to buy the latest LP by the Stones or The Who you had to pass gaggles of older girls wandering in and out of changing rooms in various stages of undress. Despite the obvious attractions of this prospect, it played havoc with your hormones. I always suspected some of the girls would wait until a young man wandered into view before deliberately emerging from behind a curtain in nothing but a pelmet skirt and brassiere. They'd always feign modesty, covering their breasts like Barbara Windsor in *Carry On Camping*, before dissolving with their friends into fits of giggles. The only way we boys could overcome our embarrassment was to go in two-by-two, like the animals in Noah's Ark, jut out our jaws, attempt to avert our gaze and pretend we hadn't noticed all this nubile female flesh as we marched purposefully towards the new releases.

Far more comfortable was the small, independent record shop in Queen Street, opposite the original Frank Perkins factory, which was almost exclusively a male preserve. Enthusiasts only, not for the casual buyer of Top 10 hits. The owner stocked minor labels, imports and obscure singles which were unobtainable elsewhere. Mostly soul and ska. If they didn't have it, they'd order it in – at a premium. I can remember paying 15s. (75p) for 'Train Tour to Rainbow City' by the Pyramids on the President label, a ska favourite that cost me almost a week's paper-round wages. An original US pressing of 'Another

Saturday Night' by Sam Cooke set me back 19s. 11d. (a penny short of £1).

There was also a specialist record salesman who set up shop on Peterborough market once a week. His stall was next to the cattle market, which was still running in those days, and there was an ever-present stench of cowshit. He travelled far and wide seeking out his stock, which was displayed in not exactly alphabetical order in old beer crates. You had to know what you were looking for. It demanded perseverence. He was rumoured to have contacts on the US airbases, and at the docks in London, Liverpool and Southampton. Again, these 45s weren't cheap but if you wanted the original Hammond label release of 'Shotgun Wedding' by Roy C, or the Jamie Records pressing of 'Boogaloo Down Broadway' by the Fantastic Johnny C (no relation) this was the only show in town.

Until London's Harry Fenton opened a Peterborough outpost in the late 1960s, the market was also the place to buy the latest fashions. Shelton's and Trollope's sold traditional shirtmakers such as Arrow and Van Heusen, but these weren't the brands my generation craved.

Ben Sherman and Brutus shirts were especially sought-after. Ben Sherman was a Brighton-based brand, started by Arthur Benjamin Sugarman, who moved after the war to America, where he changed his name. He returned to

England in the early 1960s and launched his own clothing brand. Ben Sherman produced high-quality, Ivy League-style, button-down-collar shirts, made from genuine Oxford cotton imported from the US, based on the classic Brooks Brothers design. My first Ben Sherman I coupled with a pair of Levi's Sta-Prest slacks, which Olive had sent me from America, and a pair of my dad's old black brogues, which had come full circle since he'd bought them after the war and were now the very epitome of fashionable footwear for the discerning young man around Peterborough.

Brutus Trimfit shirts, launched three years later, were similar in style to Ben Sherman, shaped and darted at the waist, but cut less generously and from cheaper material. Their outstanding feature was that they came in a variety of loud colours, predominantly Madras checks and tartans. Both companies faded during the hippy era but the style was kept alive first by the skinheads, the 2-Tone movement, Brit Pop, Madness, and, of course, the assorted Mod revivals of the seventies, eighties and nineties. There seems to be a Mod revival every five minutes these days. The original 1966 Brutus design is back on the shelves and Ben Sherman sells an extensive range of clothes from its flag-ship store in modern Carnaby Street and across Europe. The difference today is that the Brighton factory has long since closed and Ben Sherman's are mostly made in the Far East.

The market was also the only place to go to buy shoes direct from the manufacturers in nearby Northamptonshire – brogues, loafers and Dr Marten's Airwair, with their unique 'bouncing soles'. These shoes not only tended to be better made, they also undercut the High Street chains such as Freeman Hardy Willis, Saxone and Dolcis. There were three or four competing stalls on the market, all selling shoes made within a short drive away. Today, the Northants footwear industry is down to a few upscale, specialist companies, such as Church's, an inevitable consequence of globalisation. Church's is owned by the luxury Italian brand Prada.

Peterborough market, too, is a tawdry shadow of its former glory. It was once a place where respectable ladies did their shopping, filling their baskets with local produce. The stallholders used to bawl out their wares in the distinctive local dialect to drum up custom – 'Peound a plooms, me duck' – just as the sing-song east London accents of Ilford's stallholders used to provide the entertaining soundtrack at the Pioneer Market. When I revisited Peterborough market while researching this book, it was a Tower of Babel.

The sounds and smells of old East Anglia had been replaced by those of Eastern Europe and elsewhere. Most of the stalls were selling cheap mass-produced tat from the Far East and goods imported for sale to recent immigrants from the 'EU accession states'. It was a cross between a Third World bazaar and a car boot sale. The only 'locals' in evidence seemed to be layabouts drinking from cans of lager and stuffing their faces with disgusting 'fast food'.

The market still stands on Cattle Market Road, at the back of the Embassy, but the cattle market closed decades ago. Pity; the smell of cowshit might raise the tone of the place today.

When Dad worked on the railways he often had to travel to London, York and Doncaster for meetings. After he joined Perkins, his new job took him further afield, dealing with suppliers in Europe, Japan and America. He'd also bring home some of his business associates, which meant Mum had to entertain them. This she rather enjoyed, since she loved to cook, and it gave her a chance to showcase the dishes she'd learned at her 'Continental cookery' evening classes. It could also lead to clashes of cultures as our guests were often unfamiliar with the food she served.

On one occasion she presented some Americans with the newly fashionable starter of avocado pear with prawns, then watched in horror as they proceeded to cut up the avocados and eat them, including the skins. The avocado isn't known as the 'alligator' pear in some parts of the world without good reason. It took them at least fifteen minutes to chew their way through the skins, which they had the grace to pronounce delicious. Mum was worried sick she might have poisoned them. Fortunately, they didn't attempt to eat the stones.

Another time, Dad rang at short notice to say he was bringing home some representatives of a Swedish conglomerate. Mum had nothing in the house, so she had to improvise. While Dad poured generous drinks in the sitting room, she bundled me into the car and we headed off to the chippie for eight portions of plaice and chips. Smuggled in through the back door, and served on our best china with silver cutlery and lashings of Liebfraumilch, the meal was rapturously received. The head Swede even asked Mum for the recipe, since he wanted to take it home to his wife in Stockholm. She had to explain that it was a closely guarded family secret, handed from mother to daughter, and had never actually been written down. Her explanation seemed to satisfy him and a few days later he sent her a waffle iron, one of his company's sidelines, in appreciation of her splendid hospitality.

This was the era of 'cheese and wine' parties, cocktail cabinets and exotic drinks. Mum was partial to something called a 'Snowball', a mixture of lemonade and Advocaat, which for some reason I thought was made from the juice of avocados. I didn't have much interaction with the adult world in the normal course of events but I'd occasionally come home when one of my parents' cheese and wine extravangazas was still in full swing. Skip's dad, Dennis, was the life and soul of every party, telling filthy jokes and organising daft games. Dennis was great fun to be around. 'Work as a team, bugger the expense' was his motto. I never quite figured out what he did. Something to do with the motor trade, I think, since he always seemed to have a wad of cash and the latest model of car, which he changed every year. He later became a debt collector-cum-bailiff. Dennis always had some kind of scam going on.

A few years earlier, I'd joined the local Cub pack with Skip and his brother David, aka Butch. We hadn't been in the Cubs for long when one evening the door of the church hall burst open and in marched Dennis in search of the Scout leader, or 'Scouter', who oversaw the Cubs and the Boy Scouts. Having located him in his office, there was a brief exchange of words, followed by a scuffle during which Dennis decked the Scouter, collected Skip, Butch and me, and announced we were leaving, never to return. Although I had no idea what was going on, I complied. Subsequently, I discovered that Dennis had read a court report in the evening paper about the Scout leader being fined for importuning a plainclothes policeman in a public convenience. When my dad found out, too, that was the end of my career in the Boy Scouts.

The Skippers had a lovely pedigree labrador bitch called Bonnie. Her full name was Bonnie of Grange, from the Sandilands Kennels, in Bedfordshire. (When we bought a lab, Ossie, in 1990, we discovered from his pedigree certificate that he was a direct descendant of Bonnie.) Dennis realised there was a few bob to made breeding her and selling the puppies. Bonnie was introduced to a number of stud dogs but appeared to have no intention of cooperating. She'd sit down on her haunches, tuck her tail between her back legs and refuse to budge. After a few weeks, I can recall an exasperated Dennis remarking: 'If she doesn't give it up soon, I'll do her myself.'

The Skippers lived at 44 Ledbury Road, next to Foreman Bovril, a few doors down from us at 32. They'd moved there from King's Lynn shortly after we arrived. Dennis was a Norfolk boy, born and bred, and had an intimate knowledge of the beautiful North Norfolk coastline. In summer our families would go cockle picking at Old Hunstanton, Dennis leading expeditions far out across the sands of the Wash, keeping a weather eye on the tides so that we wouldn't get stranded. It was a close-run thing a few times, although the waters off Hunstanton are quite shallow. It was always claimed that at low tide it was once possible to walk across the flats from North Norfolk to Gibraltar Point near Skegness on the Lincolnshire coast. Not that we ever attempted it.

At the end of the day, we'd have buckets of fresh cockles to take home, boil and eat with vinegar and crusty bread. Before we drove home, the adults would adjourn to the seventeenth-century Le Strange Arms for a drink while we children played on the beach.

No one worried about drinking and driving in the sixties. The breathalyser wasn't introduced until 1967, by Barbara Castle when she was Transport Secretary under Harold Wilson, and even then used fairly sparingly. Dad was a generous host and no one ever left my parents' cheese and wine parties sober.

Dennis used to organise elaborate party games, one of which involved putting a pile of clothes in a heap in the middle of the room. Contestants would be blindfolded and would be invited to pull a garment from the pile, which they would then be expected to put on. One night I came home to find Dennis helping a man who used to work on the railways with my dad climb into a pair of rubber corsets made for a petite woman. Having got them on, over his trousers, he discovered he couldn't get them off. My last memory of that evening is Dennis manhandling the bloke out to his car, three sheets to the wind and still in his corsets, and pouring him into the driving seat, all the time exhorting, in his pure Norfolk accent: 'Come on, old boy. Work as a team, bugger the expense.'

Back at Deacon's, my chequered educational career was continuing to progress onwards and sideways. After three years, two classes became three to prepare us for specialist O-level examinations. We were split into 4A, 4B and 4G.

Not 4C, you will note, or even 4D. The 'bottom' stream was 4G, to leave its inhabitants in no doubt that they were little more than pond life, and to emphasise the yawning gap between them and their cleverer, more industrious contemporaries. Heaven knows what modern education-alists would make of this torture by classification. They'd have a field day bemoaning the effect being dumped in 4G would have on the poor little mites' 'self-esteem issues'.

No prizes for guessing that I went straight into 4G, my prowess at English notwithstanding. The fact that I'd represented the school on *Top of the Form* counted for nothing. Not that I gave a toss, frankly. I wore member-ship of 4G like a badge of honour. Actually, what stream you ended up in depended on your ability in Latin, math-ematics and the sciences, which were all the rage in the sixties thanks to Harold Wilson's declaration that we were living in a new age forged in the 'white heat of technology'.

Since I was only really interested in English and history and didn't fancy the law or medicine, I dropped Latin early on. So when they were handing out badges to 4A, I wasn't even in the room. My French was OK, certainly good enough to get me through a holiday in Paris in 1968. I did the talking for the family, buying everything from petrol to fresh baguettes and ordering in restaurants. We'd done a house swap with a French family and spent two wonderful weeks in an apartment in Monmartre. My parents bought some art, including portraits of Viv and me painted by a pavement artist. Dad brought back some French wine, Mum her favourite nougat, Viv a French doll and a model of the Eiffel Tower. And me? I came home with an original French pressing of an Otis Redding double album, on the ATCO label. Otis died six months earlier when his plane crashed in Wisconsin. His death had as big an effect on me as that of Buddy Holly had on an earlier generation.

My conversational French didn't do me any favours when it came to exams. I went on to fail French O-level. While I could understand the language as spoken and make myself understood in everyday French, I couldn't be bothered to conjugate verbs or bugger around learning about past participles. The 'sex' of a table didn't interest me in the slightest. As for the *plume de ma tante*, I thought that was a Biro.

It was around this time that I locked horns again with the gruesome Clelland. Until the fifth form, all Deacon's boys were supposed to wear caps as part of their uniform on their way to and from school. This was a rule observed largely in the breach. Quite apart from the obvious fashion considerations, by the age of fifteen most young men have started shaving and look ridiculous in schoolboy caps. Some of us in the fourth form were already going to pubs, and getting served. I had no intention of walking the streets looking like the Clitheroe Kid.

One day, Clelland spotted a group of us wandering

along not wearing our caps. When we got to school he took us to task. I gave him some lip. He told me he was going to cane me, not for refusing to wear a cap but for insolence. I told him where he could stick his cane. By then, I was as big as him. If he'd tried to hit me with a stick in the street, I was pretty confident he'd have come off worse.

Next thing I knew I was summoned to the headmaster's office. Upcott-Gill was an aloof, self-important man, who always wore a grey three-piece suit and an academic gown, which made him look from the back like an overweight Batman. He probably had a mortarboard somewhere and appeared to be under the illusion that he was running some kind of elite public school, not a state grammar. Despite the suit and cape, Upcott-Gill was a sartorial disaster. His tie and waistcoat were always gravy-stained, he regularly forgot to button up his flies and legend had it that he once took morning assembly wearing two different shoes, one brown and one black. I'd never had much to do with him, since I seem to recall he taught Latin and sixth-form mathematics, neither of which were my forte. He couldn't have been more different from Eric Sutton, my primary school head. Sutton was feared, but he was also respected and admired. Sutton earned your respect. Upcott-Gill seemed to think he was entitled to respect by virtue of his position and made no attempt to earn it. Eric Sutton had a cane, but

I never knew him to use it in anger. Where Mr Sutton had reminded me of Jimmy Edwards' whack-happy headmaster in *Whacko!*, Upcott-Gill fancied himself as the real thing.

My refusal to allow Clelland to cane me had brought about my audience with the head. I was informed that I'd committed a serious breach of discipline and if I wouldn't accept my punishment from Clelland, I would have to submit to a beating from the headmaster. I begged to differ, arguing that Clelland was simply looking for any excuse to cane me. I went into full barrack-room lawyer mode, maintaining that if any man beat me with a stick outside the school gates it would constitute a criminal assault. So why the hell should I have to put up with such barbaric treatment within the cloisters of Deacon's? It wasn't that I was afraid of the cane. I'd had a few strokes in my time. I just felt it was an unwarranted abuse of authority. My father didn't cane me, so why should I allow a teacher to do it? I've never believed in corporal punishment or capital punishment, either – despite my false reputation among the Guardianistas as a hanger and a flogger. Still don't. Upcott-Gill gave me an ultimatum: take the beating or I would be suspended from school until he had spoken to my parents.

In the middle of the day, I walked out of the gates and made my way home, frankly not caring whether I ever went back. Dad was away on business, out of the country if memory serves. By the time I got home, Mum had already received her summons by telephone. She sympathised with me, knowing full well Clelland's reputation. But she couldn't ignore Upcott-Gill's ultimatum and in Dad's absence abroad would have to deal with it herself. Upcott-Gill told her bluntly that if I continued to refuse the cane I would be expelled, no ifs, no buts. While she was at the school, I was at a friend's house round the corner. She returned from the meeting visibly upset, not just with me but with the school. I knew that I would have to give in, for her sake. After lunch I walked into the head's study and told him to do his worst. Upcott-Gill took down one of his canes from the wall. I held out my hand. He had other ideas. Bend over, boy. This was the ultimate humiliation but I had to comply. Four strokes, applied slowly, with relish. When it was over, Upcott-Gill offered his hand for me to shake, as was his habit. He expected his victims to thank him, like gentlemen, for their chastisement. To hell with that. If he thought I was going to thank him, he was out of luck. I just glared at him.

I left his study, vowing I would have my revenge. In the scheme of things, I wouldn't have to wait all that long.

One of the boys I most admired at Deacon's was Lloyd Watson. He was a couple of years above me and was an extraordinarily gifted musician. Lloyd had a Jamaican father and English mother, a mixed-race heritage which was fairly rare in 1960s Peterborough. He'd grown up steeped in music, spent five years learning the piano and had taught himself to play acoustic guitar. At the end of every Christmas term, Deacon's would stage house competitions, where members of the school houses – Normans, Britons, Saxons and Danes – would showcase their assorted talents in music and drama. I remember sitting mesmerised in the hall as Lloyd gave a remarkable virtuoso guitar performance. His influences ranged from blues and soul to the Beatles and the Stones and while still at school he formed his own band, the Soulmates, which quickly gained a wide following, me included.

During a gig at USAF Alconbury, Lloyd invited onstage two American airmen known as Pee Wee and Al, who sang duets on a whole range of Stax and Motown hits. They were such a success that they became full members of the band, performing as many shows as their service careers would permit. It turned out that Pee Wee was the cousin of Motown artist Stevie Wonder. Occasionally, they were supplemented by another black American serviceman, Ray Gates. With this line-up they went on to win the first ever Beat Competition staged in Peterborough, a sort of Battle of the Giants for local groups, at the long-demolished Elwes Hall.

To my mind, their most memorable gig was a live, open air concert in Cathedral Square one summer afternoon. Pee Wee and Al were simply sublime. It was like watching the legendary Stax-Volt revue, which had taken Britain by storm a few years earlier and had been headlined by Otis Redding and Sam and Dave. Musicians' Union rules restricted the ability of American recording artists to work in Britain, so we had to make do with home-grown alternatives such as Jimmy James and the Vagabonds, Zoot Money and his Big Roll Band, and Geno Washington and the Ram Jam Band, fronted by another former US serviceman, who decided to stay on.

Pee Wee and Al went home when their tour of duty ended and Lloyd formed another band, Lloyd Watson's Pocket Edition. He then joined Ma Grinder's Blues Mission, who had a residency at the Halcyon, the pub on the Netherton Estate, round the corner from Ledbury Road. Although just a local boozer, this was an important staging post on the British blues trail, featuring acts such as Champion Jack Dupree, Mississippi Fred McDowell and Chicken Shack, whose lead singer Christine Perfect (later McVie) went on to stardom with Fleetwood Mac.

All these musicians were backed by local boy made good Lloyd Watson, who later won Best Solo Artist in the Melody Maker Folk/Rock Competition, which secured him a coveted slot on BBC 2's *Old Grey Whistle Test*. Lloyd became a much-sought-after session musician and toured with David Bowie, Roxy Music and King Crimson. He's still out on the road in his own 'never ending tour' today, having gone back to his roots in the Peterborough area.

I'd have loved to have had Lloyd Watson's talent, but as I've previously explained my attempts to play musical instruments were about as successful as my aptitude for woodwork. I can remember we were once asked to fashion a naval destroyer out of a single block of wood in our second-year handicraft class. I managed to saw off the angles of bow and stern in the wrong direction, so that the ends of the ship sloped downwards rather than ascending upwards. When the woodwork teacher, 'Hank' Haybittle, a vulpine individual with a predilecton for taking nips of whisky in the store cupboard during lessons, asked what the hell I thought I'd made, I replied confidently: 'It's a tank.' It was no real surprise when I wasn't entered for woodwork O-level.

Still, despite lacking any musical dexterity, I wanted to be part of the local music scene. In the words of George Bernard Shaw, from *Man and Superman*: those who can, do; those who can't, teach. In my case it was: those who can play, play; those who can't, become disc jockeys.

A couple of times a week, I used to go to the Spinning Wheel Club, a discotheque at the back of a Grade II Listed pub called the Bull and Dolphin, in Bridge Street. Run by a couple of lads in their late teens/early twenties, called Dave Bennett and Rod Manuell, it was gaining quite a reputation. Specialising in rare soul and ska, the Spinning Wheel was a forerunner of what would become the Northern Soul scene in the 1970s. It was an early Southern outpost of Northern Soul. Steve Allen's Cloud Nine, in the ballroom of the old Grand Hotel, opposite the Town Hall, was the biggest venue in town, but the Spinning Wheel was coming up on the rails. One night, I heard they were expanding and were looking for another DJ, to host soul nights at the club and take a mobile disco on the road. They let me try out and I got the job. I was fifteen and still at school, but I thought I'd arrived in the big time.

Auntie Em died, leaving £1740, her life savings, to be divided between my dad, his brother Ken and their cousin Mick, who was a woman. After Em's death, Nanna and Grandad Littlejohn decided to sell Vine Gardens and emigrate to Australia for good. It was a wrench, especially for my dad, but in retrospect was the best thing they could have done. Nanna had always been a frail woman, ever since Ronnie died as a baby, and suffered from chronic colitis, a serious bowel disorder, which caused her to have a colostomy in her mid-sixties. If she'd stayed in Ilford, she probably wouldn't have survived much past seventy. Relocated to sunny Sydney, both Nanna and Grandad lived well into their nineties. When I visited them in Australia in 1984, Nanna was still sharp as a tack and had just reread the entire works of Agatha Christie. Grandad was by then eighty-seven years old and fit as a fiddle, living on his unchanging daily diet of bacon and eggs for breakfast and lamb chops and boiled potatoes for dinner, what he still called 'tea'. One day, he took me for his regular long walk, his morning 'constitutional', along the waterfront. I was thirty, he was almost three times my age, yet he walked the hind legs off me. I was left trailing in his wake. Not only that, but two decades after retiring from the London Docks, Grandad was still working. Part-time, anyway. For a couple of weeks a year. He'd found himself a seasonal job as Father Christmas at Australia's oldest department store, David Jones in Sydney. Every December, he'd be transported through Sydney on the back of a lorry, dressed up as Santa and waving to the cheering crowds who had turned out for the city's annual Christmas Parade. My grandad, William Henry Littlejohn VI, Australia's Father Christmas. Who'd have thought it? He'd come a long way from 'Wipers', Scruttons Meat Storage, the Royal Docks, and Grosvenor Gardens, East Ham.

We were on the move, too, although not very far. Mum and Dad sold Ledbury Road after we'd lived there for ten years and bought a run-down 1920s detached house in Westwood Park Road, one of the more sought-after streets in the area. I hated the idea of moving, even though our new home was less than a mile away on the other side of the Grange. The first time I went to the Westwood Park Road house, it was like a squat. Nothing seemed to have been done to the property since the Great Depression. It still had all its original wiring and light switches, the walls were covered in thick anaglypta paper and the plumbing looked as if it had been installed under the personal supervision of Thomas Crapper, who, contrary to popular misconception, did not invent the flush toilet. Crapper was a London plumbers' merchant who did much to popularise the indoor lavatory, but was not responsible for the piece of sanitaryware which still bears his name. He did, though, invent the ballcock, for which he received a Royal Warrant from Queen Victoria.

Unlike my parents, I didn't have the vision to realise the potential of the property. But decades before Kirsty and Phil turned up on Channel 4, Mum and Dad embraced the concept of location, location, location. All that I could grasp was that we were moving from a warm, modern house into a dump with rising damp. But with the help of some local tradesmen, my parents transformed the property into a desirable, comfortable family home, with a mature, well-stocked garden.

Some people believe there are fairies at the bottom of every garden. We didn't have any fairies, but we did have Little Ern. Our garden backed on to the home of Ernie Wise, the short, fat, hairy half of Morecambe and Wise, then just about the biggest stars on British television. After we moved in, we also bought a labrador puppy, Sherrie, from the litter born to Dennis Skipper's dog, Bonnie, who eventually submitted herself to stud. We were never sure who the father was, but as she got older I could have sworn Sherrie did look a bit like Dennis. Whenever I heard Ernie Wise out walking in his garden, I'd open the French doors and command Sherrie: 'Little Ern. See him off!' Sherrie would shoot from the house like a torpedo and bound down towards the fence, barking ferociously. When I met Ernie many years later, at a Variety Club bash, and related the story, he thought it was hilarious. 'That was your bloody dog, was it?'

The summer of 1969 changed my life. Dad had taken out an extra mortgage when we bought Westwood Park Road, to finance a holiday in America. Flying to the States wasn't all that simple in the sixties, especially for a family of four. Regular air fares were prohibitively expensive, deterring all but the wealthy or those travelling on business expense accounts. There were no budget airlines and the main routes were jealously guarded and protected by law. Price competition was non-existent. Freddie Laker's revolutionary cut-price Skytrain service between Britain and the US was still four years in the future. The standard (economy) fare between London and New York was £75, which would have meant an outlay of £250 for the four of us to make the trip, approximately £3500 today, and was way beyond our means. Currency controls, imposed by Harold Wilson, meant that no one could take more than £50 out of the country.

The only way we could afford to fly to the States was by joining an organisation called, I think, the North American Families Association. This had been set up after the war to allow the families of GI brides to visit their daughters in North America. The association chartered aircraft on some of the less busy routes, which allowed it to offer cheaper fares. Because it was essentially a private club, these flights were exempt from the tight transatlantic regulations set up to protect the big airlines. But it also meant your choice of destination was severely limited. There were no direct flights to Detroit, which meant we had to fly to Toronto in Canada. Olive and Tom collected us at the airport and drove us across the border. I'll never forget my first sight of the Detroit skyline as we crossed the Ambassador Bridge, which links Canada and the US. People who visit America for the first time always tell you it's like walking on to a movie set. They're not wrong. America was an eye-opener in every sense of the word.

This was the summer of the first Moon landing and Woodstock. We arrived in Detroit the day before Neil Armstrong set foot on the Moon on 21 July and watched it unfold on Olive and Tom's colour television. It wasn't only Neil Armstrong making a giant leap. I felt as if I'd landed on another planet.

Detroit was one of the richest cities in America, built on the success of the automobile industry, and downtown, with its fabulous Art Deco skyscrapers, was like something out of a James Stewart or Spencer Tracy film. It was also the home of Motown Records, the soul music capital of the US. When the Spinning Wheel proprietors discovered I was spending the summer there, they gave me £50 out the till to buy as many records as I could. I spent hours downtown, scouring the music shops, hoovering up rare records on obscure labels, such as Edwin Starr on Ric-Tic and Major Lance on Okeh, worth a fortune back home. I returned triumphantly with a suitcase full of valuable 45s. These days I could have downloaded all of them off the internet in a few minutes.

I mention this aspect of the holiday only because of its relevance to my life back in Peterborough. But there's no room here to do justice to my first experiences of the United States. That would fill another book. Suffice to say that America had a profound and lasting effect on me and my world outlook. What we didn't realise in 1969 was that seven years later my dad would be transferred to the USA and my parents and sister would end up living round the corner from Olive and Tom in the Detroit suburb of Birmingham. I didn't go with them, but my mum and Viv still live there. When I went out for Mum's eighty-fifth birthday in the summer of 2013, Detroit had just filed for bankruptcy, brought to its knees by bovine protectionism, rampant corruption and violent crime. The once majestic downtown is a burned-out shell and the inner suburbs have been returned to prairie. Whoever described Detroit as 'America's first ex-city' was bang on the money.

The vibrant, prosperous metropolis I first visited in 1969, the shining incarnation of the America Dream, really is a lost world.

Back in Britain, I wasn't especially looking forward to returning to the suffocating cloisters of Deacon's grammar school. The fifth form was supposed to be the most important year of your life, since it led up to the holy grail of O-level exams. I'd already banked two O-levels, English Language and English Literature, so I figured I'd done all the hard work. My priority was to concentrate on my new career as a disc jockey. In November of that year it earned me a full-page spread in the *Peterborough Evening Telegraph*, reviewing the latest record releases. The yellowing cutting shows a fresh-faced youth in a Fred Perry polo shirt and a white mac. I wonder where he went. The copy reads:

A Fifth Former at Peterborough's Deacon's Grammar School, Richard Littlejohn, is carving quite a name for himself on the local discotheque scene.

Richard is one of five DJs at the Spinning Wheel discotheque in Bridge Street and helps run the Road Show which travels throughout East Anglia taking music to the dancers.

> *With the Road Show, Richard gets around quite a bit – a*
> *few weeks ago he was at a youth centre in Louth, then at*
> *Wisbech Cricket Club and tonight the show goes to Peterborough*
> *Youth Centre. But he still found time to listen to six of the latest*
> *releases . . .*

This big build-up is followed by my expert comments on four records released that week, by Blood, Sweat and Tears; Checkmates Ltd featuring Sonny Charles; the Climax Chicago Blues Band; and Stevie Wonder.

The Stevie Wonder single in question was 'Yester Me, Yester You, Yesterday', his follow-up to 'My Cherie Amour'. With the prescience and sound judgement which was to become a hallmark of my newspaper columns from 1988 onwards, I confidently ventured the opinion that Stevie Wonder 'hadn't lived up to the expectations of his youth' and I would be surprised if it rose any higher than 'the lower part of the Top 30'. 'Yester Me' went to number two, at the time Stevie Wonder's highest ever chart placing in the UK.

For the first time, Skip and I found ourselves in the same class. Although he had always been a year above me at school, he'd been made to stay down in the fifth form to retake all the O-levels he had failed. This didn't bode particularly well, either for Deacon's or for our educational prospects. We'd always managed to bring out the worst in each other. Sticking us in the same class could only spell trouble with a capital T. We went on a mission to cause as much disruption as possible. On one occasion, I caused a diversion in a science class by setting fire to an exercise book with a Bunsen burner while he climbed out of the window. The teacher wondered what had happened to Skipper. Had anyone seen him leave? Not a clue, sir. Are you sure he was ever here in the first place? We were also caught smoking at the back of the quad. As a precaution, we always posted a lookout, but the caretaker – known to all as the Colonel – outwitted us by climbing over the roof using a ladder.

We were more interested in music than education. Although I was still soul-mad, my musical tastes were expanding. The previous year, 1968, I'd got a holiday job in the car park at the East of England Showground on the outskirts of town. At the end of every agricultural show, there would be a concert held in a giant marquee. That summer they'd booked an unknown act called Jethro Tull, presumably on the grounds that Jethro Tull was the name of the man who invented the seed drill, so there was a farming connection. We all thought it would be the usual, finger-in-the-ear English folk group, full of fol-de-rols and hey-nonny-nonnies. When the band came on stage, no one had ever seen anything like it. There was this mad, demonic figure, standing on one leg, playing the flute in front of an electric rock band. This was, of course, Ian Anderson, one of rock's more eccentric and enduring entertainers. Jethro Tull's first album, *This Was*, was released later that year and they would become one of the most successful acts across the world in the early 1970s. The next time I saw Jethro Tull onstage was at the Isle of Wight Festival in 1970.

Britain's answer to Woodstock in 1969 was the Isle of Wight Festival, headlined by Bob Dylan. I was in the States that summer and, despite the considerable freedom my parents had always given me, they would almost certainly have drawn the line at letting their fifteen-year-old son head off for a week's sex'n'drugs'n'rock'roll on an island off the south coast. There was to be another Isle of Wight Festival in August 1970. Since I'd be sixteen by then, my parents couldn't possibly object. Skip and I sent off for tickets, after answering an advert in the *Melody Maker*. We also booked tickets for the Bath Festival of Blues and Progressive Music, which was to be held in June at the showground in Shepton Mallet. Unfortunately, the date of the Bath Festival clashed with my O-level chemistry exam. Clearly, something would have to give. There was no contest. My entire future was at stake, this was a one-off opportunity. I went to Bath.

Kitted out in army surplus jackets from Millets, which also supplied our sleeping bags, we headed off to hitch-hike cross-country to Bath. We hitch-hiked everywhere in those days, to save on bus and train fares. I can't remember the last time I saw anyone hitch-hiking, but in those days it was a widely accepted mode of transport. My old man wasn't too bothered about us being abducted and murdered by nonces, but he did suggest we both carried Stanley Knives in our pockets, just in case. We got to Bath early and crashed out in a derelict Georgian building, with a crowd of other concert-goers from all over Britain. There was plenty of dope being smoked, but I never really acquired a taste for it. I've always liked a drink, so bought some local cider. It was called, I think, Knee Cracker, although I could be confusing it with the cider I bought before the Glastonbury Festival in 1982. You have to treat rough cider with great respect, since its bowel-loosening properties are legendary and pop festivals were not renowned for their exemplary – or, indeed, remotely adequate – sanitary facilities. As I was to learn, first-hand.

Breakfast the next day was a bottle of milk nicked from the house next door's front doorstep. Then it was off to the festival. The Shepton Mallet showground wasn't exactly Max Yasgur's farm in upstate New York but it was the next best thing. On the way, we passed the Babycham factory, which had sensibly closed for the duration. Arriving at the site, the first bloke we bumped into was an old mate from Deacon's, Geoff Owen, who'd left school the previous year and was now knocking out tie-dyed tee-shirts from the back of a Ford Transit.

What a line-up. Saturday featured Canned Heat, John Mayall, Steppenwolf, Johnny Winter, Pink Floyd, Fairport Convention, Colosseum, It's A Beautiful Day, Keef Hartley, and the Maynard Ferguson Big Band. Sunday was the turn of Led Zeppelin, Jefferson Airplane, Frank Zappa and the Mothers of Invention, the Byrds, Santana, Dr John the Night Tripper, Country Joe and the Fish and Hot Tuna, the Jefferson Airplane spin-off band.

Halfway through day one, the cider began to work its mysterious way through the system. I repaired to the portable chemical toilets, situated next to a health-food tent. After queueing for an eternity, it was my turn. I opened the door and was confronted with a sight which is still etched, horribly, on my memory. The chemical toilets were little more than metal dustbins, about two feet six off the ground, with a plastic seat. This particular karzi wasn't only full, it was overflowing. The level of faeces rose above the seat, like the pyramid of earth in the kitchen sink from the film *Close Encounters of the Third Kind*. The only way the more recent deposits could have been left was if the previous occupant had scaled the walls, like Spiderman, and dropped his load from above, in the manner of a Lancaster bomber. I took one look and headed off into the surrounding fields, where several dozen of my fellow concert-goers had a similar idea.

*

The Isle of Wight 1970 is widely acknowledged as the best-attended rock festival of all time. *The Guinness Book of Records* puts the crowd at between 600,000 and 700,000, even bigger than Woodstock the year before. Once again, Skip and I hitch-hiked, though this time only as far as London. We caught the Tube across town from St John's Wood, took the boat train to Portsmouth and hopped on the ferry to Ryde. When we got there this gentle offshore backwater, stuck in the early 1950s, was teeming with wannabe hippies, freaks and bikers. Having landed a couple of days before the festival was due to start, we headed out of town and pitched up for the night in some woods next to a Pontin's holiday camp. This had the added advantage that we could climb over the fence and use the communal shower facilities on site. We were rumbled when one of a group of lads from Chelmsford (who was a dead ringer for Canned Heat's rotund lead singer Bob 'The Bear' Hite) was caught coming out of the ladies' shower block, with his towel rolled up under his arm.

Hi-De-Hi!

Another fabulous, never-to-be-repeated line-up. In alphabetical order:

Arrival, Joan Baez, Black Widow, David Bromberg, Cactus, Chicago, Leonard Cohen, Miles Davis, Donovan, the Doors, Emerson, Lake and Palmer, Fairfield Parlour, Family, Gary Farr, Free, Gilberto Gil, Good News, the Groundhogs, Richie Havens,

Hawkwind, Heaven, Jimi Hendrix, Howl, Jethro Tull, Judas Jump, Kris Kristofferson.

Lighthouse, Ralph McTell, Melanie, Mighty Baby, Joni Mitchell, Moody Blues, Pentangle, Shawn Phillips, the Pink Fairies, Procol Harum, Redbone, Terry Reid, Andy Roberts' Everyone, John Sebastian, Sly and the Family Stone, Kathy Smith, Rosalie Sorrels, Supertramp, Taste, Ten Years After, Tiny Tim, the Voices of East Harlem, Tony Joe White and The Who.

To be honest, there are several artistes on that list I simply can't remember – Arrival, Black Widow, Good News, Heaven, Howl, Judas Jump, Mighty Baby, Kathy Smith and Rosalie Sorrells. Nope, sorry. But there are plenty more I'll never forget – John Sebastian, from the Lovin' Spoonful; the sensational Sly and the Family Stone; the Doors; The Who; Hendrix. Apparently Emerson, Lake and Palmer fired a cannon during their set. I slept through it, undisturbed.

The most bizarre act on the bill was Tiny Tim, a tall, effeminate, falsetto, American ukelele player – a floppy-haired throwback to the days of vaudeville, in a check *Boardwalk Empire* suit. He was helicoptered into the site, as were many of the other acts, because the surrounding country roads were gridlocked. At one stage he led half a million people in a rousing chorus of 'There'll Always Be An England', singing through a hand-held megaphone. Outside of the Last Night of the Proms, and possibly a

Madness concert, can you imagine that happening today? Me neither. The diversity police would have a fit. We now live in a country where it is considered 'racist' even to fly the Union Flag.

Although peace and love was being preached from the stage, it wasn't all harmony around the perimeter. Fights broke out after some French anarchists started pulling down the fences. Eventually, under siege from the sheer weight of numbers, the organisers declared a free festival.

Like Shepton Mallet, the sanitation left much to be desired. The men's toilet was an open sewer, the women's a discreetly screened sewer.

The communal gents' comprised a series of wooden planks, suspended above a trench, straight from the Somme, with holes cut every three feet. As I approached, there was an ominous creaking and one of the planks snapped in half, despatching a couple of dozen screaming hippies on hash cakes into the murky depths below. Their downhill scramble to the sea was like watching one of those cheese-rolling contests. No one got in the way. I turned and ran in the opposite direction. It cost me half-a-crown to get a bus back into Ryde, where I broke back into the holiday camp to use the facilities.

After three or four days of glorious sunshine, the English weather intervened and the heavens opened. We left the site at the crack of dawn in pouring rain as the American singer-songwriter Richie Havens performed an acoustic set. Back in Ryde, we had return ferry tickets but almost no money left. It was time to employ the ten bob (50p) note which my dad had made me keep in the back of my wallet 'for emergencies'. This was just such an emergency. I walked into a bookies, picked a horse and put the whole 10s. on the nose. It was a shot in the dark, since I knew, and still know, absolutely nothing about the gee-gees. To my amazement, my horse came home at 10-1. I'd won a fiver. We caught the train back to London.

Another memory of the Isle of Wight was queueing for the payphone to ring home to discover my O-level results. I'd passed three more, somehow – history, geography and maths, which I'd scraped through with a grade six – and now boasted a grand total of five, the bare minimum for entry into the sixth form. Clelland must have been astonished that I'd passed geography and will have wondered how the hell I managed it. Simple: I busked it. One of the questions, which carried enough marks to secure a pass, was worded something like: 'Describe a field survey you have carried out in a particular locality.' Since I spent the only field trip I can remember, to the Norfolk coast, bunking off for ice cream and cigarettes, I pretended I'd carried out a field survey of Peterborough, about which I knew quite a bit: population, main industries, agriculture, etc. The judges weren't going to be any the wiser and they were obviously sufficiently impressed to award me a grade-two pass.

As I mentioned, even in 1970 the Isle of Wight seemed to be stuck in the fifties. It has remained so ever since. The Isle of Wight ferry isn't so much a Ticket to Ryde as a one-way journey Back to the Future. A couple of years ago, plans were announced to drag it screaming and kicking into the present century. *The Economist* magazine reported that the Isle of Wight had been designated as Britain's first 'eco' island. The plan was to make the island self-sufficient in energy by smothering it with wind farms and solar panels. It was the brainchild of an outfit called Ecoisland (geddit?), described as 'so green that the invitations it sent to an event at Britain's House of Commons were printed on recycled paper embedded with meadow-flower seeds (just plant, water and watch them grow)'.

The report continued: 'Ecoisland plans to . . . insulate houses better, make greater use of geothermal, wind and tidal energy, and generate power from waste. There are also plans for electric vehicles that residents and visitors alike can hire. Locally grown food would be delivered through island-wide supply hubs. A concerted effort is under way to reduce water use and capture more rainwater (about one-third of the island's fresh water at present is pumped from the mainland).' All very commendable, you might think. But they weren't doing this simply for the sake of saving the polar bears. Someone had worked out there was a nice drink in it for them – which is why the project was being sponsored by multi-national companies such as IBM and Toshiba. While the idea of generating all our energy supplies from natural, sustainable sources is hugely attractive in theory – and would certainly have found favour with the 1970 Isle of Wight pop festival crowd – the problem is that it doesn't work in practice and is hideously expensive.

By 2020, every household in Britain will be paying £280 a year over the odds for gas and electricity to fund the government's 'green' agenda, which amounts to little more than bunging foreign firms billions of pounds to clutter up our beautiful, World Heritage site countryside and our outstanding natural coastline with utterly useless *War of the Worlds* windmills.

I wonder if anyone bothered to ask the inhabitants of the Isle of Wight whether they wanted to be forced to drive rented electric cars, knit their own toilet paper and have their scenery desecrated by hopelessly inefficient solar panels and wind turbines sprouting like triffids. And having to pay through the nose for the privilege. What had they done to deserve being singled out for an expensive eco-experiment?

In future, the only tourists prepared to travel to the island would have been woolly-headed *Guardian* readers posing for pictures in front of an artificial forest of aluminium windmills before retreating to their overpriced, wood-fired Stoke Newington slums, where they could revel in the snapshots of their eco-friendly vacation on their nuclear-powered iPads over bowls of meadow-flower muesli. By the time the wind farms were whirring at full speed, the Isle of Wight would have weighed anchor and sailed off into the mid-Atlantic sunset like a competitor in the annual round-the-island yacht race.

It was, perhaps, significant that the plans for the island's exciting eco-future were announced in the same week that Jimi Hendrix, who topped himself shortly after topping the bill at the Isle of Wight pop festival, was voted the best guitarist of all time.

Mercifully, the plans collapsed like a wind turbine in a gale and the company behind it went into liquidation. And in a spooky echo of the early demise of Jimi Hendrix, in October 2013 the director of the failed eco-island corporation was found dead at his home. David Green, fifty-two, had previously been arrested on fraud allegations in connection with the disappearance of £115,000 of taxpayers' money which had been allocated to the project. Police said his death was not suspicious. Despite the collapse of the Isle of Wight scheme, ministers have confirmed that they intend to go ahead with covering what remains of our green-and-pleasant with thousands more of these hideous, cripplingly expensive and utterly useless wind farms.

Incidentally, Tiny Tim's only other hit was a dreadful cover version of 'Tiptoe Through the Tulips', a song written for the 1929 talkie *Gold Diggers of Broadway*. Somehow, 'Tiptoe Through the Turbines' doesn't have the same ring to it.

There'll always be an England? Not at this rate, there won't.

A couple of footnotes: I've already mentioned watching Jethro Tull at the Isle of Wight. They were sandwiched between the Moody Blues and Jimi Hendrix, who reprised his electrifying version of 'The Star Stangled Banner' at Woodstock by segueing into a demented version of 'God Save the Queen', perhaps the only time the national anthem has been performed by a man playing the guitar with his teeth.

Forty-odd years later, my wife and I were sitting round a swimming pool in Florida with our friends John and Kirsten Lodge. Over several bottles of pinot noir, we were reminiscing about our schooldays and John and I realised that we were both at the Isle of Wight Festival in 1970. 'You should write a book about all this,' John said. This is that book. Actually, when I said we were both at the Isle of Wight, I should perhaps make something clear: I was in the audience and John was up on stage. John Lodge is the bass guitarist in the Moody Blues, still touring, still going strong in their fifth decade. A bit like me, no one's ever told him to stop.

After another sensational summer, I signed up for the sixth form at Deacon's, although my heart wasn't really in it. My mind was set on a media career: newspapers first, radio second. It was just a case of waiting for the right opportunity. To say I neglected my studies would be an understatement. By now, I was pretty much full-time at the Spinning Wheel and its associated activities. Having played the youth-club circuit, I was getting a few more grown-up gigs. The young farmers always paid well. I've never seen drinking like it – and I've spent thirty-five years in Fleet Street's various incarnations. All you had to do to get them going was put on 'Hi Ho Silver Lining', by Jeff Beck, or 'Oh, Pretty Woman', by Roy Orbison and they'd go berserk: tipping beer everywhere, punching the air, stamping their sturdy boots and stripping to the waist. And that was just the women. One night I went outside a village hall at some remote hamlet in the Fens, to get a spare mic from the van, only to discover a young farmer giving a young farmeress a good seeing-to over the bonnet, his trousers round his ankles and his rustic backside going fifteen to the dozen. 'Don't mind me,' I said. 'I won't, me duck,' he replied, rutting away furiously, without missing a beat.

Another night in the summer of 1970 I was hosting

a concert at the Isle of Ely College, featuring a semi-acoustic underground folk-rock group fronted by singer Marc Bolan and his percussionist sidekick Mickey Finn. Halfway through the set, they were joined onstage by some other musicians carrying electric instruments. Bolan strapped on an electric guitar and steamed into 'Ride a White Swan', a song none of us had ever heard before. He'd just recorded it and this was, if not the first, then certainly one of its first public outings. The name of the band was shortened to T Rex, 'Ride a White Swan' was released in the October and the record became the first of a string of hits. Bolan went on to become one of the defining figures of the 'glam rock' era. He died in a car crash in 1977.

Shortly after joining the Spinning Wheel roster, I had accompanied Dave Bennett on a visit to the headquarters of Island Records in Notting Hill, west London. Notting Hill wasn't the gentrified, middle-class suburb it is today. Back then it was a run-down, bohemian area with a large West Indian population. Island's founder Chris Blackwell had signed up most of the top Jamaican reggae, ska and blue beat acts, including Desmond Dekker, whose 1967 rock steady single '007 (Shanty Town)' was a favourite in the clubs. Originally released on the Pyramid label, it got to number seventeen in the charts and became the first Jamaican record to make the UK Top 20. Dave had heard that Dekker was soon to tour England and was anxious to book him. We secured Dekker's services for £90, provided we also agreed to take one of Island's new 'progressive' acts, a horn-heavy, jazz-rock outfit called If, who went on to enjoy success in Europe and America in the early 1970s. The week Desmond Dekker was due to appear in Peterborough, his latest record, 'Israelites', went to number one. We were worried he wouldn't turn up, or would at least demand a substantial increase in his fee to reflect his new-found success. On the night Dekker was due to appear, there must have been a thousand people queueing to get into a venue which only held a couple of hundred at most. If Dekker didn't show up, they'd have torn us and the building apart. We needn't have worried. Dekker arrived on time and was a real gentleman. He gave a scorching show, we paid his management the £90 as promised and bid him a fond farewell. I can't help wondering whether a modern pop star would bother fulfilling a long-standing commitment to play a small provincial club for a paltry £90 (just over a grand today) in the week his record went to number one.

In the event, If, featuring the brilliant Dick Morrisey on flute and tenor sax, went down a storm. Dave and Rod figured that, since 'prog-rock' was increasingly popular, we might as well start a dedicated rock night on Sundays. Among the many acts who appeared at the Spinning

Wheel were the Strawbs, a British folk-inspired group who had recently gone electric and added a young organist called Rick Wakeman to their ranks. This was one of Wakeman's early appearances with the Strawbs. He had previously been playing in a pub band in Ilford, so we had history in common. Rick later joined Yes, went solo and became one of the biggest 'prog-rock' stars of the 1970s.

The Strawbs went on to enjoy chart success with 'Part of the Union'. This well-known song about the working man was interpreted by the trades union movement as a proud celebration of solidarity and was adopted by the TUC as an unofficial anthem. In one of my earlier newspaper incarnations as an industrial and labour correspondent, I often heard it played at rallies and on picket lines. But if you listen to it carefully, you soon realise that it is a sarcastic ditty, which was originally called 'The Brothers', aimed at mocking the damage the intransigent, strike-happy unions were doing to the economy in the 1970s. Rick Wakeman became a prominent supporter of the Conservative Party during the Thatcher years.

We also booked an up-and-coming Birmingham heavy metal band called Black Sabbath, fronted by a singer called Ozzy Osbourne. Some readers may have heard of him. When we'd originally made the booking the band was relatively obscure, but had since released their first LP, which had gone to number eight in the charts. They were due to play the Spinning Wheel just as their second album,

Paranoid, was released. There hadn't been such an eagerly anticipated show at the Spinning Wheel since the night Desmond Dekker came to town. The 'prog-rock' crowd was completely different from the Spinning Wheel's regular meat-and-drink, soul-and-ska punters. They took their music very seriously indeed, carrying their favourite album covers under their arms wherever they went as a symbol of their intellectual superiority. Whereas the soul crowd would dance their socks off in joyous celebration, the 'prog-rock' brigade would sit cross-legged on the floor, nodding their heads earnestly, like Tibetan monks at prayer. Both crowds held each other in utter contempt.

On the evening of the Black Sabbath gig, it was standing room – or, rather, sitting room – only. The band was out the back, getting ready to come onstage in what passed for a dressing room, a cramped cellar stacked with beer crates. They'd turned up late and the natives were getting restless.

After their roadie indicated they were ready, I went onstage to introduce them. First, though, I decided to have some fun. I took the mic and said: 'Ladies and gentlemen, sorry about the delay and thank you for your patience. We've just had a telephone call from Black Sabbath's road manager. Unfortunately, their Transit has broken down on the A1 and they won't be able to perform tonight.' Groans of disappointment filled the room.

'But it's not all bad news. We have managed at the

last minute to secure a substitute band. So will you all please put your hands together and welcome back to the Spinning Wheel stage, the fabulous Desmond Dekker and his Aces . . .'

The whole place erupted with unbridled fury and Black Sabbath emerged from their dressing room to a chorus of boos and catcalls. Some missiles were thrown. As he took the stage, Ozzy Osbourne grabbed me by the arm and said in a menacing, but deadpan, Brummie accent: 'Oi s'powse yow think that's fooking foony.'

Every Thursday night, the Spinning Wheel road show hosted a disco in a room above a pub called the Bell, in Deeping St James, a Lincolnshire village a few miles north of Peterborough. The gig usually fell to me. I knew most of the regular crowd, but one evening my eye was caught by a newcomer, a gorgeous, tall blonde girl about my age. Towards the end of the evening she appeared to be about to leave and I wasn't going to miss the opportunity to introduce myself. I put on the first record which came to hand, stepped down off the stage, strode over and asked her to dance. This wasn't quite as romantic as it sounds. The record in question was 'War' by Edwin Starr, a thumping, raucous anti-Vietnam anthem, originally written for the Temptations but rejected by them on the grounds that it was too controversial. It's nobody's idea of music to chat up a woman by.

Oh, well, in for a penny. I discovered that her name was Wendy Bosworth and she'd just moved to the area from Luton with her parents, who had opened a bakery on a new estate.

'Have you got a boyfriend?' I asked.

No, she replied.

'Would you like one?'

Did I have anyone in mind?

'How about me?'

OK, she said, forgetting to add: 'You smooth-talking devil.'

We went out for a while, lost touch, got back together and married on Wendy's twenty-first birthday. On 18 October 2014, we are due to celebrate our fortieth wedding anniversary. Since it's a ruby wedding, we'll probably go out for a curry.

On 25 June 1988 we went to see Bruce Springsteen's Tunnel of Love Tour at Wembley Stadium. Ten songs into the set Springsteen brought on a surprise special guest – Edwin Starr. Backed by the E Street Band, Bruce and Edwin performed a duet: 'War'. What else? I turned to Wendy and said: 'They're playing our song.' We burst out laughing.

Five years later, Edwin Starr pitched up as a guest on my morning radio show on LBC. What a lovely man. I told him about my trip to Detroit in 1969, about buying his single 'Agent Double-O-Soul' on Ric-Tic records in a long demolished downtown record store. 'Oh, and by the way,' I added, almost as an aside: 'You're the man who introduced me to my wife.' He thought it was hilarious.

My time at Deacon's was careering towards an inevitable conclusion. But before we parted company, I was determined to take my revenge on Upcott-Gill, the headmaster who had made me submit to a caning on pain of expulsion. The annual house competitions would afford me the opportunity. I've already mentioned Lloyd Watson's mesmerising guitar solos. Each house would also put on a play and the best acts were always chosen to perform at a special parents' evening before the school broke up for Christmas. That term, I was put in charge of producing the Saxons' play and selected one written in the inter-war years and set in a minor public school, a cross between Mr Chips and Billy Bunter's Greyfriars. I cast myself as the headmaster. The play was a great success, we won the competition and would close the show on parents' night.

There must have been around four hundred mums and dads present that evening, including my own. It was Upcott-Gill's habit to have his desk and chair brought from his study into the room and sited in the centre aisle about halfway back, chair perched on the desktop. He would sit there like a Buddha, master of all he surveyed.

During the first performance, in front of my fellow pupils, I'd played it straight. In the couple of days between the end of the house competitions and parents' night, I made a few minor alterations to the script. When the curtain rose, my character was centre stage and had been transformed into 'Mr Upshott-Bill'. I'd padded out a suit with cushions, to resemble Upcott-Gill's well-upholstered frame, left the flies gaping open and was even wearing one brown shoe and one black shoe, in line with school legend. I then proceeded, to the best of my ability, to give a twenty-minute impersonation of our headmaster, portraying him as an incompetent, blustering, comedy bully.

Nobody was left in any doubt about whom my character was based upon. There were roars of laughter and four hundred pairs of smiling eyes turned to Upcott-Gill, marooned on his self-inflicted pedestal in the middle of the hall. He could only glower in my direction.

The following day, my parents received a letter from Upcott-Gill stating that I wasn't taking my studies seriously and he could see no useful purpose in my remaining at the school. He was too late. I'd already made up my mind to leave. One of the two local weekly papers, the *Peterborough Standard*, had advertised for a trainee reporter. I'd been for an interview and our neighbour Paul Mowforth, a former sports editor of the *Standard* now working as a press officer at Perkins, put in a good word for me. I got the job and would start in January.

Whatever else Deacon's taught me – and, frankly, it

gave me a pretty good education, one which, since the abolition of the grammars, most parents would have to pay for privately – I came away from that last night with two valuable lessons. The first cemented the old adage that revenge is a dish best served cold. The second was that if you want to cut someone down to size, so that it really hurts, ridicule is always so much more effective than angry polemic.

If I was glad to see the back of Deacon's, there was certainly no doubt that Deacon's was equally glad to see the back of me. When I was researching this book, I asked my mum to dig out some of my old reports. Here's a quote from my final history report, a fitting epitaph for someone who would go on to carve out a career as a newspaper columnist:

'It is clear from your work this term that you are not doing the necessary reading to enable you to write or discuss logically and in an informed manner. Assumptions and generalities will, in the end, get you nowhere.'

And that was where this book was supposed to end. But on the day I was writing the final chapter I turned on the local London television news to discover that a Romanian prostitute had been stabbed to death in Ilford Lane. The murder took place just round the corner from Vine Gardens and my grandparents' old house, where I was born. She is believed to have been knifed on a piece of waste ground where prostitutes take their clients and managed to stagger to a nearby fast-food restaurant, where she collapsed and died. The restaurant is called Pizza and Chicken 4 U, and appears to be in the same parade where Bill Fraser once ran his famous sweet shop.

In the wake of the stabbing, police issued logbooks to local residents to keep a record of all sightings of prostitutes and kerb crawlers in Ilford Lane. Although there have been 'ongoing issues' with illegal drug use and prostitution in Ilford Lane, the local council leader warned against a 'knee-jerk reaction' – perhaps an unfortunate choice of phrase in the circumstances.

Heaven knows what Bill and Min Littlejohn would have made of what a sewer their old, safe, respectable neighbourhood has become. Lost world, indeed.